Critical Acclaim for other books from PC Learning Labs

PC Learning Labs Teaches DOS 5

"[This] book is designed to help you attain a high level of DOS 5 fluency in as short a time as possible.

   ...a solid foundation of skills in DOS file management..."

—**Woody Liswood,** *MicroTimes Magazine*

"It's like having a personal teacher...you will emerge a confident user of personal computers...

   This book from an organization with 10 years classroom teaching of personal-computer operation under its belt makes the learning process both easier and organized."

—**Hugh Anderson,** *The Gazette*

PC Learning Labs Teaches WordPerfect 5.1

"...a tightly focused book that doesn't stray from its purpose...it concentrates on the beginner, and it stays with the beginner."

—**William J. Lynott,** *Online Today*

"Excellent keystroke-by-keystroke instruction is provided by this handsome book."

—**Computer Book Review**

PC LEARNING LABS TEACHES WORD FOR WINDOWS 2.0

a b c d e

k l m n o p

g r s t u v

y z a b c d

PC LEARNING LABS
TEACHES WORD
FOR WINDOWS 2.0

LOGICAL OPERATIONS

Ziff-Davis Press
Emeryville, California

Curriculum Development	Logical Operations
Writers	Richard P. Scott and Robert Nichols Kulik
Editor	Valerie Haynes Perry
Technical Reviewer	Mark Hall
Project Coordinator	Bill Cassel
Proofreader	Cort Day
Cover Design	Ken Roberts
Cover Illustration	Carrie English
Book Design	Laura Lamar/MAX, San Francisco
Technical Illustration	Cherie Plumlee Computer Graphics & Illustration and Steph Bradshaw
Word Processing	Howard Blechman and Cat Haglund
Page Layout	Tony Jonick, Bruce Lundquist, and M. D. Barrera
Indexer	Elinor Lindheimer

This book was produced on a Macintosh IIfx, with the following applications: FrameMaker®, Microsoft® Word, MacLink®*Plus*, Aldus® FreeHand™, Adobe Photoshop™, and Collage Plus™.

Ziff-Davis Press
5903 Christie Avenue
Emeryville, CA 94608

ISBN 1-56276-065-3
Manufactured in the United States of America
10 9 8 7 6 5

CONTENTS AT A GLANCE

TABLE OF CONTENTS

INTRODUCTION

Welcome to *PC Learning Labs Teaches Word for Windows 2.0*, a hands-on instruction book designed to help you attain a high level of Word for Windows competency in as short a time as possible. And congratulations on choosing Microsoft Word for Windows 2.0, a powerful and feature-rich program that will greatly enhance your creation and editing of written documents.

We at PC Learning Labs believe this book to be a unique and welcome addition to the ranks of "how-to" computer publications. Our instructional approach has evolved during a decade's worth of successful teaching in a hands-on classroom environment. We mix theory consistently with practice throughout; we present a topic and then immediately let you practice it in a hands-on activity. These activities use the included Data Disk, which contains over two dozen sample Word files.

When you're done working your way through this book, you will have a solid foundation of skills in the following areas of Word for Windows 2.0:

- *Documents*   The creation, editing, printing, storage, and retrieval of text documents

- *Formatting*   The modification of a document's appearance (type-styles and sizes, page layout, and so on)

- *Proofing*   The checking of documents for spelling, grammar, style, and wording errors

- *Glossaries*   The creation, modification, printing, storage, and retrieval of glossaries (Word glossaries hold frequently used text you can insert in your documents without retyping)

- *Tables*   The creation, modification, and enhancement of tables

- *Newspaper-style columns*   The creation and modification of multicolumn text

- *Graphics*   The insertion, sizing, moving, and modification of graphics (on-screen pictures)

- *Form letters*   The creation and generation of form letters

- *Templates and styles*   The use of templates and styles to simplify the creation of documents

WHO THIS BOOK IS FOR

This book was written with the beginner in mind. While experience with word processing and personal computers is certainly helpful, none is required. You should know how to turn on your computer, monitor, and printer, how to use your keyboard, and how to move your mouse. Everything beyond that will be explained in the text.

READ THIS BEFORE BEGINNING CHAPTER 1!

We strongly advise you to read through this entire Introduction before beginning Chapter 1. If, however, you are anxious to dive in, you must first work through the section below entitled "Creating Your Work Directory," as it is crucial to your successful completion of the hands-on activities in this book.

HOW TO USE THIS BOOK

This book is designed to be used as a learning guide, a review tool, and a quick reference.

AS A LEARNING GUIDE

Each chapter covers one broad topic or set of related topics. Chapters are arranged in order of increasing Word proficiency; skills you acquire in one chapter are used and elaborated on in subsequent chapters. For this reason, you should work through the chapters in successive order.

Each chapter is organized into explanatory topics and step-by-step activities. Topics provide the theoretical overview you need to master Word; activities allow you to immediately apply this understanding to specific, hands-on examples.

 AS A REVIEW TOOL

Any method of instruction is only as effective as the time and effort you are willing to invest in it. For this reason, we encourage you to regularly review the more challenging topics and activities presented in this book.

 AS A QUICK REFERENCE

General procedures (such as printing a document or copying selected text) are presented as a series of bulleted steps; you can find these bullets (•) easily by skimming through the book.

At the end of every chapter, you'll find a quick reference listing the mouse/keyboard actions needed to perform the techniques introduced in that chapter.

WHAT THIS BOOK CONTAINS

The contents of this book are divided into the following thirteen chapters:

Chapter 1   Word Basics

Chapter 2   Navigating in Word

Chapter 3   Editing Text

Chapter 4   Character Formatting

Chapter 5   Paragraph Formatting

Chapter 6   Page Formatting

Chapter 7   Proofing Your Documents

Chapter 8   Advanced Formatting and Editing Techniques

Chapter 9   Using Glossaries to Store Frequently Used Text

Chapter 10   Working with Tables

Chapter 11   Newspaper-Style Columns and Graphics

Chapter 12   Creating Form Letters

Chapter 13   Using Templates and Styles to Automate Your Work

In addition, there are four appendices:

Appendix A Installation

Appendix B Keystroke Reference

Appendix C Differences between Word 2.0 and Word 1.0

Appendix D Exchanging Documents with Other Programs

To attain full Word for Windows 2.0 fluency, you should work through all 13 chapters. The appendices are optional.

The following features of this book are designed to facilitate your learning:

- Carefully sequenced topics that build on the knowledge you've acquired from previous topics

- Frequent hands-on activities designed to sharpen your Word skills

- Numerous illustrations showing how your screen should look at key points during these activities

- The Data Disk, which contains all the files you will need to complete the activities

- A quick reference at the end of each chapter, listing in easy-to-read table form the mouse/keyboard actions you need to use the techniques introduced in the chapter

- A keystroke reference in Appendix B listing the keystroke shortcuts you need to navigate through a document and to issue commands

WHAT YOU NEED

To run Word for Windows 2.0 and complete this book, you need a computer, monitor, keyboard, and mouse. A printer is strongly recommended, but optional.

 COMPUTER AND MONITOR

You need an IBM or IBM-compatible personal computer and monitor that can run Microsoft Windows. Windows must be installed on the computer; if it is not, see a Windows reference manual for instructions. Word for Windows 2.0 must also be installed; for help, see Appendix A.

 KEYBOARD

IBM-compatible computers come with various styles of keyboards; these keyboards work in the same way, but have different layouts. Figures I.1, I.2, and I.3 show the three main keyboard styles and their key arrangements.

Figure I.1   **IBM PC–style keyboard**

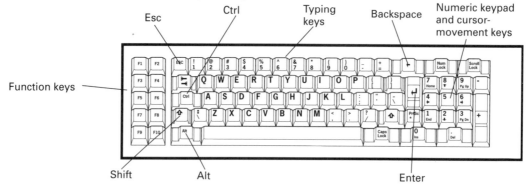

Figure I.2   **XT/AT–style keyboard**

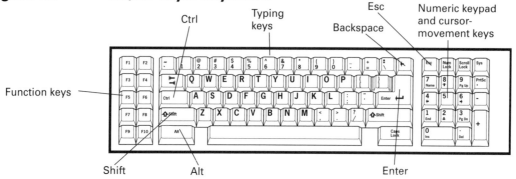

Figure I.3   **PS/2–style Enhanced Keyboard**

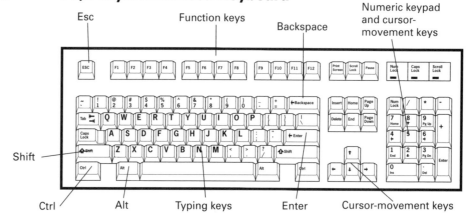

Word uses three main areas of the keyboard:

- The *function keys*, which enable you to access Word's special features. On the PC-, XT-, and AT-style keyboards, there are ten function keys on the left side of the keyboard; on the PS/2-style Enhanced Keyboard, there are 12 at the top of the keyboard.

- The *typing keys*, located in the main body of all the keyboards. These include letters, numbers, punctuation marks and in addition, the Shift, Ctrl, and Alt keys, which you will need to access several of Word's special features.

- The *numeric keypad*, which groups the numbers (the same ones found across the top row of the typing keys) for convenient numeric data entry. The numeric keypad also contains the screen-movement keys: Up, Down, Left, and Right Arrows; Home; End; Pg Up (Page Up); and Pg Dn (Page Down). To enter numeric data using the numeric keypad, *Num Lock* must be on. (Pressing the Num Lock key will toggle Num Lock on and off.) To use the screen-movement keys on the keypad, Num Lock must be off. To enter numeric data when Num Lock is off, use the number keys on the top row of the typing area.

  The Enhanced Keyboard has an additional screen-movement keypad to the left of the numeric keypad. This allows you to use the numeric keypad for numeric data entry (that is, to keep Num Lock on) and still have access to screen-movement keys.

 MOUSE

You need a mouse to work through the activities in this book. Any of the standard PC mice will do.

 PRINTER

Although you aren't required to have a printer to work through the activities, we strongly recommend it. A Postscript-type laser printer is ideal, but a non-Postscript laser or a dot-matrix printer is acceptable. For your printer to work with Word, you must select it during the Word installation procedure; for help, see Appendix A.

The printed examples shown in this book were all printed on a Postscript laser printer. Your printouts may differ somewhat, depending on which printer you are using. Printer choice also affects how text appears on your screen. If you are using a non-Postscript printer, your screen typestyles and sizes may differ from those shown in this book's figures.

If you have no printer, simply skip over the steps that involve printing. We do recommend, however, that you read through these steps to acquire some familiarity with the printing process.

CREATING YOUR WORK DIRECTORY

In the course of this book, you will be storing several Word files on your hard disk. In order to keep these files together, you need to create a *work directory* for them. A directory is like a drawer of a filing cabinet: you store a group of related files in it. Your work directory will also hold the sample files contained on the Data Disk at the back of this book.

Follow these steps to create your work directory:

1. Turn on your computer. After a brief internal self-check, your *operating environment* will automatically load. If you are in Windows, please go to step 2. If you are in DOS, please go to step 3. If you are in another (non-Windows, non-DOS) operating environment, exit from this environment to DOS and go to step 3. For help exiting to DOS, see the reference books for your operating environment.

2. Within Windows, use the mouse to move the on-screen pointer to the small box in the upper-left corner of the screen. Double-click on the dash (press the left mouse button two times in rapid succession while pointing to the dash) in this box. A box entitled *Exit Windows* will appear in the middle of the screen. Click the mouse pointer once on the OK within this box. You have now exited from Windows to DOS. Skip steps 3 through 8, and go to step 9.

3. You may see this prompt:

```
Current date is Tue 1-01-1980
Enter new date (mm-dd-yy):
```

(Your current date will be different.) If you do not see a date prompt, skip to step 6.

4. If the current date on your screen is wrong, type the correct date. Use a dash (-) to separate the month, day, and year (for example, 3-25-93).

5. Press **Enter**. After you type a command, you must press the Enter key to send this command to the computer.

6. You may see this prompt:

```
Current time is 0:25:32:56
Enter new time:
```

(Your current time will be different.) If you do not see a time prompt, skip to step 9.

7. If the current time on your screen is wrong, type the correct time. Use the format *hh:mm*. Most versions of DOS use a 24-hour clock (for example, 10:30 for 10:30 a.m., and 22:30 for 10:30 p.m.).

8. Press **Enter** to send the time you specified to the computer's internal clock.

9. The DOS prompt will appear:

```
C>
```

(Your DOS prompt may differ from this.)

10. Type **md \winword\wrkfiles**. Be sure to type backslashes (\) and not forward slashes (/), and to insert a space after the "d" in "Md," before the first backslash.

11. Press **Enter** to create your work directory, named WRKFILES. It is in this directory that you will store all the files you create during the course of this book.

12. If the message *Unable to create directory* appears, repeat steps 10 and 11; if not, skip to step 13. If the *Unable to create directory* message appears again, after you repeat steps 10 and 11, this means that your Word for Windows 2.0 program directory is not named WINWORD. (This is the name that is normally chosen when you install Word 2.0.) You'll have to issue a slightly different command to create your WRKFILES directory. Type **md \winname\wrkfiles** (leaving a space between the "d" and the first backslash), where *winname* stands for the name of your Word for Windows 2.0 program directory. For example, if your Word directory were named *winword2*, you would type *md \winword2\wrkfiles*. (For help finding out the name of your Word directory, please consult your DOS reference manuals.) Press **Enter** to create your WRKFILES work directory.

13. Insert the enclosed Data Disk (label up) into the appropriate floppy disk drive. Determine whether this is drive A or drive B. On a single floppy disk system, the drive is generally designated as A. On a double floppy disk system, the upper drive is generally designated as A and the lower as B. If you need help, refer to your computer reference books.

14. Close the drive doors, if necessary.

15. If your Word program directory is named WINWORD (if you did not get an *Unable to create directory* message in step 12), type **copy a:*.* \winword\wrkfiles** (if the Data Disk is in drive A) or type **copy b:*.* \winword\wrkfiles** (if the Data Disk is in drive B). Be sure to insert a space between the second asterisk and the first

backslash. Press **Enter** to copy all the files stored on the Data Disk to your hard disk WRKFILES directory.

16. If your Word program directory is not named WINWORD (if you got an *Unable to create directory* message), perform step 15, substituting *winname* for *winword*, where *winname* is the name of your Word for Windows 2.0 program directory.

17. A list of file names will appear one by one on the screen as the copying proceeds. If this does not occur, make sure that the floppy disk is correctly inserted, that you have chosen the correct drive (A or B), and then repeat step 15 or 16.

Please perform the following steps to ensure that your configuration (setup) of Word for Windows 2.0 matches the configuration used for the hands-on activities in this book:

1. Type **cd \windows** (don't forget the space between "d" and the backslash) and then press **Enter** to locate yourself in the disk directory that contains the Windows program.

2. Type **win** and then press **Enter** to start Windows.

3. When Windows appears, look for an on-screen item entitled *Word for Windows 2.0*. If this item is an icon (a small box about .5" square), continue with step 4 below. If the item is a window (a larger, framed box with icons inside it), continue with step 5.

4. Use your mouse to move the on-screen pointer to the **Word for Windows 2.0** icon. Double-click (press the **left mouse button** two times in rapid succession) on the icon to turn it into a window.

5. Move the mouse pointer to the **Microsoft Word** icon, and double-click (press the **left mouse button** two times in rapid succession) on the icon. The Word program is loaded into memory, and a blank document appears on-screen.

6. Press the **F5** key and quickly observe the screen. If a box entitled *Help for WordPerfect Users* appears, continue with step 7. If not, press **Esc** and skip to step 10.

7. Wait a few seconds for the *Help for WordPerfect Users* box to disappear. A smaller box entitle *List* appears in its place. Press the **Esc** key to remove this box from the screen. Click on **Tools** (in the menu bar), and then click on **Options** (in the drop-down Tools list). A box entitles *Options* appears.

8. Click on the **General** icon in the Category section on the left side of the options box. Observe the *WordPerfect Help* and *WordPerfect Document Navigation Keys* options. If either of these options is selected (that is, if the box to the left of the option name contains an X), click on the option box to deselect it (to remove the X). Both options must be deselected before you begin the hands-on activities in this book.

9. Click on **OK** to accept your changes.

10. Click on **File** (in the menu bar), and then click on **Exit** to exit from Word to DOS.

CONVENTIONS USED IN THIS BOOK

The conventions used in this book are designed to help you learn Word easily and efficiently. Each chapter begins with a short introduction and ends with a summary that includes a quick-reference guide to the techniques introduced in the chapter. Main chapter topics (shown in large, capitalized headings) and subtopics (headings preceded by a three-dimensional cube) explain the theory behind Word features. Hands-on activities allow you to practice these features in realistic word-processing situations.

To help you distinguish between steps presented for your general knowledge and steps you should carry out at your computer as you read, we have adopted the following system:

- A bulleted step, like this, is provided for your information and reference only.

1. A numbered step, like this, indicates one in series of steps that you should carry out in sequence at your computer.

In these activities, menu choices, keystrokes, and anything you are asked to type are all presented in boldface. Here's an example from Chapter 2:

4. Click on **Edit** to display the drop-down Edit menu.

Activities follow a *cause-and-effect* approach. Each step tells you what to do (cause) and then what will happen (effect). From the example above,

- Cause: Click on Edit.

- Effect: The drop-down Edit menu is displayed.

A plus sign (+) is used with the Shift, Ctrl, and Alt keys to denote a multi-key keystroke. For example, *press Shift+F7* means, "Press and hold down the Shift key, then press the function key F7, then release both."

BEFORE YOU START

The activities in each of the following chapters are designed to proceed sequentially. In many cases, you cannot perform an activity until you have performed one or more of the activities directly preceding it. For this reason, we recommend that you allot enough time to work through an entire chapter in each session.

You are now ready to begin. Good learning and... *bon voyage!*

CHAPTER ONE: WORD BASICS

To help you distinguish between steps presented for your general knowledge and steps you should carry out at your computer as you read, we have adopted the following system:

- A bulleted step, like this, is provided for your information and reference only.

1. A numbered step, like this, indicates one in a series of steps that you should carry out in sequence at your computer.

Welcome to Word for Windows 2.0 and the exciting world of word processing! From here on we'll refer to Word for Windows 2.0 simply as Word. In this first chapter, we'll lead you through one complete Word work session; you'll start the Word program, create and edit a document, save and print this document, create and save a new document, and finally exit Word. This, in a nutshell, is the procedure you'll use in your day-to-day word processing work with Word.

When you're done working through this chapter, you will know

- How to start Word

- How to enter text

- How to insert, delete, and replace text

- How to save and name a document

- How to print and close a document

- How to create a new document

- How to exit Word

INTRODUCTION TO WORD

A *word processor* (such as Word) is a computer program or application that enables you to create, edit, print, and save documents for future retrieval and revision. (The terms *program* and *application* are synonymous.) You enter text into the computer using a keyboard. As you type, your words are displayed on a *monitor*, or screen, and are stored in computer memory rather than on paper.

One of the chief advantages of a word processor over a conventional typewriter is that a word processor enables you to make changes to a document without retyping the entire document. For example, you can create a letter in a word processor and then, after you are finished, go back and change margins, add sentences, delete words, move paragraphs, correct spelling errors, and so on. All of this is done without retyping the original text.

 STARTING WORD

To start Word, you must load the program from your hard disk into computer memory. Word will remain in memory for as long as you continue running it, as will any documents you are currently working on. When you exit Word, it will remove itself from memory, thus freeing space for other programs to use.

Let's begin. As the name implies, Word for Windows 2.0 runs in the Microsoft Windows environment; this means that you have to start Windows before you can start Word.

Note: If you did not complete the activity in the "Creating Your Work Directory" section of the Introduction, please do so now. Otherwise, you will not be able to perform the tasks in this book.

Follow these steps to start Word:

1. Turn on your computer; your operating environment will automatically load. If you are already in Windows, you may skip steps 2 through 7 and continue with step 8. If you are in DOS, you should continue with step 2. If you are in another operating environment (DOS Shell or GeoWorks, for example), exit to DOS and continue with step 2. For help with exiting to DOS, see your operating environment's reference manuals.

2. Next, you may be prompted for the current date; if not, skip to step 4. If the date is incorrect, type today's date. Use the format *mm-dd-yy* or *mm/dd/yy* (for example, 10/18/91 or 10-18-91).

3. Press **Enter**. Remember that the Enter key must be pressed to send a command to your computer.

4. You may then be prompted for the current time; if not, skip to step 6. If the time is incorrect, type the current time. Use the 24-hour format *hh:mm* (for example, 10:30 for 10:30 a.m. and 22:30 for 10:30 p.m.).

5. Press **Enter** to set the computer's internal clock.

6. Type **win** and then press **Enter** to start Windows.

7. When Windows is loaded, look for an on-screen object entitled *Word for Windows 2.0*. If this object is an icon (a small box about .5" square), continue with step 8. If this object is a window (a larger, framed box with icons inside of it), continue with step 9.

8. Use your mouse to move the on-screen pointer to the **Word for Windows 2.0** icon. Double-click (press the **left mouse button** two times in rapid succession) on the icon to turn it into a window.

9. Move the mouse pointer to the **Microsoft Word** icon and double-click (press the **left mouse button** two times in rapid succession) on the icon. The Word program is now loaded into memory and a blank document window appears on-screen (see Figure 1.1). Document windows are discussed in the next section.

Figure 1.1 **Word upon startup**

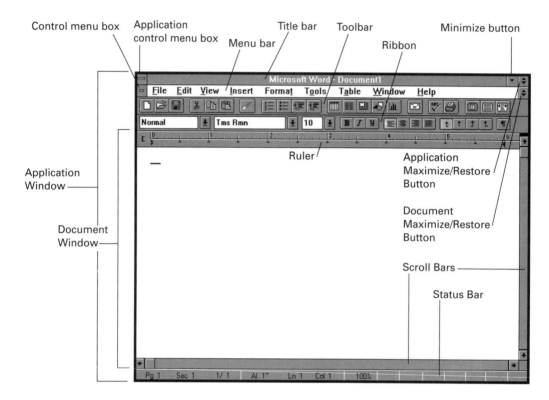

Word is a user-customizable program. Users can specify, for example, whether certain on-screen icons are to be displayed or hidden. To ensure that your Word screens and the screens in this book's figures look alike, please do the following:

1. Move the mouse pointer to the word **View** near the top of your screen, and then click the mouse button (press and release the **left mouse button** once). A list of View options appears.

2. Observe the options Toolbar, Ribbon, and Ruler. They should all be selected (preceded by a check). If any of these options is not checked, move the mouse pointer to the option and click on it. Once all the options are checked, click the mouse pointer on the word **View** to remove the View options from the screen.

THE WORD APPLICATION AND DOCUMENT WINDOWS

Word is structured around a set of *interactive windows*—rectangular, on-screen boxes in which information is passed between the user (you) and the program (Word). When you start Word, two windows appear on the screen, one within the other. The larger of these, called the *application window*, frames the entire screen; you use it to communicate with the Word program. (Remember, the terms program and application can be used interchangeably.) The smaller window, called the *document window*, fits seamlessly within the application window; you use it to create and edit your Word documents.

Table 1.1 defines the screen elements with which you need to be familiar when using Word. (Figure 1.1 illustrates where each of these elements is located.)

Table 1.1   **Word Screen Elements**

Term	Definition
Application window	The larger of the two start-up windows; it provides an interface between the user and Word
Document window	The smaller of the two start-up windows; it holds the currently active Word document
Control menu boxes	Located in the upper-left corner of the screen; they control the size and position of the application window (upper box) and document window (lower box)
Title bar	Located at the top of the screen, it displays the name of the application (Microsoft Word) and document (Document1, in this case)
Maximize/ Restore buttons	Located in the upper-right corner of the screen, they control the size of the application window (upper box) and document window (lower box)
Minimize button	Located to the left of the application Maximize/ Restore button, it reduces the application window to an icon

Term	Definition
Menu bar	Located below the title bar; it lists the Word menu options
Toolbar	Located below the menu bar; it provides quick access to Word's most frequently used commands and utilities
Ribbon	Located below the toolbar; it provides quick access to Word's most frequently used formatting commands
Ruler	Located below the ribbon; it provides ongoing page measurement as well as quick access to margins, tabs, and indents
Scroll bars	Located along the right side and bottom of the document window; they are used to display different areas of the active document (each scroll bar contains directional scroll boxes denoted by arrows)
Status bar	Located along the bottom of the screen, it displays a variety of information relating to the active document

Let's take a closer look at some of these screen elements. (The remaining elements will be discussed in detail over the next few chapters.)

1. Use the mouse to move the on-screen pointer to the **Control menu box** of the application window (the higher of the two boxes containing a horizontal bar in the upper-left corner of your screen). Click the mouse (press and release the **left mouse button** once) to open the box; do not double-click, as this would cause you to exit Word. Note the Control menu box options: Restore, Move, Size, Minimize, and so on. Click on the **Control menu box** again to close the box.

2. Use the mouse to move the on-screen pointer to the **Control menu box** of the document window (the lower of the two boxes in the upper-left corner of the screen). Note the similarities in document and application window Control menu box options.

3. Use the mouse to point to the application window **Maximize/ Restore button** (the higher of the two boxes containing an up/ down indicator in the upper-right corner of the screen). Click the mouse to *restore* (shrink) the application window; an inch of space appears at the bottom of the screen. Note that the Maximize/Restore button now contains an up indicator alone, indicating that its function is to maximize (rather than restore) the window. Click on the Maximize/Restore button again to remaximize the application window.

4. Repeat step 3, substituting the document Maximize/Restore button (the lower of the two boxes in the upper-right corner of the screen) for the application Maximize/Restore button. Note that when you click on the document Maximize/Restore button the first time, the button moves to the upper-right corner of the restored (shrunk) document window; this is the button you click on to maximize the window. Note also that when the document window is restored, it gets its own title bar.

USING THE MENU BAR TO ISSUE COMMANDS

In order to perform your daily word processing tasks (such as retrieving a document from disk, setting new margins, and so on), you must issue the appropriate Word commands. You can do this by

- Using the mouse to choose the command from the menu bar

- Using the mouse to choose the command from the toolbar, ribbon, or ruler

- Using the keyboard to enter a command keystroke

For example, to print a document, you could

- Choose the *Print* command from the File option on the menu bar

- Click on the *toolbar* Print button

- Press *Ctrl+Shift+F12* from your keyboard (press and hold the Ctrl key, press and hold the Shift key, press the F12 key, then release all three keys)

Please do not perform any of these actions now.

The menu bar is the only method that allows you to issue every available Word command. The toolbar, ribbon, and ruler provide a subset of the most frequently used commands, as does the keyboard. For this reason, we'll begin our exploration of Word commands by using the menu-bar approach.

Let's issue some commands using the menu bar:

1. Move the mouse pointer to the **File** option on the menu bar, then press and hold down the **left mouse button**. (Do not release this button until indicated in step 4.) The File menu drops down, displaying a set of file-related commands: New, Open, Close, Save, Save As, and so on.

2. Observe the text in the status bar at the bottom of your screen. Word displays a brief description of the currently selected item—in this case, the File menu.

3. Without releasing the button, drag the mouse pointer down to highlight the **Save As** command. (When you *highlight* an item in Word, the item is displayed in inverse video.) The status bar now displays a brief description of the File, Save As command.

4. Release the mouse button to open the Save As dialog box (see Figure 1.2). *Dialog boxes* prompt you to enter information relating to the selected command (File, Save As, in this case). You will work extensively with dialog boxes during the course of this book.

5. Click the mouse pointer on the **Cancel** button in the upper-right corner of the Save As dialog box to close the box.

6. Click on the **Edit** option of the menu bar. The Edit menu drops down, displaying Word's editing commands. Note that you can either press and hold the mouse button (as in steps 1 through 4), or press and release (click) the button to display a drop-down menu.

7. Observe that several Edit commands are *dimmed* (Cut, Copy, Paste, Paste Special, and so on). Word dims menu commands to show that they are unavailable in the current context. For example, the Copy command is dimmed because you have not selected any text to copy. (You'll learn how to select text later in this chapter under "Editing a Document.")

8. Observe also that several commands are followed by ellipses (Find..., Replace..., Go To..., and so on). Word appends ellipses to menu commands that display dialog boxes. To keep this book easy to read, we chose not to print ellipses

when referencing these commands. For example, in step 3 of this listing, we ask you to drag the mouse pointer to the *Save As* command, though *Save As...* is how the command actually appears on your screen.

9. Click on **Edit** again to close the Edit menu.

Figure 1.2   **The Save As dialog box**

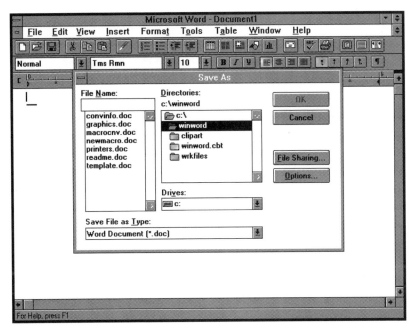

THE BASICS OF ENTERING TEXT

Word is a *WYSIWYG* (What-You-See-Is-What-You-Get) word processor; the screen shows you how the text will look when you print your document. Most users prefer WYSIWYG programs because they remove the arcane codes and inaccurate page layouts that plague non-WYSIWYG programs. Word's WYSIWYG feature encourages you to work in a "visual-intuitive" style in which you treat the word processor as a computerized extension of a typewriter.

In the next several sections, we'll discuss the basics of entering text in a Word document.

THE TEXT AREA

When you start Word, a new document window automatically appears, providing you with a blank area for typing called the *text area*. Word assumes certain settings for margins, page length, line spacing, tab stops, and several other document attributes. Because of these assumptions, called *defaults*, you can begin to type immediately, without first having to specify any of the settings yourself.

As you type, characters are inserted in front of a blinking vertical bar called the *insertion point*. To change the location of the insertion point, you simply click the mouse pointer at the desired place in the text.

Let's examine Word's text area (see Figure 1.3):

Figure 1.3   **The text area**

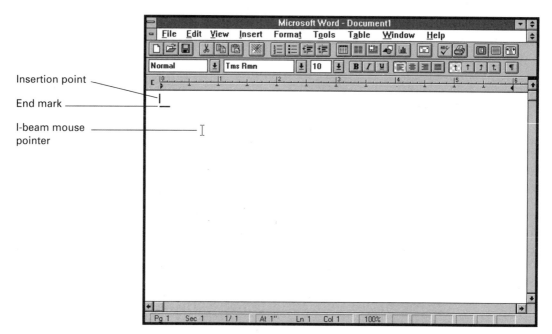

1. Observe the **insertion point** (the blinking vertical bar). Its location determines where the next character you type will be entered into your document. Note that the insertion point of a

new document always appears in the upper-left corner (that is, at the beginning) of the document window.

2. Observe the **end mark**. This is the broad horizontal line that indicates the end of the document. The end mark cannot be formatted or deleted (erased) and you cannot place the insertion point beyond it.

3. Observe the **mouse pointer**. The pointer changes to an *I-beam* (see Figure 1.3) when it is within the text area. When moved outside the text area, it becomes an arrow. Take a moment to verify this.

WORD-WRAP AND THE ENTER KEY

The Enter key on your keyboard is analogous to the Return key on a typewriter. When using a typewriter, you need to hit the Return key whenever you want to end a line. In word processing, when a word does not fit on a line, it automatically flows to the beginning of the next line. This feature is called *word-wrap*. However, you *do* need to press Enter to accomplish the following:

- End a short line (one that does not extend to the right margin)

- End a paragraph

- Create a blank line

Let's type some text in our new document window and practice using the Enter key. (Word-wrap will be demonstrated under "Using the Backspace Key to Delete Text," later in this chapter.)

1. Observe the **status bar**. The vertical page position measurement (*At*) and the line number (*Ln*) reflect the current position of the insertion point.

2. Type **Nancy Wright** to enter the characters at the insertion point and then press **Enter** to end the line. Note that the status bar At and Ln indicators show the new insertion point position.

3. Type **3325 Fillmore Avenue** and then press **Enter**.

4. Type **North Hills, NY 14052** and then press **Enter**.

5. Press **Enter** to create a blank line.

6. Type **Dear Janet:** and then press **Enter** twice to end the line and create one blank line. Your screen should now match Figure 1.4.

Figure 1.4   **Entering text in a document**

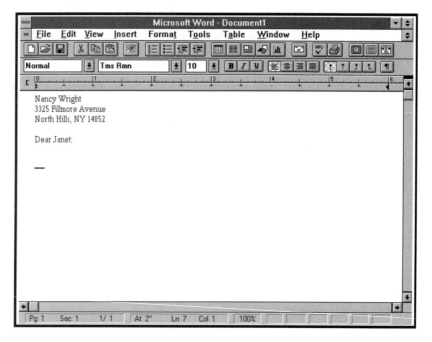

NONPRINTING CHARACTERS

You can choose to have Word display a number of special characters on the screen that show the places in the text where you pressed the spacebar, or the Enter and Tab keys. These *nonprinting characters* (so called because they do not appear on paper when you print the document) are often useful to see. This is particularly true when you are working with heavily formatted documents and need to keep track of your tabs, spaces, blank lines, and so on.

To display Word's nonprinting characters you will click on the Show/Hide button in the ribbon.

Let's display the nonprinting characters of your active document:

1. Examine the screen. Each line of text is short, not reaching the right margin. Note that there are no characters marking the ends of these lines.

2. Click on the **Show/Hide** button to display Word's special formatting characters; the Show/Hide button is the rightmost button in the ribbon, identified by a paragraph mark (¶).

3. Examine the screen. Each time you pressed Enter, Word placed a paragraph mark (¶) in the document. Each time you pressed the spacebar, Word placed a space mark (·) in the document. These nonprinting characters only appear on the screen when the Show/Hide button is set to Show; they will not appear on your printed document.

USING THE TAB KEY TO ALIGN TEXT HORIZONTALLY

Tabs enable you to align text horizontally. These lines are properly aligned:

Line 1 ....

Line 2 ....

These are not:

Line 1 ....

  Line 2 ....

Pressing the Tab key moves the insertion point to the next tab stop to the right. *Tab stops* are fixed horizontal positions within a line. By default, Word's tab stops are set at .5" increments. Pressing Tab once moves the insertion point .5" to the right; pressing Tab again moves it another .5", for a total of 1" (.5" + .5") from the left margin; and so on. (We created the properly aligned example just shown by pressing Tab once at the beginning of each line. We created the improperly aligned example by using the spacebar to insert blank spaces at the beginning of each line.)

USING THE BACKSPACE KEY TO DELETE TEXT

You can use the Backspace key to delete text one character at a time. Simply press Backspace to delete the single character immediately to the left of the insertion point.

Let's experiment with Word's Tab, Backspace, and word-wrap features:

1. Press **Tab** to insert a tab at the beginning of the line. This moves the insertion point to the first tab stop, .5" to the right. Note that Word displays the tab mark (→), since Show/Hide is still set to Show from our last exercise. As with the paragraph and space marks, this tab mark will not appear on the printed page.

2. Press **Tab** again to insert another tab. This moves the insertion point to the second tab stop, 1" from the left margin.

3. Press **Backspace** to remove the second tab character.

4. Type **I have been happy with the service provided by Global Travel**. (Include the period.) Then press the **spacebar** to insert a space before the next sentence.

5. Type **I would like additional information** and then examine the screen. Notice that the word *information* automatically wraps to the next line, even though you did not press Enter. This is an example of word-wrap.

6. Complete the paragraph as shown in Figure 1.5. When you've typed the last period, press **Enter** twice to end the paragraph and add one blank line.

PRACTICE YOUR SKILLS

Complete the entire letter as shown in Figure 1.5.

EDITING A DOCUMENT

As mentioned in the Introduction to this chapter, one of the strongest arguments for switching from a typewriter to a word processor is the greatly increased ease of editing your documents. In the time it would take you just to pencil in your desired changes to a typewritten document (without actually retyping it), you could incorporate these changes into a word-processed document, print it out, and save it on a hard or floppy disk for future revision.

In the next several sections, we'll discuss the rudiments of text editing in Word.

Figure 1.5 **Completed letter in Show mode**

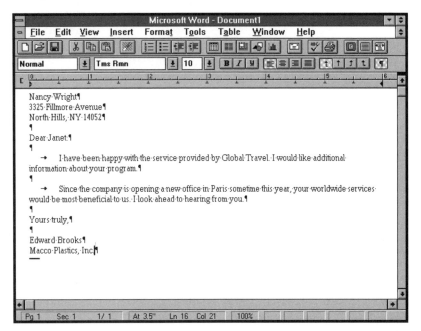

INSERTING TEXT

By default, Word runs in *insert mode*; as you type, text to the right of the insertion point is pushed further to the right to make room for your new text. Inserting text in a document requires two basic steps:

- Placing the insertion point (use the mouse to position the I-beam and click) where you want to add text

- Typing the new text

Let's practice inserting text in a document:

1. Point to the left of the *p* in *program*, which is located in the second sentence of the paragraph beginning with *I have*. Click the mouse button to place the insertion point directly before the *p* in *program*. (Do not place the insertion point before the space preceding the *p*.) This is where you will insert your new text.

2. Type **corporate travel** and press the **spacebar**. Note that the existing text is pushed to the right of the inserted text.

SELECTING TEXT

It is often easier to work with a block of text rather than with a single character. For example, if you needed to underline a sentence in a paragraph, you would not want to underline each and every character separately (a multistep, tedious task); rather, you would want to underline the entire sentence at once (a single-step, straight-forward task).

In order to work with a block of text, you must first *select* it. In the next exercise (in the section "Deleting Text") you'll select text using the following method:

• Point to the first (or final) character of the text to be selected

• Press and hold the mouse button

• Drag across the text to the final (or first) character to be selected

• Release the mouse button

Note: As just indicated, you can select text downward (from the first to the last character) or upward (from the last to the first character). Both methods are equally effective; use whichever you feel more comfortable with.

DELETING TEXT

As you know, Backspace deletes the character to the *left* of the insertion point. To delete the character immediately to the *right* of the insertion point, press the Del key on the numeric keypad. If you have a PS/2-style *Enhanced Keyboard*, you may press the Delete key on the auxiliary keypad to the left of the numeric keypad. Pressing either of these keys has the identical effect on the text being deleted.

Note: If you intend to use the numeric keypad Del key to perform your deletions, make sure that Num Lock is off (press the Num Lock key until the light goes out). If Num Lock is on, Del functions as a decimal point key; when you press it, Word displays a period (.) on the screen instead of performing the deletion.

To delete a block of selected text

• Select the text

• Press *Del* (or *Delete*)

Let's begin by deleting text one character at a time:

1. Place the insertion point directly to the left of the *A* in *Avenue*, which is located in the heading at the top of the page.

2. Press **Del** (or **Delete**) six times to delete the word *Avenue*. (To keep things simple, we'll only mention the Del key from here on. Feel free, however, to use the Delete key instead, if you wish.)

3. Type **Circle**.

4. Place the insertion point to the right of the *y* in *happy,* located in the paragraph beginning with *I have.*

5. Press **Backspace** five times to delete the word *happy.*

6. Type **very pleased**.

Now let's delete a block (in this case, a single word) of selected text:

1. Point to the left of the *m* in *most* in the first sentence of the paragraph beginning *Since the company.*

2. Press and hold the mouse button. Then drag over **most** and the *trailing space* (the space that follows the *t* of *most*) to select the text. Do not select the space before *most.*

3. Release the mouse button.

4. Press **Del** to delete the selected text.

REPLACING TEXT

You already learned how to insert new text within a document. At times, however, you may want to replace existing text with new text. For example, you may want to replace the standard letter salutation *Dear Sir or Madam* with *To Whom It May Concern*. One way you can do this is by inserting the new text and then deleting the old text. This, however, doubles your work and can grow very tiresome, particularly when you are replacing many blocks of text. Fortunately, Word provides a more convenient solution.

Replacing existing text with new text requires two steps:

• Select the text to be replaced

• Type the new text

Let's use this technique to replace some text in our letter:

1. Select the name **Janet** in the salutation *Dear Janet:*.

2. Type **Nancy** to replace *Janet* with *Nancy*.

PRACTICE YOUR SKILLS

Make additional corrections to our letter, referring to Figures 1.6 and 1.7.

Note: Replacement text in Figure 1.6 (such as **Circle** or **Nancy**) is bold for emphasis only. Do not enter this text in bold. You'll learn about bold formatting in Chapter 4.

1. Delete *the* (in the paragraph *Since the company*). Then type **our**.

2. Delete *ahead* (in the paragraph *Since our company*). Then type **forward**.

3. Delete *Yours truly* in the closing, then type **Sincerely**.

4. Check your work against Figure 1.7.

SAVING A DOCUMENT IN A DISK FILE

Before it is saved, a document exists only in computer memory, a temporary storage area. For permanent storage, you must save the document in a disk file (hard or floppy). Word has two commands that are used to save disk files: File, Save As and File, Save.

THE FILE, SAVE AS COMMAND

You use the File, Save As command to save a disk file for the first time, to save a disk file with a new name, or to save a disk file in a different location (on another disk or in a different directory).

To save a disk file using File, Save As

• Choose *File, Save As* (that is, choose the Save As command from the File menu) to open the Save As dialog box

• In the Drives and Directories list boxes, select the location (drive and directory) in which you wish to save the disk file, if this location is not already selected

• In the File Name text box, type the name of the file

Figure 1.6   **Corrections to letter**

Nancy Wright
3325 Fillmore ~~Avenue~~ **Circle**
North Hills, NY 14052

Dear ~~Janet~~ **Nancy**:

I have been ~~happy~~ **very pleased** with the service provided by Global Travel. I would like additional information about your **corporate travel** program.

Since ~~the~~ **our** company is opening a new office in Paris sometime this year, your worldwide services would be ~~most~~ beneficial to us. I look ~~ahead~~ **forward** to hearing from you.

~~Yours truly,~~ **Sincerely,**

Edward Brooks
Macco Plastics, Inc.

Figure 1.7   **Final (corrected) letter**

Nancy Wright
3325 Fillmore Circle
North Hills, NY 14052

Dear Nancy:

    I have been very pleased with the service provided by Global Travel. I would like additional information about your corporate travel program.

    Since our company is opening a new office in Paris sometime this year, your worldwide services would be beneficial to us. I look forward to hearing from you.

Sincerely,

Edward Brooks
Macco Plastics, Inc.

- Click on *OK*

- If desired, fill in the Summary Info dialog box

- Click on *OK*

When you save a disk file, Word adds the .DOC file-name extension to identify the file as a document file.

Note: Your hard disk or floppy disks can hold many other types of files, such as .EXE program files, .NUM spreadsheet files, .DBF database files, and so on. Do not add the .DOC (or any other) extension yourself; let Word do it automatically.

THE FILE, SAVE COMMAND

You use the File, Save command (rather than File, Save As) to save a disk file with its current name and in its current location. File, Save *updates* a disk file; it replaces the last-saved version of the disk file with the new version of the document on your screen. For example, let's say you'd used File, Save As to save a business report to your reports directory as REPORT1, and then you'd gone back and revised the report by adding an extra closing paragraph. If you then chose File, Save, the new (extra paragraph) report version would replace the last-saved (no extra paragraph) version on the disk. Once you've used File, Save As to name and save a disk file, you should generally use File, Save for all subsequent updates of that disk file. However, if you later want to rename it or save it in a different location, you should use File, Save As.

It's very important to save your active documents as disk files frequently. That way, if something happens to the disk file in memory (for example, a power failure, which erases the contents of computer memory), you will have a recent copy of the document safe on the disk. This precaution will keep retyping to a minimum.

General rules for saving are

- Save at least once every 15 minutes

- Save before printing

- Save before spell-checking

NAMING A DOCUMENT

When you save a disk file for the first time, you must name it. Follow these guidelines when naming disk files

- A file name can contain from one to eight letters, numbers, or the following special characters: (! @ # $ % ( ) - { } ' ~)

- A file name cannot contain spaces

- A file name should be descriptive so that you can remember the file's contents (for example, JANREPT rather than X117-A)

SUMMARY INFO

The first time you save a new disk file, Word displays a Summary Info dialog box. This box prompts you for supplementary information about the disk file, including the subject, author, keywords, comments, and a descriptive title. Summary Info allows for great detail in describing a disk file; you can enter up to 255 characters for each information category. You can also choose to skip any, or all, of these categories. Summary Info is especially useful for keeping track of author names and for storing comments and notes relating to a document.

Let's save the active document as a disk file:

1. Choose **File, Save As** (click on **File** and then click on **Save As**) to open the Save As dialog box.

2. Double-click on **wrkfiles** in the Directories list box to select the WRKFILES directory. This is the work directory you created in the Introduction; it is here that you will store and retrieve all of the disk files you work with in this book.

3. Click the mouse pointer in the File Name text box and type **mychap1a** to name the document **MYCHAP1A** (capitalization is not important when you type document names). Your screen should now look like Figure 1.8.

4. Click on **OK** to save the document as a disk file.

5. Observe the **Summary Info** dialog box. As mentioned earlier, this box appears the first time you save a new document.

Figure 1.8   **Saving MYCHAP1A to the WRKFILES directory**

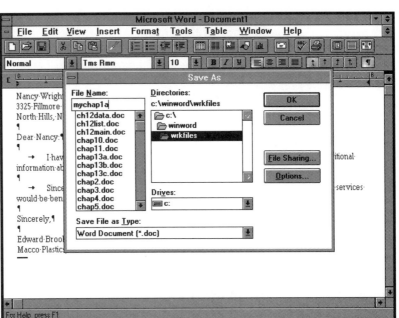

6. In the Title text box, type **My first document**. (You can enter spaces in a Summary Info text box.) Then press **Tab** twice to move down and select the text in the Author text box. Type your name to replace the selected text.

Note: During the installation of Word you are asked to enter your name. The name that you entered is displayed in the Author text box, so you may or may not need to change this text based on the contents of the box.

7. Click on **OK** to finish saving the disk file.

8. Observe the **title bar**. It has changed to display the document's name, MYCHAP1A.DOC. (As mentioned in a previous Note, when you save a disk file, Word automatically adds the extension .DOC to its name.)

PRINTING A DOCUMENT

When you're ready to print your document, Word is set up to print one copy of the entire document by default. You can, however, choose to print the current page, multiple pages, multiple copies, or selected text. You can also print to a disk file rather than to a printer, or print nondocument items such as Summary Info. (These print options will be discussed in Chapter 6.)

To print the active document

- Choose *File, Print*
- Select any desired options from the Print dialog box
- Click on *OK* to print the document

Now let's print MYCHAP1A.DOC:

1. Choose **File, Print** to open the Print dialog box (see Figure 1.9).

Figure 1.9   **The Print dialog box**

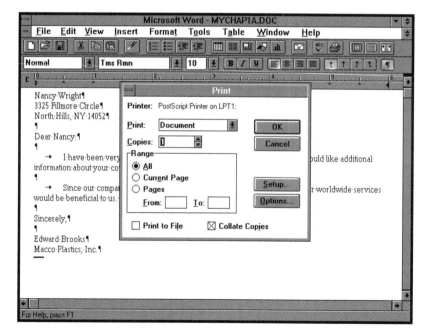

2. Click on **OK** to print the document. (Or, if you do not have a printer, click on **Cancel** to cancel the print command and return to your document.) Compare your printout with Figure 1.7. Depending on the printer you are using, your printout may vary slightly from the one depicted in the figure.

3. If your document failed to print, make sure your printer is on-line, then repeat step 1. If it still won't print, refer to Appendix A for help with selecting your printer.

CLOSING A DOCUMENT

When you're finished working with a document—that is, after you've completed, saved, and (if desired) printed it—you should close the document window. To do this, choose File, Close (or double-click on the document Control menu box).

Let's close MYCHAP1A.DOC, since we've saved and printed it:

1. Choose **File, Close** to close the document and remove it from memory.

2. Observe the screen. Word remains loaded, but there is no active document. The title bar displays only *Microsoft Word*; the menu bar contains only the File and Help choices; and the ruler and scroll bars have disappeared.

CREATING A NEW DOCUMENT

After you've closed the active document, you're ready to create a new document. To do this

- Choose *File, New*
- Click on *OK*

Word will open a new, blank document window.

Let's create a new document:

1. Choose **File, New** and then click on **OK** to open a new, blank document window.

2. Type **This is my second document**.

3. Choose **File, Save As** to open the Save As dialog box.

4. Type **mychap1b** to name the document. Note that the desired directory (WRKFILES) is still selected; Word remembered it from the last time you chose it.

5. Observe that the OK button has a dark border. This means that OK is the *default button*. To choose a default button, you simply press Enter. Do this now; press **Enter** as an alternative to clicking on OK.

6. Press **Enter** again (or click on **OK**) to bypass the Summary Info dialog box.

Let's view the default Summary Info for the document you just created:

1. Choose **File, Summary Info** to open the Summary Info dialog box.

2. Click on **Statistics** to open the Document Statistics dialog box. Observe the document statistics.

3. Click on **OK** to close the Document Statistics dialog box.

4. Click on **OK** to close the Summary Info dialog box.

5. Double-click on the document **Control menu box** (the lower of the two boxes in the upper-left corner of the screen) to close the document. Do not double-click on the application Control menu box (the higher of the two boxes), as this would cause you to exit Word. You can choose File, Close or you can double-click on the Control menu box to close a document window.

EXITING WORD

Your final step of every Word session is to exit Word. Never turn off your computer before doing so, as this could result in the loss of one or more documents. To exit Word and return to the Windows Program Manager, choose File, Exit.

As a safeguard, if you have not saved the latest version of an active document, Word will prompt you to do so before exiting.

Let's exit Word. Choose **File, Exit**. The Word application and document windows disappear, and the Windows Program Manager is displayed.

PRACTICE YOUR SKILLS

You've learned a great deal in this first chapter. The following two activities allow you to apply this knowledge to practical word-processing tasks. Please don't think of these activities as tests, but rather as opportunities to hone your Word skills. It is only through repetition that you'll internalize the techniques you've learned.

In this activity, you will create and edit the document shown in two different stages in Figures 1.10 and 1.11. Then you'll produce the final document shown in Figure 1.12.

1. Start Word.

2. Enter the text shown in Figure 1.10. (Where the text *(today's date)* appears in Figure 1.10, enter the current date.)

3. Edit the letter as shown in Figure 1.11.

4. Save the document (as a disk file) to your WRKFILES directory under the name **myprac1a**. Bypass Summary Info.

5. Print the document and compare the results to Figure 1.12.

6. Close the document window.

In the next activity, you will create and edit the document shown in two stages in Figures 1.13 and 1.14 to produce the final document shown in Figure 1.15.

1. Open a new document window.

2. Enter the text shown in Figure 1.13.

3. Edit the letter as shown in Figure 1.14.

4. Save the document (as a disk file) to your WRKFILES directory under the name **myprac1b**. Bypass Summary Info.

5. Print the document and compare the results to Figure 1.15.

6. Close the document window.

7. Exit Word.

SUMMARY

In this chapter, you learned the basics of the document creation-revision-saving-printing cycle, a procedure you'll use frequently in

Figure 1.10   The first draft of MYPRAC1A.DOC

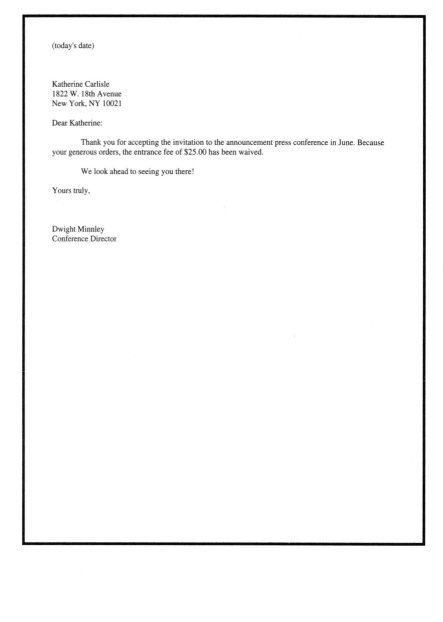

(today's date)

Katherine Carlisle
1822 W. 18th Avenue
New York, NY 10021

Dear Katherine:

     Thank you for accepting the invitation to the announcement press conference in June. Because your generous orders, the entrance fee of $25.00 has been waived.

     We look ahead to seeing you there!

Yours truly,

Dwight Minnley
Conference Director

Figure 1.11   **Editing MYPRAC1A.DOC**

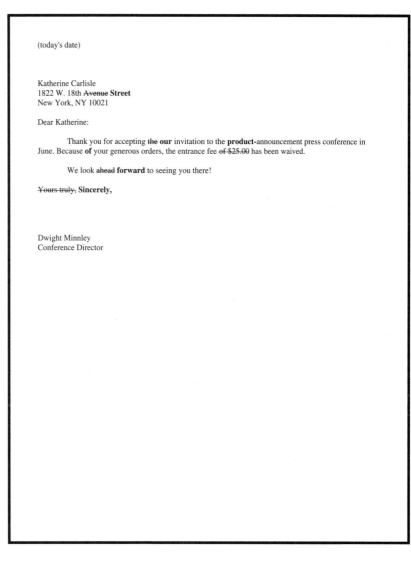

(today's date)

Katherine Carlisle
1822 W. 18th ~~Avenue~~ **Street**
New York, NY 10021

Dear Katherine:

      Thank you for accepting ~~the~~ **our** invitation to the **product**-announcement press conference in June. Because **of** your generous orders, the entrance fee ~~of $25.00~~ has been waived.

      We look ~~ahead~~ **forward** to seeing you there!

~~Yours truly,~~ **Sincerely,**

Dwight Minnley
Conference Director

Figure 1.12   **The corrected MYPRAC1A.DOC**

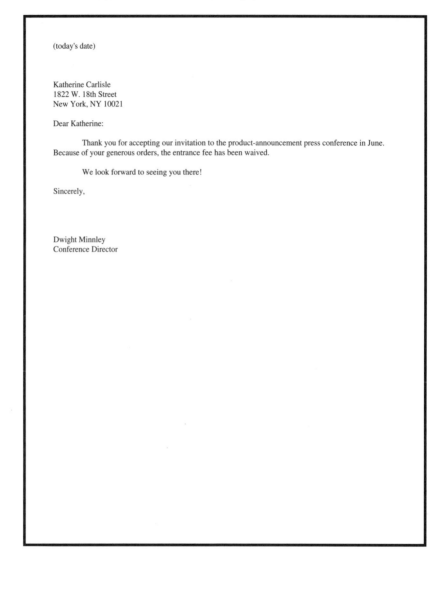

(today's date)

Katherine Carlisle
1822 W. 18th Street
New York, NY 10021

Dear Katherine:

      Thank you for accepting our invitation to the product-announcement press conference in June.
Because of your generous orders, the entrance fee has been waived.

      We look forward to seeing you there!

Sincerely,

Dwight Minnley
Conference Director

Figure 1.13   **The first draft of MYPRAC1B.DOC**

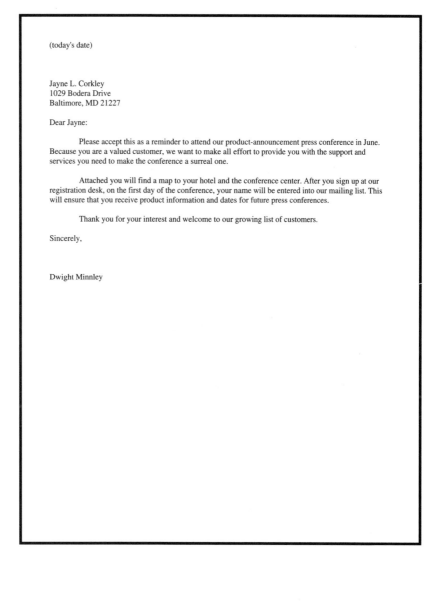

(today's date)

Jayne L. Corkley
1029 Bodera Drive
Baltimore, MD 21227

Dear Jayne:

Please accept this as a reminder to attend our product-announcement press conference in June. Because you are a valued customer, we want to make all effort to provide you with the support and services you need to make the conference a surreal one.

Attached you will find a map to your hotel and the conference center. After you sign up at our registration desk, on the first day of the conference, your name will be entered into our mailing list. This will ensure that you receive product information and dates for future press conferences.

Thank you for your interest and welcome to our growing list of customers.

Sincerely,

Dwight Minnley

Figure 1.14   **Editing MYPRAC1B.DOC**

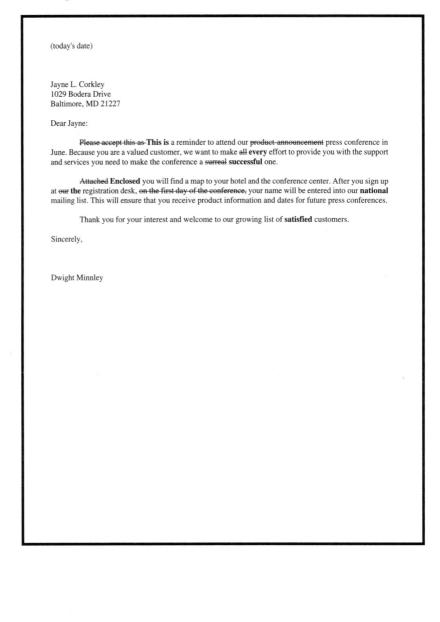

(today's date)

Jayne L. Corkley
1029 Bodera Drive
Baltimore, MD 21227

Dear Jayne:

Please accept this as **This is** a reminder to attend our ~~product announcement~~ press conference in June. Because you are a valued customer, we want to make ~~all~~ **every** effort to provide you with the support and services you need to make the conference a ~~surreal~~ **successful** one.

~~Attached~~ **Enclosed** you will find a map to your hotel and the conference center. After you sign up at ~~our~~ **the** registration desk, ~~on the first day of the conference,~~ your name will be entered into our **national** mailing list. This will ensure that you receive product information and dates for future press conferences.

Thank you for your interest and welcome to our growing list of **satisfied** customers.

Sincerely,

Dwight Minnley

Figure 1.15   **The corrected MYPRAC1B.DOC**

(today's date)

Jayne L. Corkley
1029 Bodera Drive
Baltimore, MD 21227

Dear Jayne:

    This is a reminder to attend our press conference in June. Because you are a valued customer, we want to make every effort to provide you with the support and services you need to make the conference a successful one.

    Enclosed you will find a map to your hotel and the conference center. After you sign up at the registration desk, your name will be entered into our national mailing list. This will ensure that you receive product information and dates for future press conferences.

    Thank you for your interest and welcome to our growing list of satisfied customers.

Sincerely,

Dwight Minnley

your daily word-processing work. You now know how to start and exit Word; how to enter, insert, delete, and replace text; how to save, name, print, and close a document; and how to create a new document. Congratulations! You're well on your way to mastering Word.

Here's a quick reference guide to the Word features introduced in this chapter:

Desired Result	How to Do It
Start Word	Start **Windows**, double-click on the **Microsoft Word** icon in the Word for Windows 2.0 group
Maximize/Restore a window	Click on the document or application **Maximize/Restore** button
Minimize an application window	Click on the **Minimize** box
Choose a menu command	Click on the menu-bar entry to display the drop-down menu; click on the command; or, press and hold the mouse button on the menu-bar entry; drag down to the command; release the mouse button
End a paragraph or short line	Press **Enter**
Create a blank line	Press **Enter**
Display/remove nonprinting characters	Click on the ribbon **Show/Hide** button
Align text horizontally	Use the **Tab** key
Delete character to the left of the insertion point	Press **Backspace**
Select text	Point to the first (or final) character of the text; press and hold the mouse button; drag across the text to the final (or first) character; release the mouse button

Desired Result	How to Do It
Delete character to the right of the insertion point	Press **Del**
Delete selected text	Select text, press **Del**
Replace selected text	Select text, type the new text
Save a disk file for the first time	Choose **File, Save As**
Rename a document or save a document as a disk file in a new location	Choose **File, Save As**
Save a previously saved disk file with the same name/location	Choose **File, Save**
Print the active document	Choose **File, Print**
Close the active document	Choose **File, Close**; or, double-click on the document **Control menu box**
Create a new document	Choose **File, New**
Choose a default button	Press **Enter**
View Summary Info for the active document	Choose **File, Summary Info**
Exit Word	Choose **File, Exit**

In the next chapter, we'll show you how to navigate in Word. You'll learn how to open a document, display different portions of a document, search for text in a document, control document magnification, and how to obtain on-line help.

A NOTE ON HOW TO PROCEED

If you wish to stop here, feel free to do so. If you wish to press onward, please proceed directly to the next chapter. Remember to allot enough time to work through an entire chapter at one sitting.

CHAPTER TWO: NAVIGATING IN WORD

Using File, Open to
Open a Document

Scrolling through a
Document

Moving through a
Document

Using Edit, Find to
Search for Text

Using Zoom to
Control Document
Magnification

Using Word Help to
Obtain On-Line
Help

Saving the
Modified File

To help you distinguish between steps presented for your general knowledge and steps you should carry out at your computer as you read, we have adopted the following system:

- A bulleted step, like this, is provided for your information and reference only.

1. A numbered step, like this, indicates one in a series of steps that you should carry out in sequence at your computer.

In Chapter 1 you learned how to use the mouse to move around within a one-page document. In this chapter, you'll learn how to use the mouse *and* the keyboard to navigate through a multipage document. It's essential for you to master these navigational techniques as early as possible in your Word career. The more comfortable you feel moving around within a document, the more you'll be able to concentrate on the contents of the document itself.

When you're done working through this chapter, you will know

- How to open a document

- How to use the mouse to scroll through a document

- How to use the keyboard and menus to move through a document

- How to use Edit, Find to search for text

- How to use Zoom to control document magnification

- How to use Word Help to obtain on-line Help

USING FILE, OPEN TO OPEN A DOCUMENT

In Chapter 1 you learned how to create, modify, and save a document as a disk file. Here you'll learn how to *open* (retrieve) a document that is stored as a disk file. This way, you'll be able to revise previously saved disk files and then reprint and resave them.

To open a document

- Choose *File, Open* to display the Open dialog box

- Select the desired drive (in the Drives list box) and directory (in the Directories list box), if necessary

- Click on the desired file (in the File Name list box) and then click on OK; or, simply double-click on the desired file

When you open a document, a copy of the disk file is placed in a document window on your screen. Because this is a *copy* of the disk file, and not the disk file itself, you can revise it to your heart's content without changing the original document stored on your disk. (You will, however, change the original document if you save your revised document as a disk file with the same name, and in the same location, as the original. For this reason, if you want to preserve the original document, make sure to give your revised disk file a new name.)

Word also provides a convenient file-opening shortcut; it keeps track of the last four files that you worked on and places their names as choices at the bottom of the File menu. To open one of these documents, choose File and click on the desired document name.

If you are not running Word, please follow the steps listed in Chapter 1 under "Starting Word" to load the program.

Let's begin by opening a document that is stored in your WRKFILES directory:

1. Choose **File, Open** to display the Open dialog box (see Figure 2.1).

Figure 2.1   **The Open dialog box**

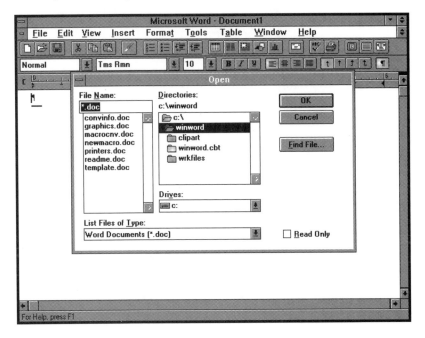

2. If your WRKFILES directory is not already selected, select it now (double-click on **wrkfiles** in the Directories list box). You must tell Word where to find a document stored as a disk file before you open it.

3. In the File Name list box, click once on **chap2.doc**. Note that this file name is automatically inserted in the File Name text box. (A *list box* displays a list of options; a *text box* contains text that is either entered automatically or that you can enter when prompted.)

4. Click on **OK** (or press **Enter**) to open the document. A copy of the disk file appears in an active document window. Note the title bar, CHAP2.DOC (see Figure 2.2).

Figure 2.2   **CHAP2.DOC, newly opened**

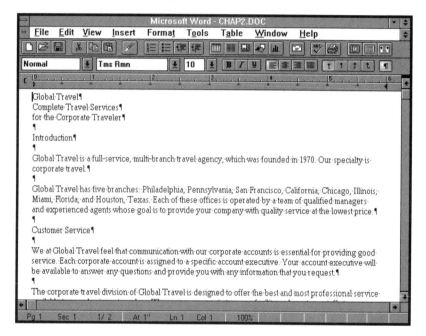

5. Double-click on the document window (*not* the application window) **Control menu box** to close CHAP2.DOC.

Now let's try the shortcut method for opening this document:

1. Click (once) on **File** to display the drop-down File menu. Note that CHAP2.DOC appears in the recently accessed files section at the bottom of the menu.

2. Click on **CHAP2.DOC** to open this document.

SCROLLING THROUGH A DOCUMENT

A Word document window can only display about half of a standard business-size (8.5" by 11") page at any one time. To view the remainder of the page (or other pages within the document), you can use the mouse in conjunction with the vertical and horizontal scroll bars to *scroll* through the document—that is, to display different areas of the document. The vertical scroll bar controls up-down scrolling; the horizontal scroll bar controls side-to-side scrolling.

Scrolling through a document changes the document display, but does *not* change the position of the insertion point. For example, if the insertion point is at the top of page 2 and you use the vertical scroll bar to scroll down to page 8, the contents of page 8 will be displayed on the screen, but the insertion point will still be at the top of page 2. If you then begin to type, your text is entered at the insertion point on page 2, not on page 8. (You'll learn how to change both the document display *and* the insertion point position in the next section.)

Table 2.1 lists Word's vertical and horizontal scrolling options and how to perform them. Figure 2.3 identifies relevant screen elements used for scrolling.

Table 2.1   **Vertical and Horizontal Scrolling Options**

To Scroll	Do This
Up or down one line at a time	Click on the up or down scroll arrow
To the top, bottom, or middle of a document	Drag the vertical scroll box to the top, bottom, or middle of the scroll bar
Up or down a screen at a time	Click in the shaded area above or below the vertical scroll box
Left or right a column at a time	Click on the left or right scroll arrow
To the left edge, right edge, or middle of a document	Drag the horizontal scroll box to the left, right, or middle of the scroll bar
Left or right a screen at a time	Click in the shaded area to the left or right of the horizontal scroll box

Figure 2.3   **Scrolling terminology**

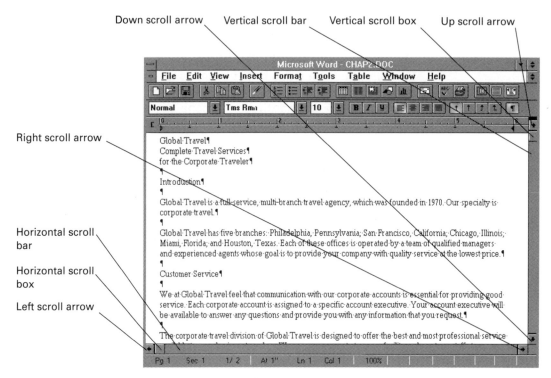

Let's practice using the mouse and scroll bars to scroll through the active document, CHAP2.DOC:

1. Click on the **down scroll arrow** several times to scroll down through the document one line at a time. Note that the insertion point does not move.

2. Click on the **up scroll arrow** several times to scroll up through the document.

3. Drag the **vertical scroll box** to the bottom of the scroll bar to scroll to the bottom of the document.

4. Drag the **vertical scroll box** to the middle of the scroll bar to scroll to the middle of the document.

5. Observe the *page break*—the dotted line that indicates where one page ends and the next begins. (You may have to scroll to see this.) Because CHAP2.DOC is a two-page document, the page break is located about halfway through the document.

6. Drag the **vertical scroll box** to the top of the scroll bar to scroll to the top of the document. Note that, throughout all of your scrolling, the insertion point has remained at the top of the document.

7. Click in the vertical scroll bar below the vertical scroll box to scroll one screen length down through the document.

8. Repeat step 7 as many times as necessary to scroll to the bottom of the document.

9. Click in the vertical scroll bar above the vertical scroll box to scroll one screen length up through the document.

10. Repeat step 9 as many times as necessary to scroll to the top of the document.

Let's take a moment to observe a common scrolling mistake. Assume you wanted to enter your initials at the end of the active document:

1. Drag the **vertical scroll box** to the bottom of the scroll bar to display the end of the document.

2. Type your initials. The text is inserted at the top of the document (where your insertion point is located), not at the end (where you scrolled to). Note that Word automatically repositions the document to display the inserted text. To avoid making such a mistake, remember these two things: Text that you type is always inserted at the insertion point; and, the insertion point does not move when you use the mouse to scroll through your document.

3. Use **Backspace** to erase your initials.

4. Scroll back down to the end of the document and look at the page indicator in the status bar. It shows the position of the insertion point (page 1), not the current document display (page 2). Observing the status bar from time to time can help you keep track of your insertion point position.

MOVING THROUGH A DOCUMENT

When you *scroll* through a document, you change the document display but not the insertion point. When you *move* through a document, you change both the document display *and* the insertion point. For this reason, you should scroll when you just want to view different parts of a document, and you should move when you want to view and modify a document.

 USING THE KEYBOARD TO MOVE THROUGH A DOCUMENT

Table 2.2 lists several ways to move through a document by using the keyboard.

Table 2.2   **Keyboard Movement Techniques**

To Move	Press
Up one screen	Pg Up (or Page Up on Enhanced Keyboards)
Down one screen	Pg Dn (or Page Down)
To the top of the document	Ctrl+Home
To the end of the document	Ctrl+End
To the beginning of a line	Home
To the end of a line	End

Now let's practice using the keyboard to move—rather than to scroll—through a document.

Note: If you intend to use the Pg Dn and Pg Up keys on the numeric keypad, make sure that Num Lock is off.

1. Press **Pg Dn** (or **Page Down**) twice to move two screen lengths down through the document. Note that the insertion point has moved along with the document display.

2. Press **Pg Up** (or **Page Up**) twice to move two screen lengths up through the document. Note that the insertion point has moved.

3. Press **Ctrl+End** to move to the end of the document.

4. Press **Ctrl+Home** to move to the beginning of the document.

Let's redo our initial-writing task, this time using the correct method:

1. Press **Ctrl+End** to move to the end of the document.

2. Type your initials. They now appear in the desired location, because you used Ctrl+End (not the scroll bar) to move the insertion point along with the document display.

 USING EDIT, *GO TO* TO MOVE TO A PAGE

You can use the Edit, Go To command to move to the top of a specified page in the active document. This technique is particularly useful when you are moving through long (multipage) documents.

To move to the top of a page

- Choose *Edit, Go To*

- Type the page number

- Click on *OK* (or press Enter)

Instead of choosing Edit, Go To from the menu, you can also use the F5 shortcut key to issue a Go To command. *Shortcut keys* allow you to issue frequently used commands directly from the keyboard. (For a list of Word's shortcut keys, see Appendix B.)

To use the F5 shortcut key to move to the top of a page

- Press F5; Word displays a "Go To" prompt in the status bar

- Type the page number and press Enter

Let's use the Edit, Go To command to move through a document:

1. Choose **Edit, Go To** to open the Go To dialog box (see Figure 2.4).

2. In the Go To text box, type **2** to specify the destination page. Then press **Enter** to move (the document display and the insertion point) to the top of page 2.

3. Choose **Edit, Go To**. *Enter* 1—that is, type **1** and then press **Enter**—to move to the top of page 1. (From here on we'll use "enter text" to mean "type *text* and then press *Enter.*")

4. Click on **Edit** to display the drop-down Edit menu. Observe the shortcut key for the Go To command. It is F5. Click on **Edit** again to close the Edit menu.

Figure 2.4   **The Go To dialog box**

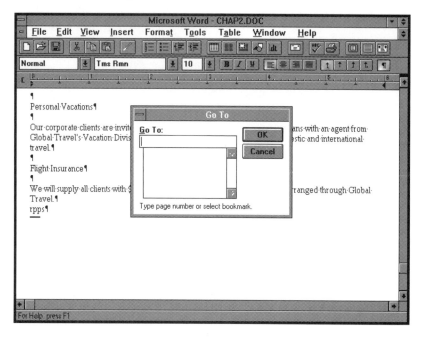

5. Press **F5** (Go To). Instead of opening the Go To dialog box, Word displays a *Go To* prompt in the status bar.

6. Enter **2** (type **2** and press **Enter**) to move to the top of page 2.

7. Press **F5** and then enter **1** to move to the top of page 1.

PRACTICE YOUR SKILLS

1. Use Edit, Go To to move to the top of page 2.

2. Use F5 to attempt to move to the top of page 3. Since CHAP2.-DOC does not have a page 3, you are moved to the top of the final page (2).

USING EDIT, FIND TO SEARCH FOR TEXT

One of Word's most powerful features is its ability to quickly locate a specific word or phrase in a document. You can use this feature to move rapidly to any desired document location. For example, you can move to the sentence containing the phrase "We would like to establish ...," even if you have no idea on which page this sentence appears.

To use Edit, Find to search for text within a document

- Place the insertion point where you wish to begin the search. By default, Word searches from the insertion point downward to the end of the document. To search the entire document, place the insertion point at the top.

- Choose *Edit*, *Find* to open the Find dialog box.

- In the Find What text box, type the *search text* (the text that you want to find).

- Select any desired search options (covered next).

- Click on *Find Next* (or press *Enter*); Word highlights the first occurrence of your search text.

- Repeat the previous step as many times as necessary until you have searched through the entire document. Or cancel your search at any time by clicking on Cancel. When Word has reached the end of your document, it displays a message informing you so.

- Click on *OK* (or press *Enter*) to close this message box.

- Close the *Find* dialog box.

Edit, Find provides several options which allow you to refine your text searches. By choosing the *Match Whole Word Only* option, you can tell Find to locate only whole words that match your search text. By choosing the *Match Case* option, you can locate only words that exactly match the case (capitalization) of your search text. By selecting the *Up* option, you can search from the insertion point upward, instead of in the default downward direction.

Let's experiment with the Edit, Find command:

1. Press **Ctrl+Home** to move the insertion point to the top in preparation for searching the entire document.

2. Choose **Edit**, **Find** to open the Find dialog box (see Figure 2.5).

3. In the Find What text box, type **vacation**. Verify that the Match Whole Word Only and Match Case options are not selected; when an option is selected, an X appears in the box.

Figure 2.5   **The Find dialog box**

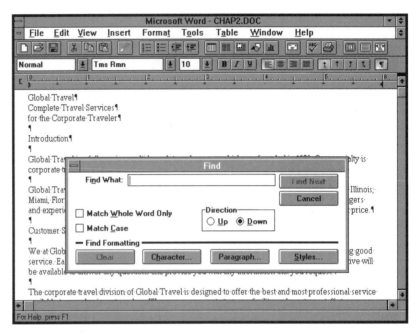

4. Click on **Find Next** (or press **Enter**) four times, pausing each time to examine the found word; when a word is found, it is highlighted in the document. Word finds the following occurrences of *vacation*:

```
Vacations
vacation
Vacation
Vacation
```

Word found the second occurrence just listed—*vacation*—because it exactly matches your search text. It found the last two occurrences (Vacation), because by leaving the Match Case option unselected, you told it to ignore capitalization. It found the first occurrence (Vacations) because by leaving the Match Whole Word Only option unselected, you also told it to ignore whole-word matching (*vacation* is a partial match of *Vacations*).

5. Click on **Find Next** (or press **Enter**) again. A *message box* appears, informing you that Word has completed its search

through the end of the document. Click on **OK** (or press **Enter**) to close this box.

6. Click on **Cancel** (or press **Esc**) to close the Find dialog box.

Now let's refine our search by using the Match Whole Word Only and Match Case options:

1. Move the insertion point to the top of the document (press **Ctrl+Home**).

2. Choose **Edit**, **Find** to open the Find dialog box.

3. *Check* (select) the **Match Whole Word Only** option by clicking inside the box; an X appears. In Word, selecting a checkbox-type option (such as Match Whole Word Only or Match Case) is formally called *checking* the option.

4. Click on **Find Next** (or press **Enter**) three times, pausing to examine each found word. Three occurrences are found: *vacation*, *Vacation*, and *Vacation*. *Vacations* is not found, because you told Word to find only whole-word matches of *vacation*.

5. Click on **Find Next** (or press **Enter**) again; the end-of-document message box appears. Click on **OK** to close this box and then click on **Cancel** to close the Find dialog box.

6. Move the insertion point back to the top of the document (press **Ctrl+Home**).

7. Check (select) the **Match Case** option (Both Match Case and Match Whole Word Only should now be checked. Click on **Find Next** (or press **Enter**) two times. Only one occurrence of your search text is found: *vacation*. *Vacation* is not found, because you told Word to find only case-matching occurrences of *vacation*.

8. Click on **OK** to close the end-of-document message box and then click on **Cancel** to close the Find dialog box.

PRACTICE YOUR SKILLS

1. Uncheck the Match Whole Word Only and Match Case options and then search your entire active document for **news**. (**Hint**: Remember to move the insertion point to the top before beginning the search.) There are three matches.

2. Check Match Whole Word Only and repeat the search. There is one match.

3. Uncheck Match Whole Word Only, check Match Case, and repeat the search. There are two matches.

4. Repeat step 3, this time searching from the bottom up to the top of the document. (**Hint:** Remember to move the insertion point to the bottom before beginning.)

USING ZOOM TO CONTROL DOCUMENT MAGNIFICATION

The Zoom feature enables you to control the level of magnification at which a document is displayed on your screen. By default, Zoom is set to 100% magnification (where the screen display matches the actual document size), but you can adjust this magnification to anywhere from 25% to 200%.

A magnification of 25% shrinks the on-screen document to ¼ of its actual size, allowing you to view all (or most of) an entire page without having to scroll. A magnification of 200% enlarges the on-screen document to twice its actual size, allowing you to view text and graphics close up to perform detail work. (Word allows you to edit a document's text at any Zoom magnification level.)

To specify an exact Zoom magnification (such as 68% or 124%), you must use the View, Zoom command. To do this

• Choose *View, Zoom*

• Type the desired magnification in the Custom box

• Click on *OK* (or press *Enter*)

For most situations, however, you can use the Zoom buttons in the toolbar to quickly *zoom in* (increase the magnification) and *zoom out* (decrease the magnification) of a document. These buttons include *Zoom Whole Page, Zoom 100 Percent*, and *Zoom Page Width*. They are, respectively, the last three buttons on the right side of the toolbar.

To use the Zoom buttons to control document magnification

• Click on *Zoom Whole Page* to shrink a page to fit on the screen

• Click on *Zoom 100 Percent* to display a page at 100% magnification (actual size)

- Click on Zoom Page Width to shrink a page with extra-wide text lines to fit these lines on the screen

Note: Zoom Page Width fits the full page width on the screen; you may still have to scroll vertically to view the entire length of the page. Zoom Whole Page fits the full page width *and* length on the screen; scrolling is unnecessary.

The Zoom buttons can also be used as a navigational tool, allowing you to quickly move the insertion point to the part of the page you wish to edit. To do this

- Click on *Zoom Whole Page* to view the entire page

- Place the insertion point where you want to edit text

- Click on *Zoom 100 Percent* to return to 100% magnification

The document window will automatically reorient to the new position of the insertion point.

Let's try using Zoom as a navigational tool to edit an entry in the tabbed table at the bottom of the first page.

1. Move the insertion point to the top of the document (press **Ctrl+Home**).

2. Observe the status bar. Located to the right of the column indicator, the magnification indicator displays 100%.

3. Click on the **Zoom Whole Page** button (third from the right in the toolbar, it shows a page within a larger frame). Word displays a miniature view of the page (see Figure 2.6). Observe the status bar. The current magnification is 30%.

4. Move the mouse pointer to the first line of the tabbed table at the bottom of page 1. Click to position the insertion point.

5. Click on the **Zoom 100 Percent** button (second from the right in the toolbar, it shows a whole page) to return to 100% magnification.

6. Delete **/Motel** (you might need to scroll) in the first line of the tabbed table.

Figure 2.6   **Page 1 of CHAP2.DOC in Zoom Whole Page view**

Zoom Whole   Zoom 100 Percent   Zoom Page Width
Page button   button   button

USING WORD HELP TO OBTAIN ON-LINE HELP

Word Help is an extensive on-line help system that provides you with "how-to" information on every aspect of the Word program. The beauty of Word Help is its accessibility. No matter what you are doing in Word (choosing a command from the menu, editing a document, filling in a dialog box, and so on), Help is only a keystroke—or mouse click—away.

USING THE HELP INDEX TO OBTAIN HELP

The Word Help index provides an overview of the topics (similar to a table of contents) for which Help information is available. To use the Help index

• Choose *Help, Help Index* to open the Help index

- To get help for a specific topic, click on any underlined word or phrase in the index

- To jump to a new Help window, click on any solid-underlined word or phrase

- To pop up a definition of a word or phrase without moving from the current screen, point to a dotted-underlined word or phrase, then press and hold the mouse button

- To close the Word Help window, double-click on the window's Control menu box

Let's practice using the Word Help index:

1. Choose **Help**, **Help Index** to display the Word Help index (see Figure 2.7).

Figure 2.7 **The Word Help index**

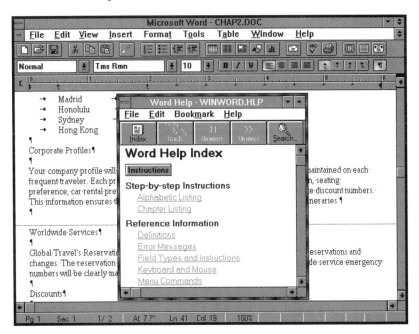

2. Move the mouse pointer to the entry **Alphabetic Listing**. Note that the pointer changes to a hand. Click to view an alphabetical list of step-by-step instructions.

3. Scroll down through the list and click on the entry **Closing windows**. Then click on **Closing a window** to view Word Help on closing a window.

4. Read the Help text. The text explains a variety of methods for closing windows.

5. Close the Word Help window by double-clicking on its **Control menu box**. (Do not double-click on the application or document window Control menu boxes, as this would close the Word program or active document.)

USING THE F1 KEY TO OBTAIN CONTEXT-SENSITIVE HELP

In addition to its list of index topics, Word Help offers you *context-sensitive* help: information related to your current working context. For example, if a dialog box is open and you ask for context-sensitive help, Help displays information about that particular dialog box. Used in this manner, Help can quickly provide information about specific dialog boxes, menu commands, or areas of the screen. You can use either of the following methods to obtain context-sensitive help:

• Press *F1*; Word displays the Help window related to your current working context

• Press *Shift+F1*; the mouse pointer changes to an arrow with a question mark attached

• Make any menu choice or click on the desired part of the application window and Word will open the related Help window

Let's use the F1 (Help) key to obtain context-sensitive help:

1. Choose **Edit**, **Go To** to open the Go To dialog box.

2. Press **F1** (Help) to open the Help window for the Go To command (see Figure 2.8). This is an example of context-sensitive Help, in which Word provides help relative to your current working context.

3. Close the Help window (double-click on its **Control menu box**).

4. Click on **Cancel** to close the Go To dialog box.

Figure 2.8   **Help window for the Go To command**

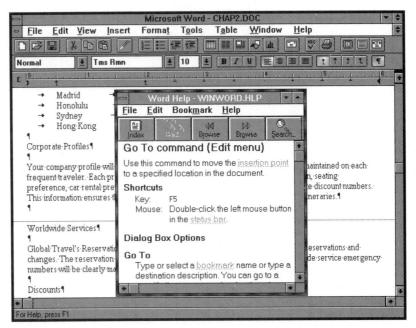

Now let's use the Shift-F1 method to obtain context-sensitive Help:

1. Press **Shift+F1** to activate context-sensitive Word Help. Note that the mouse pointer now has a question mark attached to it (see Figure 2.9).

2. Choose **File, Summary Info** to open the Help window on the Summary Info command.

3. Close the Help window (double-click on its **Control menu box**).

4. Press **Shift+F1** to reactive context-sensitive help.

5. Click the mouse pointer on a blank area of the toolbar (an area between buttons) to open the Word Help window for the toolbar.

6. Close the Help window.

Figure 2.9   **Context-sensitive Help pointer**

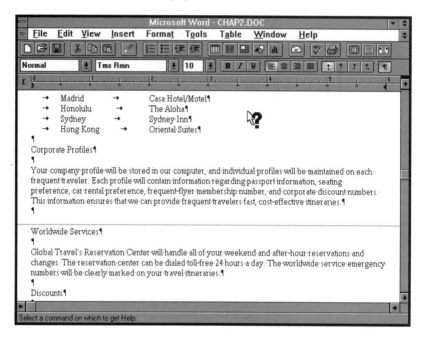

SAVING THE MODIFIED FILE

Let's end this work session by using File, Save As to rename the active document and save it (as a disk file) to your WRKFILES directory. By using the File, Save As command, you preserve the original version of the document (CHAP2.DOC) along with your revised version. If you instead used the File, Save command to save the active document, you would preserve the revision (as CHAP2.DOC), but delete the original.

1. Choose **File**, **Save As** to open the Save As dialog box.

2. In the File Name text box, type **mychap2** to rename the document.

3. If your WRKFILES directory is not already selected, select it now.

4. Click on **OK** (or press **Enter**) to save your modified CHAP2-.DOC document under the name MYCHAP2.DOC.

5. Click on **OK** (or press **Enter**) to bypass the Summary Info dialog box. Note the title bar (MYCHAP2.DOC).

6. Double-click on the document window (*not* the application window) **Control menu box** to close the document.

SUMMARY

In this chapter, you learned the basics of navigating in Word. You now know how to open a document, scroll and move through a document, search for text, control document magnification, and how to obtain on-line help.

Here's a quick reference guide to the Word features introduced in this chapter:

Desired Result	How to Do It
Open a document	Choose **File**, **Open**; select the drive and directory; click on the disk file and then click on OK (or double-click on the file)
Open a recently used document	Choose **File**; click on the document name at the bottom of the File menu
Scroll up or down one line	Click on the **up** or **down scroll arrow**
Scroll to the top, bottom, or middle of a document	Drag the **vertical scroll box** to the top, bottom, or middle of the scroll bar
Scroll up or down a screen	Click in the vertical scroll bar above or below the vertical scroll box
Scroll left or right a column	Click on the **left** or **right scroll arrow**
Scroll to the left edge, right edge, or middle of a document	Drag the **horizontal scroll box** to the left, right, or middle of the scroll bar
Scroll to the left or right a screen at a time	Click in the horizontal scroll bar to the left or right of the horizontal scroll box

Desired Result	How to Do It
Move up one screen	Press **Pg Up**
Move down one screen	Press **Pg Dn**
Move to the top of the document	Press **Ctrl+Home**
Move to the end of the document	Press **Ctrl+End**
Move to the beginning of a line	Press **Home**
Move to the end of a line	Press **End**
Move to the top of a page	Choose **Edit, Go To**; type the page number; click on **OK** or press **Enter**; or press **F5** and enter the page number
Search for text	Place the insertion point where you want to begin searching, choose **Edit, Find**; type the search text, select any desired search options; click on **Find Next** (or press **Enter**)
Specify an exact Zoom magnification	Choose **View, Zoom**; type the desired magnification in the Custom box; click on **OK** (or press **Enter**)
Use the Zoom buttons to control magnification	Click on **Zoom Whole Page** to fit a page on screen; click on **Zoom 100 Percent** to display a page at actual size; click on **Zoom Page Width** to fit full page width on the screen
Use the Zoom buttons as a navigational tool	Click on **Zoom Whole Page**; position the insertion point; click on **Zoom 100 Percent**
Open the Help index	Choose **Help, Help Index**
Get help from the index	Click on any underlined word or phrase

Desired Result	How to Do It
Jump to a new Help window	Click on any solid-underlined word or phrase
Pop up a definition of a word or phrase	Point to a dotted-underlined word or phrase; press and hold the mouse button
Obtain context-sensitive help	Press **F1** or press **Shift+F1**; make any menu choice or click on the desired part of the application window
Close the Word Help window	Double-click on the window's Control menu box

In the next chapter, you'll learn how to edit text. The editing process includes replacing found text, moving text, and copying text. You'll also be introduced to a handy way to undo an action when you change your mind about an editing decision.

IF YOU'RE STOPPING HERE

If you need to break off here, please exit Word (for help, see "Exiting Word" in Chapter 1). If you want to proceed directly to the next chapter, please do so now.

CHAPTER THREE: EDITING TEXT

To help you distinguish between steps presented for your general knowledge and steps you should carry out at your computer as you read, we have adopted the following system:

- A bulleted step, like this, is provided for your information and reference only.

1. A numbered step, like this, indicates one in a series of steps that you should carry out in sequence at your computer.

In Chapter 1, you learned the basics of editing—how to insert, select, replace, and delete text. In this chapter we'll introduce you to some of Word's more advanced editing techniques. You'll learn sophisticated ways to select text and then move and copy this text to other locations in your document. You'll find out how to use the Edit, Replace command (Edit, Find's more powerful cousin) to find text and replace it with new text of your choice. Finally, we'll show you how to use the Undo command to rescue yourself from a potentially catastrophic word-processing mistake.

When you're done working through this chapter, you will know

- How to use the mouse, the keyboard, and menus to select text
- How to use the Edit, Replace command to replace found text
- How to move and copy text
- How to use the Undo command to reverse your last operation

TECHNIQUES FOR SELECTING TEXT

Before you can move or copy text, you must select it. You can do this by using the mouse, the keyboard, or menus. Table 3.1 lists Word's text selection techniques.

Table 3.1 **Text Selection Techniques**

Selection Technique	How to Do It
Dragging	Point at one end of the text you want to select. Press and hold the mouse button. Move (*drag*) the mouse pointer to the other end of the text. Release the mouse button. All the text between the two ends is selected.
Using Shift	Place the insertion point at one end of the text. Press and hold Shift, then click at the other end of the text you want to select (do not drag). Release Shift. All the text between the two ends is selected.
Selecting a word	Point anywhere inside the word and double-click the mouse button. The trailing space is automatically selected along with the word.
Selecting a sentence	Point anywhere inside the sentence. Press and hold the Ctrl key, then click the mouse button. Release Ctrl. End punctuation and trailing spaces are automatically selected along with the sentence.

Selection Technique	How to Do It
Selecting a line	Point in the *selection bar* area (the blank vertical bar on the left side of the document window) next to the line and click the mouse button. All the text on that line is selected.
Selecting multiple lines	Point in the selection bar next to the first or last line of text you want to select. Press and hold the mouse button, then drag down or up. Release the mouse button. All the lines you "dragged" are selected.
Selecting a paragraph	Point in the selection bar next to the paragraph and double-click the mouse button. The ending paragraph mark is selected along with the paragraph.
Selecting an entire document	Choose *Edit, Select All*. Or, point anywhere in the selection bar, press and hold Ctrl, click the mouse button, then release Ctrl.
Extending an existing selection	While holding Shift, click beyond the existing selection. The selection extends to that point.
Shortening an existing selection	While holding Shift, click inside the existing selection. The selection shortens to that point.
Deselecting an existing selection	Make another selection, or click the mouse button in the text area anywhere outside the existing selection.

If you are not running Word, please start it now (for help, see "Starting Word" in Chapter 1). Let's begin this chapter's activities by opening a new document file and then using the mouse-dragging method to select text:

1. Click on the **Open** button (second from the left in the toolbar; it shows a file folder being opened) to display the Open dialog box. Clicking on the Open button is equivalent to choosing the File, Open command from the menu.

2. If your WRKFILES directory is not already selected, select it now.

3. In the File Name list box, double-click on **chap3.doc** to open the document file. Double-clicking on a list-box item is often equivalent to clicking once on the item and then clicking on OK (or pressing Enter).

4. Point to the left of the *C* in *Corporate* in the third line of the document.

5. Drag to the right to select **Corporate** and the trailing space.

6. Release the mouse button. Your screen should resemble Figure 3.1.

Figure 3.1　　**Dragging the mouse to select text**

Open button

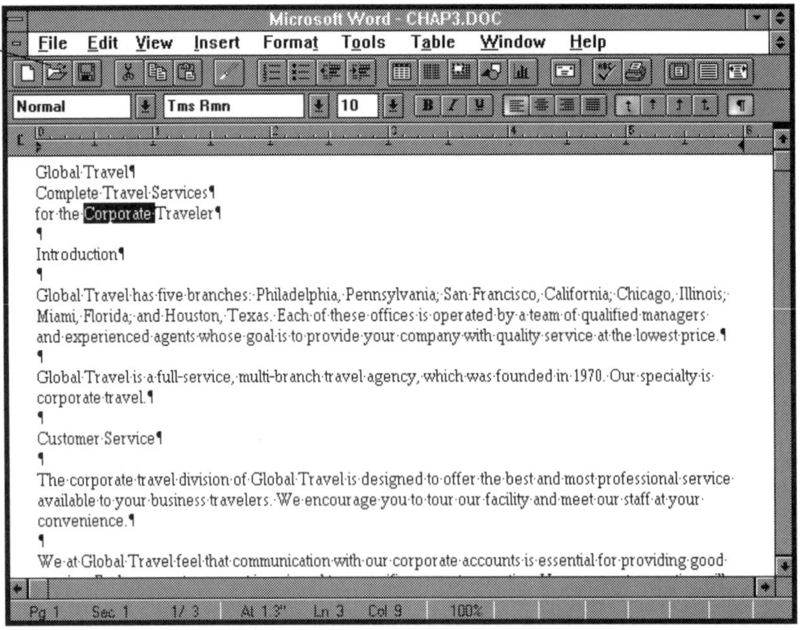

Now let's use the whole-word selection technique:

1. Point to the word **five** in the first paragraph of the document.

2. Double-click the mouse button to select the entire word **five**. Note that selecting *five* deselects *Corporate*.

3. Examine the selected text. The trailing space after *five* is also selected.

Now let's use the selection bar to select text:

1. Move the mouse pointer into the selection bar—the blank vertical bar between the left edge of the document window and the left edge of the document text (see Figure 3.2). Note that the pointer changes from an I-beam into an arrow.

Figure 3.2   **The selection bar**

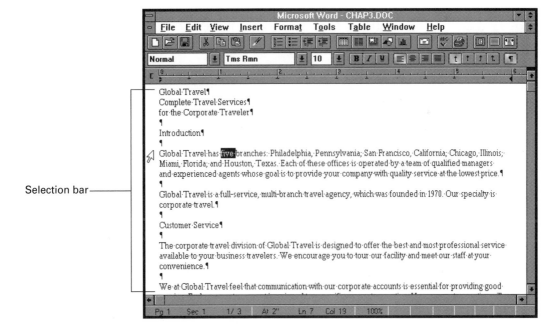

Selection bar

2. Point in the selection bar next to the line beginning with *Global Travel is a full-service*. Click the mouse button to select the entire line.

3. Point in the selection bar next to *Global Travel has five branches*. Double-click the mouse button to select the entire paragraph.

4. Point in the selection bar next to *Introduction*. Press and hold the mouse button, then drag down to the paragraph mark before *Customer Service* to select multiple lines of text. Release the mouse button.

Let's use the Shift key to select a block of text and then extend and shorten this selection:

1. Place the insertion point before the *C* in *Corporate* in the third line of the document.

2. Press and hold **Shift**, then click the mouse pointer in the space after *five* to select all the text from *Corporate* to *five*. Release **Shift** (see Figure 3.3).

Figure 3.3   **Selecting text with the mouse and the Shift key**

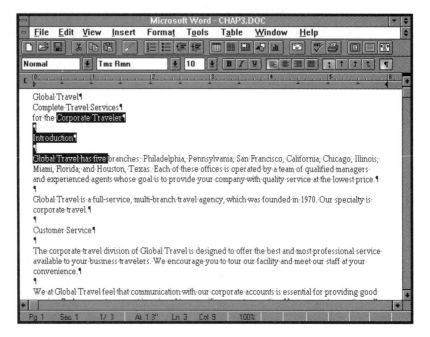

3. Point to the right of the *s* in *Texas* in the next line down. Press and hold **Shift**, then click the mouse button to extend the selection through to the end of *Texas*. Release **Shift**.

4. Point to the left of the *P* in *Philadelphia*. Note that the pointer appears as an arrow (instead of an insertion point) when you

point to selected text. Press and hold **Shift**, then click the mouse button to shorten the selection. Release **Shift**.

Finally, let's use the menu to select the entire document:

1. Choose **Edit, Select All** to select the entire document.

2. Click anywhere within the text area to *deselect*.

PRACTICE YOUR SKILLS

1. Select the first sentence of the paragraph beginning with *Global Travel is a full-service*, using the mouse-dragging technique.

2. Deselect.

3. Select the same sentence as in step 1, this time using the mouse in conjunction with Ctrl to select the entire sentence without dragging. (For help, refer to Table 3.1, earlier in this chapter.)

4. Use the double-clicking technique to select each of the following words in the first paragraph: **Global**, **Philadelphia**, **Texas**, **qualified**, **price**. Note that double-clicking selects the trailing space after a word, but not the trailing comma (as in *Philadelphia,*) or period (as in *Texas.* and *price.*).

5. Use the selection-bar technique to select the first line of the document. Extend the selection to include the first four lines. Shorten the selection to include the first two lines.

USING EDIT, REPLACE TO REPLACE FOUND TEXT

In Chapter 2, you learned how to use Edit, Find to search for text in a document. Here you'll learn how to use the Edit, Replace command to search for text and replace it with new text of your choice.

Edit, Replace is one of Word's most powerful commands. Let's say you typed a 100-page document that made frequent reference to a man named *Pablo Sitauskus* and then you found out that the correct spelling was *Sitauskis*. Normally you'd have to find each occurrence of *Sitauskus* and retype it—an ugly task considering the length of the document. Using Edit, Replace, however, you could issue a single command that would automatically (and rapidly) replace every occurrence of *Sitauskus* with *Sitauskis*.

To use Edit, Replace to replace found text in a document

- Place the insertion point where you wish to begin the search/replace operation (Edit, Replace—unlike Edit, Find—only permits you to search from the insertion point downward); to search an entire document, place the insertion point at the top of the document

- Choose *Edit, Replace* to open the Replace dialog box

- In the Find What text box, type the *search text* (the text you wish to find)

- In the Replace With text box, type the *replace text* (the text you wish to replace the search text)

- If necessary, check your desired search option(s)—Match Whole Word Only or Match Case

- Click on *Find Next* (or press *Enter*); Word highlights the first occurrence of your search text

- Click on either *Replace* (to replace the found text and search for the next occurrence), *Find Next* (to leave the found text unchanged and search for the next occurrence), or *Replace All* (to replace all occurrences of the search text throughout the rest of the document)

- Repeat the previous step as many times as necessary until you have searched through the entire document, or cancel your search at any time by clicking on *Cancel*

- Close the Replace dialog box

Let's use the procedures just described to find and replace some text in the active document:

1. Press **Ctrl+Home** to move the insertion point to the top of your document in preparation for searching the entire document.

2. Choose **Edit, Replace** to open the Replace dialog box (see Figure 3.4).

3. In the Find What text box, type **20**. This is the text we will search for and replace.

4. Press **Tab** to select the Replace With text box and then type **50**. This is the text that will replace the search text (20).

Figure 3.4   **The Replace dialog box**

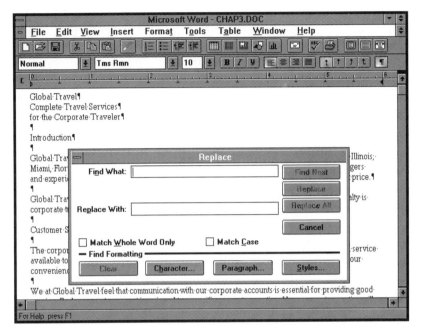

5. Uncheck (deselect) the **Match Whole Word Only** and **Match Case** options, if necessary.

6. Click on **Find Next** to find the first occurrence of *20*.

7. Click on **Replace** to replace *20* with *50* and to search for the next occurrence of *20*.

8. Click on **Find Next** to leave *20-30%* unchanged and search for the next occurrence of *20*.

9. Click on **Replace** to replace *20* with *50* and search for the next occurrence of *20*. Because there are no more occurrences of *20*, the insertion point moves back to the top of the document.

10. Click on **Cancel** to close the Replace dialog box.

You'll have a chance to use the Replace All command in the "Practice Your Skills" section at the end of this chapter.

MOVING AND COPYING TEXT

Another of Word's powerful editing features is its ability to move and copy text within a document. You can, for example, quickly and easily move a table of numbers from the top of the fifth page of a business report to the bottom of the eleventh page, or copy a four-line address to several different locations within the body of a letter.

 ### THE CLIPBOARD

Windows provides a temporary storage area called the *Clipboard* for those times when you move or copy text. When selected text is *cut* (removed) or copied, it is placed on the Clipboard. *Pasting* inserts a copy of the Clipboard contents before the insertion point. You'll notice that the Paste button, which is the sixth from the left on the toolbar, resembles a clipboard. Entries remain on the Clipboard, either until you cut or copy another entry to it or until you exit from Windows.

 ### MOVING TEXT

To move text within a document

- Select the text to be moved.

- Choose *Edit, Cut* (or click on the *Cut* button—fourth from the left in the toolbar; it shows a pair of scissors) to cut the selected text from the document and place it on the Clipboard. See the previous section for a discussion of the Clipboard.

- Place the insertion point where you want to move this text.

- Choose *Edit, Paste* (or click on the *Paste* button) to paste the cut text before the insertion point.

Let's practice moving text from one location to another within a document:

1. Drag in the selection bar to select the paragraph beginning with *Global Travel is a full-service* and the trailing blank line.

2. Choose **Edit, Cut** to remove the selected text from the document and place it on the Windows Clipboard.

3. Place the insertion point before the *G* in *Global Travel has five.*

4. Choose **Edit, Paste** to paste a copy of the Clipboard contents before the insertion point (see Figure 3.5).

Figure 3.5   **Page 1 of CHAP3.DOC, after pasting**

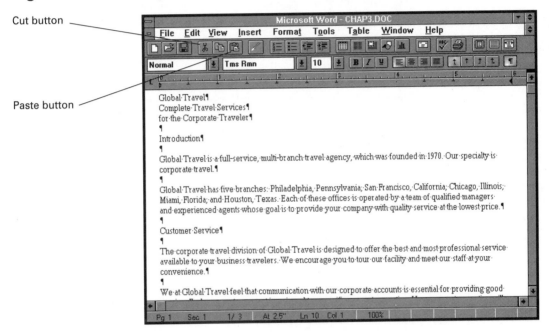

Cut button

Paste button

COPYING TEXT

To copy text within a document

- Select the text to be copied

- Choose *Edit, Copy* (or click on the *Copy* button—fifth from the left in the toolbar; it shows two identical pages) to *copy* the selected text to the Clipboard

- Place the insertion point where you want to copy this text

- Choose *Edit, Paste* (or click on the *Paste* button) to paste the Clipboard text before the insertion point

Now let's practice copying text within a document:

1. Select the first four lines of the document (the three-line page heading and the trailing blank line).

2. Choose **Edit, Copy** to place a copy of the selected text on the Clipboard. Note that the selected text is not removed from the document, as it is when you choose Edit, Move.

3. Use **F5** (Go To) to place the insertion point at the top of page 2.

4. Choose **Edit, Paste** to paste a copy of the Clipboard contents before the insertion point (see Figure 3.6).

Figure 3.6　　**Page 2 of CHAP3.DOC, after pasting**

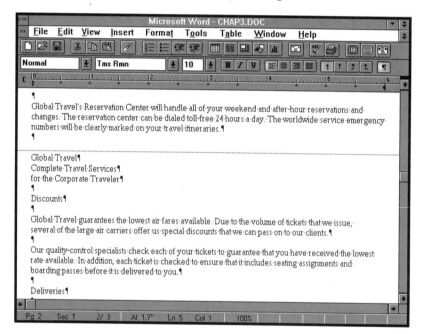

As demonstrated earlier, you can also use the toolbar to paste text from the Clipboard. Let's try this out:

1. Place the insertion point at the top of page 3.

2. Click on the **Paste** button (the one showing a clipboard). Because a copy of the text is still on the Clipboard, you do not need to copy the text again before pasting.

3. Use **File, Save As** to save the document as **mychap3**.

4. Click on **OK** (or press **Enter**) to bypass the Summary Info dialog box. Or, feel free to enter information into this box if you wish, and then click on **OK**.

USING UNDO TO REVERSE YOUR LAST OPERATION

Word provides an Undo command that allows you to reverse (undo) the last operation that you performed. Because Undo can only reverse your *last* operation, you must use it immediately after performing the operation.

Use either of the following Undo methods to reverse your last operation:

- Choose *Edit, Undo*

- Click on the *Undo* button (seventh from the left in the toolbar, it shows a pencil with an eraser)

Let's delete a block of text from MYCHAP3.DOC and then use the Undo feature to undelete this text:

1. Select the heading *Flight Insurance* near the top of page 3.

2. Press **Del** to delete the text. (Because you used Del rather than Edit, Cut or Edit, Copy, the text has *not* been placed on the Clipboard.)

3. Click on **Edit** to display the Edit drop-down menu. Observe the Undo option at the top; it reads *Undo Edit Clear.* The Edit, Undo option changes to reflect the operation to be undone.

4. Click on **Undo Edit Clear** to restore your deleted text.

Now let's use the toolbar Undo button to reverse a potentially catastrophic text-replacement mistake:

1. Select the entire document. (Choose **Edit, Select All.**)

2. Type your first initial. Word prompts:

```
Are you sure you want to replace the current
selection?
```

This prompt is intended as a safeguard to prevent you from accidentally replacing (thus deleting) the entire contents of your document. For now, we'll choose to ignore its warning.

3. Press **Enter** (or click on **Yes**) to replace the entire document with your first initial. Surprise! All that's left in the document window is a single letter. We should have taken Word's warning more seriously.

4. Click on the **Undo** button (the one showing a pencil eraser) to restore the original text. All is well.

5. Deselect to avoid deleting the entire document again.

6. Choose **File, Save** to update the document—that is, to save it with the same name and in the same location.

7. Close the document window.

PRACTICE YOUR SKILLS

In Chapters 2 and 3, you've learned how to navigate within a document, and how to select, replace, move, and copy text. The following two Practice Your Skills activities give you the opportunity to apply these techniques to realistic word-processing situations. After each activity step, a chapter reference is provided (in parentheses) to inform you where the relevant technique for that step was introduced.

Follow these steps to produce the final document shown in Figures 3.7 and 3.8 from the original document PRAC3A.DOC:

1. Open **PRAC3A.DOC** (Chapter 2). (You'll have to scroll through your WRKFILES directory.).

2. Replace all occurrences of *Mayco* with **Macco** (Chapter 3). (**Hint:** Select *Replace All* in the Replace dialog box.)

3. Move the second paragraph on page 1 (beginning with *Congratulations to all*), and the trailing blank line, to before the first paragraph on page 1 (beginning with *As we expected*) (Chapter 3).

4. Copy the three-line heading and the trailing blank line on the top of page 1 to the top of page 2 (Chapter 3).

5. Save the document as myprac3a (Chapter 2).

6. Print the document and compare it to Figures 3.7 and 3.8 (Chapter 1).

7. Close the document (Chapter 1).

Figure 3.7   **Page 1 of the completed document MYPRAC3A.DOC**

Macco Plastics Inc.
Quarterly Sales Report
First Quarter

1. Introduction

Congratulations to all of you! An initial review of the sales figures for the nation reveals a surge in sales in all of Macco's sales areas. Major new clients have been added and many new products are on the way.

As we expected when we entered the field, computer-related products, such as keyboard housings and protective carrying cases, are accounting for a major portion of this upswing.

2. Regional Updates

Midwestern Territory

After several years of falling sales due to the slump in the auto industry, Blair Williams and his folks have something to celebrate. The recent boom in auto manufacturing has led to renewed demand of Macco products in Detroit.

Northeastern Territory

John Martinson and his group are doing a great job in Nashua. They have secured major contracts for a wide range of new and existing products. Much of this business is coming from Computer Equipment Corporation, a major client of Macco's.

Southern Territory

Mark Daley and his group have done a fine job of maintaining relations with Becker's Product Development Division in Boca Raton. They have been working closely with Becker to decrease manufacturing costs.

3. Computer Study

A companywide study will begin in March, under the direction of Cathy Donaldson and Bill Schuster in data processing, to determine how to most effectively implement automation in our firm. We will be making a large commitment to productivity gains via computerization sometime late this year.

Figure 3.8   **Page 2 of the completed document MYPRAC3A.DOC**

Macco Plastics Inc.
Quarterly Sales Report
First Quarter

4. Quarterly Meeting

The quarterly meeting will take place in Memphis this time. You will find the agenda attached to this report.

5. Conclusion

If the recovery continues at the current pace, this year should be a banner year for all of us at Macco. We want to thank all of you for the outstanding jobs you have done and, most important, for standing by Macco in hard times. Keep up the good work!

John Smith
Regional Coordinator
Macco Plastics Inc.

Follow these steps to produce the final document shown in Figures 3.9 and 3.10 from the original document PRAC3B.DOC:

1. Open **PRAC3B.DOC** (Chapter 2).

2. Replace all case-matching occurrences of *Territory* with **Region** (Chapter 3).

3. Move the heading *3. Computer Study* and the subsequent paragraph and paragraph marks on page 1 to before the heading *2. Regional Updates* (Chapter 3).

4. Change *3. Computer Study* to **2. Computer Study** (Chapter 1).

5. Change *2. Regional Updates* to **3. Regional Updates** (Chapter 1).

6. Add the current date as a fourth line to the three-line heading on the top of page 1 (Chapter 1).

7. Copy the entire date line into the heading on the top of page 2 (Chapter 3).

8. Save the document as **myprac3b** (Chapter 2).

9. Print the document and compare it to Figures 3.9 and 3.10 (Chapter 1).

10. Close the document (Chapter 1).

SUMMARY

In this chapter, you learned how to use the mouse, keyboard, and menus to select text; how to use the Edit, Replace command to replace found text; how to move and copy text; and how to use the Undo command to reverse your last operation.

Here's a quick reference guide to the Word features introduced in this chapter:

Desired Result	How to Do It
Select text by dragging	Point at one end of the text to be selected; press and hold the mouse button; drag the mouse pointer to the other end of the text; release the mouse button

Figure 3.9   **Page 1 of the completed document MYPRAC3B.DOC**

Macco Plastics Inc.
Quarterly Sales Report
First Quarter
(today's date)

1. Introduction

Congratulations to all of you! An initial review of the sales figures for the nation reveals a surge in sales in all of Macco's sales regions. Major new clients have been added and many new products are on the way.

As we expected when we entered the field, computer-related products, such as keyboard housings and protective carrying cases, are accounting for a major portion of this upswing.

2. Computer Study

A companywide study will begin in March, under the direction of Cathy Donaldson and Bill Schuster in data processing, to determine how to most effectively implement automation in our firm. We will be making a large commitment to productivity gains via computerization sometime late this year.

3. Regional Updates

Midwestern Region

After several years of falling sales due to the slump in the auto industry, Blair Williams and his folks have something to celebrate. The recent boom in auto manufacturing has led to renewed demand of Macco products in Detroit.

Northeastern Region

John Martinson and his group are doing a great job in Nashua. They have secured major contracts for a wide range of new and existing products. Much of this business is coming from Computer Equipment Corporation, a major client of Macco's.

Southern Region

Mark Daley and his group have done a fine job of maintaining relations with Becker's Product Development Division in Boca Raton. They have been working closely with Becker to decrease manufacturing costs.

Figure 3.10   **Page 2 of the completed document MYPRAC3B.DOC**

Macco Plastics Inc.
Quarterly Sales Report
First Quarter
(today's date)

4. Quarterly Meeting

The quarterly meeting will take place in Memphis this time. You will find the agenda attached to this report.

5. Conclusion

If the recovery continues at the current pace, this year should be a banner year for all of us at Macco. We want to thank all of you for the outstanding jobs you have done and, most important, for standing by Macco in hard times. Keep up the good work!

John Smith
Regional Coordinator
Macco Plastics Inc.

Desired Result	How to Do It
Select text by using Shift	Place the insertion point at one end of the text; press and hold Shift; click at the other end of the text; release Shift
Select a word	Point anywhere inside the word and double-click the mouse button
Select a sentence	Point anywhere inside the sentence; press and hold Ctrl; click the mouse button; release Ctrl
Select a line	Point in the selection bar next to the line and click the mouse button
Select multiple lines	Point in the selection bar next to the first or last line of text to be selected; press and hold the mouse button; drag down or up; release the mouse button
Select a paragraph	Point in the selection bar next to the paragraph and double-click the mouse button
Select an entire document	Choose **Edit, Select All**; or, point anywhere in the selection bar; press and hold Ctrl, click the mouse button; then release Ctrl
Extend an existing selection	While holding Shift, click beyond the existing selection
Shorten an existing selection	While holding Shift, click inside the existing selection
Deselect an existing selection	Make another selection; or, click the mouse button in the text area anywhere outside the existing selection

Desired Result	How to Do It
Replace found text in a document	Place the insertion point where you wish to begin; choose **Edit, Replace**; type the search text in the Find What text box; type the replace text in the Replace With text box; select your desired search options; click on **Find Next** (or press **Enter**) to find the first occurrence; then click on either **Replace, Find Next**, or **Replace All**; repeat the above step as many times as necessary until you have searched through the entire document (or cancel your search at any time by clicking on **Cancel**); close the Replace dialog box
Move text within a document	Select the text to be moved; choose **Edit, Cut** (or click on the toolbar **Cut** button); place the insertion point where you want to move this text; choose **Edit, Paste** (or click on the toolbar **Paste** button)
Copy text within a document	Select the text to be copied; choose **Edit, Copy** (or click on the toolbar **Copy** button); place the insertion point where you want to copy this text; choose **Edit, Paste** (or click on the toolbar **Paste** button)
Undo your last operation	Choose **Edit, Undo** (or click on the toolbar **Undo** button)

In the next chapter, you'll learn the basics of character formatting—how to apply and remove character styles (such as **bold** and *italic*) and how to change fonts (typestyles) and point sizes for your text.

IF YOU'RE STOPPING HERE

If you need to break off here, please exit from Word. If you want to proceed directly to the next chapter, please do so now.

CHAPTER FOUR: CHARACTER FORMATTING

Applying
Character Styles

Applying Fonts and
Point Sizes

To help you distinguish between steps presented for your general knowledge and steps you should carry out at your computer as you read, we have adopted the following system:

- A bulleted step, like this, is provided for your information and reference only.

1. A numbered step, like this, indicates one in a series of steps that you should carry out in sequence at your computer.

The overall effectiveness of a document is directly related to the way it looks. A brilliantly written business report, for example, can be severely undermined by an inappropriate typestyle, print too small to read comfortably, a dizzying barrage of italics or under-lining, tables whose columns don't line up, an overbusy page layout, and so on. These next three chapters are devoted to *formatting*—controlling the way your documents look. We'll proceed logically: This chapter covers Word's smallest formatting units, *characters*; Chapter 5 covers its intermediate units, *paragraphs*; and Chapter 6 covers its largest units, *pages*.

When you're done working through this chapter, you will know

- How to apply and remove character styles
- How to change fonts and point sizes

APPLYING CHARACTER STYLES

You can enhance the appearance of your documents and emphasize selected text through the application of *character styles* (bold, italic, underline, and so on). In this book, for example, we chose to bold certain headings (such as **Desired Result** and **How to Do It**, which appear in each chapter's Summary) and italicize new terms (such as *character styles*). Word provides two methods for applying character styles: the Character dialog box (accessed by issuing the Format, Character command) and the character style buttons in the ribbon.

 USING THE CHARACTER DIALOG BOX TO APPLY CHARACTER STYLES

To use the Character dialog box to apply character styles

- Select the desired text
- Choose *Format, Character* to open the Character dialog box
- Select your desired character style options
- Click on *OK* (or press *Enter*) to apply your chosen styles

To use the Character dialog box to remove character styles, follow the procedure just described to deselect the style options you wish to remove.

If you are not running Word, please start it now. Let's begin by opening a new document and modifying its character styles:

1. Click on the **Open** button (the toolbar button showing an open file folder) to display the Open dialog box.

2. If your WRKFILES directory is not already selected, select it now.

3. In the File Name list box, double-click on **chap4.doc** to open the document.

4. Select **Introduction**, near the top of the document.

5. Choose **Format, Character** to open the Character dialog box (see Figure 4.1).

Figure 4.1   **The Character dialog box**

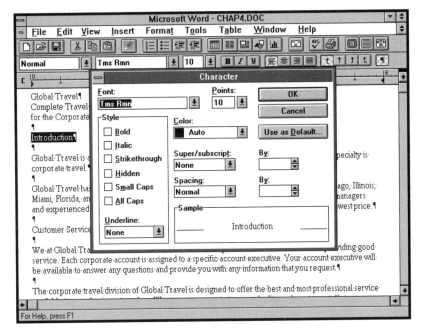

6. Check (click on) the **Bold** option. Note that the Sample box shows you how your style choice (Bold) will look.

7. Click on **OK** (or press **Enter**) to bold your selected text and return to the document.

8. Deselect **Introduction** to verify that it is bolded. You can see character styles better when the text is deselected.

9. Select **Customer Service**, the next heading on page 1.

10. Choose **Format**, **Character** to open the Character dialog box. Check Bold and then click on **OK** (or press **Enter**) to bold *Customer Service*.

Now let's see how to remove the character style that you just applied and then restore it:

1. If **Customer Service** is not selected, select it now.

2. Choose **Format**, **Character**.

3. Uncheck **Bold** and then click on **OK** (or press **Enter**) to unbold *Customer Service*.

4. Choose **Edit**, **Undo Formatting** to reverse step 3—that is, to rebold *Customer Service*.

Let's use the Character dialog box to apply multiple styles (italic and underline) to your document's first line:

1. Select **Global Travel**, the first line.

2. Choose **Format**, **Character**.

3. Check **Italic**. Observe the Sample box text; the text is italicized.

4. Click on the **down arrow** next to the Underline list box to display Word's underline options. Click on **Single** to apply a single underline. Observe the Sample box; the text is italicized and underlined.

5. Click on **OK** (or press **Enter**) to italicize and underline your selected text, *Global Travel*. Deselect the text to see the multiple styles more clearly.

6. Select **Global Travel** again.

7. Choose **Format**, **Character**.

8. Uncheck **Italic** and then click on **OK** to remove the italic character style. Deselect *Global Travel* to verify that the italics (but not the underline) have been removed, as shown in Figure 4.2.

 ## USING THE RIBBON TO APPLY CHARACTER STYLES

Located just under the toolbar, the ribbon provides quick access to character style options, including bold, italic, and underline.

To use the ribbon to apply character styles

- Select the desired text
- Click on the desired ribbon character style button

To use the ribbon to remove character styles

- Select the desired text
- Click on the ribbon button of the character style you wish to remove

Figure 4.2   **Global Travel, after removing italics**

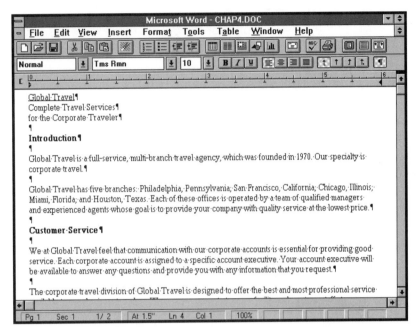

When you wish to remove all character styles from your selected text, use this shortcut: Press *Ctrl+Spacebar*.

Let's practice using the ribbon to apply character styles:

1. Move to the top of the document.

2. Select the paragraph beginning with *Global Travel has five branches* (double-click in the selection bar). Do not include the trailing blank line.

3. Click on the **Bold** button (the button with a bold **B**, in the middle of the ribbon) to bold the entire paragraph. Note that the button now appears to be pushed in.

4. Choose **Format**, **Character**. Note that Bold is checked. Regardless of how you apply character styles—by using the ribbon or the Character dialog box—these styles are reflected in both places.

5. Uncheck **Bold** and then click on **OK**. Observe the Bold button; it no longer looks pushed in.

6. Click on the **Bold** button to rebold the selected text.

7. Click on the **Italic** button (the button with an italicized *I* to the right of the Bold button) to italicize the text.

8. Click on the **Underline** button (the button with an underlined <u>U</u> to the right of the Italic button) to single-underline the text (see Figure 4.3).

Figure 4.3 **Selected text, after applying bold, italic, and underline character styles**

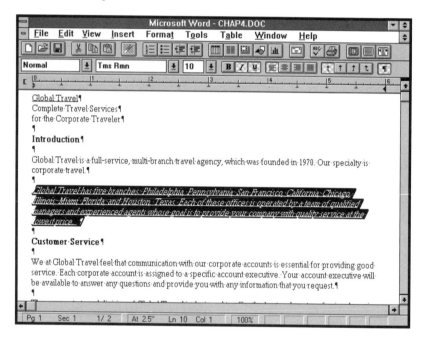

Now let's use the Ctrl+Spacebar technique to remove all character styles from your selected text:

1. If the paragraph *Global Travel has five branches* is not selected, select it now.

2. Press **Ctrl+Spacebar** to remove all character styles from the selected text. Note that this removal is reflected in the ribbon character style buttons.

PRACTICE YOUR SKILLS

1. Verify that your character style removal is also reflected in the Character dialog box.

2. Select the entire document and then italicize it.

3. Use the Undo command to reverse step 2.

4. Remove the underline from the first line (*Global Travel*), then bold and italicize it.

REPEATING CHARACTER STYLES

Once you have applied one or more character styles to your selected text, you can easily reapply (repeat) these styles to newly selected text. To do this

- Select the new text

- Choose *Edit, Repeat Character*, or press the *F4 (Repeat)* short-cut key

Note: If you wish to use the technique just described to repeat multiple character styles (for example, bold *and* italic), you must have applied these character styles through the Character dialog box. If you attempt to repeat multiple character styles that you applied by using the ribbon, only the last character style will be repeated.

Let's use the F4 key to repeat character styles:

1. Scroll to the bottom of the document. (Drag the **vertical scroll box** to the bottom of the scroll bar.)

2. Select **Flight Insurance**.

3. Choose **Format, Character**.

4. Check **Italic**. In the Underline list box, click on **Single**. Click on **OK** to italicize and underline the selected text.

5. Select **Telex**.

6. Open the Edit menu (click on **Edit**). Observe the shortcut key for the Repeat Character command—it is F4. Close the Edit menu (click on **Edit** again).

7. Press **F4** (Repeat) to repeat your last character style. Note that the selected text (*Telex*) is italicized and underlined.

8. Use F5 (Go To) to move to the top of page 2.

9. Select **Complete Travel Services**. Click on the **Bold** button, then click on the **Italic** button to bold and italicize the selected text.

10. Move to the top of the document and select **Complete Travel Services**.

11. Press **F4** (Repeat) to attempt to repeat your bold/italic styles. Deselect and observe the text. Because you used the ribbon, pressing F4 repeated only the *last* character style: italic. To ensure that *all* character styles are repeated, you should apply multiple character styles through the Character dialog box.

12. Reselect **Complete Travel Services** and click on the **Bold** button to correct the style.

13. Use File, Save As to save the disk file as **mychap4**.

PRACTICE YOUR SKILLS

1. Bold the heading **International Travel**.

2. Use **F4** (Repeat) to bold the remaining headings: **Corporate Profiles, Worldwide Services, Discounts, Deliveries, Auto Rentals, Hotel Accommodations, Additional Services, Personal Vacations, Flight Insurance**, and **Telex**.

3. Remove the italics and underlining from **Flight Insurance** and **Telex**.

4. Use the Character dialog box to bold and italicize **for the Corporate Traveler** at the top of page 1.

5. Use F4 to repeat these multiple styles to **Global Travel** and **for the Corporate Traveler** at the top of page 2.

6. Compare your document to the printouts depicted in Figures 4.4 and 4.5.

7. Update the disk file (use File, Save).

Figure 4.4   **Page 1 of MYCHAP4.DOC**

Global Travel
Complete Travel Services
for the Corporate Traveler

Introduction

Global Travel is a full-service, multi-branch travel agency, which was founded in 1970. Our specialty is corporate travel.

Global Travel has five branches: Philadelphia, Pennsylvania; San Francisco, California; Chicago, Illinois; Miami, Florida; and Houston, Texas. Each of these offices is operated by a team of qualified managers and experienced agents whose goal is to provide your company with quality service at the lowest price.

Customer Service

We at Global Travel feel that communication with our corporate accounts is essential for providing good service. Each corporate account is assigned to a specific account executive. Your account executive will be available to answer any questions and provide you with any information that you request.

The corporate travel division of Global Travel is designed to offer the best and most professional service available to your business travelers. We encourage you to tour our facility and meet our staff at your convenience.

International Travel

We offer complete international itinerary assistance. We maintain a supply of passport and visa applications so that we can provide the necessary papers to our clients with minimum delay. Our International Rate Program guarantees you fast and accurate pricing, no matter how complicated the itinerary.

Corporate Profiles

Your company profile will be stored in our computer, and individual profiles will be maintained on each frequent traveler. Each profile will contain information regarding passport information, seating preference, car rental preference, frequent-flyer membership number, and corporate discount numbers. This information ensures that we can provide frequent travelers fast, cost-effective itineraries.

Worldwide Services

Global Travel's Reservation Center will handle all of your weekend and after-hour reservations and changes. The reservation center can be dialed toll-free 24 hours a day. The worldwide service emergency numbers will be clearly marked on your travel itineraries.

Figure 4.5   **Page 2 of MYCHAP4.DOC**

Global Travel
Complete Travel Services
for the Corporate Traveler

Discounts

Global Travel guarantees the lowest air fares available. Due to the volume of tickets that we issue, several of the large air carriers offer us special discounts that we can pass on to our clients.

Our quality-control specialists check each of your tickets to guarantee that you have received the lowest rate available. In addition, each ticket is checked to ensure that it includes seating assignments and boarding passes before it is delivered to you.

Deliveries

Our courier makes daily deliveries, both in the morning and afternoon, to offices within 20 miles of our local branch. All of our offices, each located across from the local airport, have drive-up windows. If you make last minute travel plans with us you can pick up your ticket right at the drive-up window.

Auto Rentals

We guarantee the lowest prices on all car rentals. We will match the type of car with the information provided in the profile for each of your frequent travelers. Each car that is rented through Global Travel carries an extra $50,000 worth of liability insurance.

Hotel Accommodations

Our Corporate Hotel Program is the most competitive and comprehensive program in the world, offering corporate travelers cost savings and extra amenities in most business locations. Global Travel has access to more than 10,000 hotels worldwide, with a range of rooms from economy to luxury. This selection offers your corporate travelers the accommodations they want with a cost savings of 10-30% off the regular rates

Additional Services

Global Travel also provides the following services for our corporate customers:

Personal Vacations

Our corporate clients are invited to discuss their vacation and personal travel plans with an agent from Global Travel's Vacation Division. Our Vacation Division is skilled in both domestic and international travel.

Flight Insurance

We will supply all clients with $250,000 worth of flight insurance for every trip arranged through Global Travel.

Telex

Service is available for international hotel confirmations.

APPLYING FONTS AND POINT SIZES

You can change the shape and size of your selected text by changing the text's *font* and *point size*. The font determines the shape (typestyle) of the text; the point size determines the size of the font (one point equals 1/72 of an inch). The sentence you are reading, for example, is printed in 10-point Univers font. You can use the Character dialog box or the ribbon to apply fonts and point sizes.

Note: The specific fonts and point sizes that Word makes available for your use are dependent upon your currently selected printer. Postscript-type laser printers, for example, offer a large variety of fonts and point sizes, whereas low-end dot-matrix printers offer a much more limited selection.

USING THE CHARACTER DIALOG BOX TO APPLY FONTS AND POINT SIZES

To use the Character dialog box to apply fonts and point sizes

- Select the desired text

- Choose *Format, Character* to open the Character dialog box

- Select your desired font and/or point size

- Click on *OK* (or press *Enter*)

Let's select some text and use the Character dialog box to change its font and point size:

1. Move to the top of the document.

2. Select the lines **Complete Travel Services** and **for the Corporate Traveler** in the heading at the top of page 1.

3. Choose **Format, Character**.

4. Click on the **down arrow** next to the Font list box to display your available fonts. Note that the font names are listed in alphabetical order. Observe the current font (*Tms Rmn*, short for Times Roman) and the representative text in the Sample box.

5. Select **Helv** (short for Helvetica). You may need to scroll up through the list to find Helv. Observe the change in the Sample box text.

6. Click on the **down arrow** next to the Points list box to display the available point sizes for Helvetica.

7. Select **12**. Observe the change in the Sample box text.

8. Click on **OK** to apply your chosen font and point size to the selected text. Deselect and compare your screen to Figure 4.6.

Figure 4.6   **Lines 2 and 3 of the heading, after changing the font and point size**

Save button

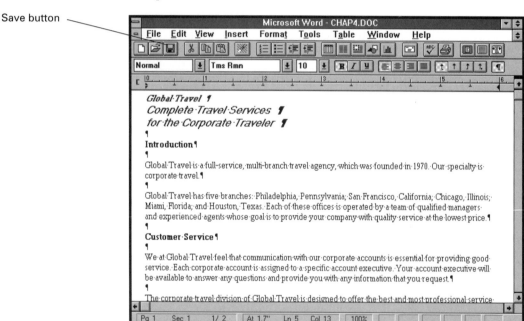

In a previous activity, you used F4 (Repeat) to repeat character styles. Now let's use F4 to repeat the font and point size:

1. Move to the top of page 2.

2. Select **Complete Travel Services** and **for the Corporate Traveler**, lines 2 and 3 in the page heading.

3. Press **F4** to repeat your last character style. Because you used the Character dialog box instead of the ribbon when you applied the font and point size on page 1, the selected text changes to Helv *and* 12 point.

4. Click on the **Save** button (the third from the left in the toolbar, it shows a floppy disk) to update the document.

USING THE RIBBON TO APPLY FONTS AND POINT SIZES

To use the ribbon to apply fonts and point sizes

* Select the desired text

* Click on the down arrow of the *Font* or *Point Size* list boxes (respectively, the second and third boxes from the left in the ribbon)

* Select your desired font or point size

Let's use the ribbon to change the font and point size:

1. Select **Global Travel**, the first line on page 2.

2. Open the Font list box in the ribbon (click on the **down arrow** to the right of the box). Note that the box currently displays *Tms Rmn*. Select **Helv**.

3. Open the Points list box in the ribbon. Note that the box currently displays *10*. Select **24** (you may need to scroll).

PRACTICE YOUR SKILLS

1. Move to the top of page 1.

2. Change the font and point size of the first line, *Global Travel*, to **Helv** and **24**. (**Hint:** Use the F4 key.)

3. Deselect and compare your screen to Figure 4.7.

4. Save the disk file and close the document.

SUMMARY

In this chapter, you learned the basics of character formatting. You now know how to apply and remove character styles, and how to change fonts and point sizes.

Figure 4.7   **Global Travel, after changing the font and point size**

Font list box

Point size list box

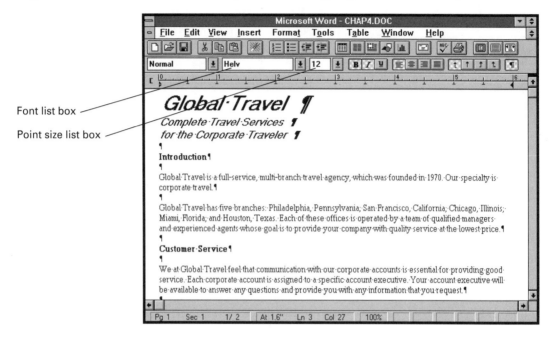

Here's a quick reference guide to the Word features introduced in this chapter:

Desired Result	How to Do It
Use the Character dialog box to apply character styles	Select the desired text; choose **Format**, **Character**; select your desired character style options; click on **OK** (or press **Enter**)
Use the Character dialog box to remove character styles	Follow the procedure just described to deselect the style options you wish to remove
Use the ribbon to apply character styles	Select the desired text; click on the desired ribbon character style button
Use the ribbon to remove character styles	Select the desired text; click on the ribbon button of the character style you wish to remove

Desired Result	How to Do It
Remove all character styles from your selected text	Press **Ctrl+Spacebar**
Repeat character formatting	Select the new text; choose **Edit**, **Repeat Character** (or press **F4***)*
Use the Character dialog box to apply fonts and point sizes	Select the desired text; choose **Format**, **Character**; select your desired font and/or point size; click on **OK** (or press **Enter**)
Use the ribbon to apply fonts and point sizes	Select the desired text; click on the down arrow of the Font or Point Size boxes; select your desired font or point size

In the next chapter, you will learn the basics of paragraph formatting. You'll find out how to work with tab stops and paragraph indents, create new lines within a paragraph, align paragraphs, and set line spacing.

IF YOU'RE STOPPING HERE

If you need to break off here, please exit Word. If you want to proceed directly to the next chapter, please do so now.

CHAPTER FIVE: PARAGRAPH FORMATTING

Working with Tabs

Setting Indents and Line Breaks

Using Shift+Enter to Create a New Line

Setting Paragraph Alignment

Setting Line Spacing

In Chapter 4, you learned the basics of character formatting. In this chapter, we'll move on to Word's intermediate unit of formatting: the paragraph. Many important document layout features are controlled at the paragraph level, including tab stops, indents, text alignment, and line spacing. Mastering paragraph formatting will greatly assist you in presenting professionally laid out, attractive documents.

When you're done working through this chapter, you will know

- How to set, change, and clear tab stops
- How to set and repeat paragraph indents
- How to create new lines within a paragraph
- How to align paragraphs
- How to set line spacing

WORKING WITH TABS

As you learned in Chapter 1, you use tabs to align text at preset tab stops across the page. This type of alignment is particularly important in tables, where several categories of information must line up in precise columns. In the first part of this chapter, you'll learn how to set, change, and clear custom tab stops.

 ## SELECTING PARAGRAPHS FOR PARAGRAPH FORMATTING

Before you set custom tab stops, you must first select the desired paragraph or paragraphs. As you learned in the last chapter, when you select a paragraph for character formatting (character styles, font, point size, and so on), you must select the entire paragraph. However, when you select a paragraph for *paragraph formatting* (tab stops, indents, line spacing, and so on), you *do not* have to select the entire paragraph. To select a *single* paragraph for paragraph formatting, place the insertion point anywhere in the paragraph. You do not have to select (highlight) any characters. To select *multiple* paragraphs for paragraph formatting, select (highlight) a portion of each paragraph.

The techniques just described are paragraph selection shortcuts. If you feel more comfortable selecting entire paragraphs for paragraph formatting, please do so.

 ## TAB TYPES

There are four types of tab stops available in Word. Figure 5.1 illustrates how tab stops align on your computer screen, and Table 5.1 defines each tab type.

Figure 5.1   **Four types of tab stops**

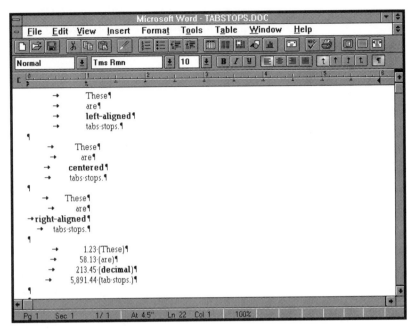

Table 5.1   **The Four Tab Types**

Type	How Tab Affects Text
Left-aligned	Text flows to the right of the tab stop
Centered	Text is centered on the tab stop
Right-aligned	Text flows to the left of the tab stop
Decimal	Text aligns on the decimal point (used for numbers)

Note: By default, left-aligned tab stops are set at .5" increments between the margins (.5", 1", 1.5", and so on). These default tab stops are displayed as small upside-down T's on the ruler.

SETTING CUSTOM TAB STOPS

Word allows you to create your own custom tab stops, and in doing so, to clear its default tab stops. To set custom tab stops

- Select the desired paragraph(s)

- Select the desired tab type by clicking on the appropriate Tab button in the ribbon: the *Left-Aligned* button, the *Centered* button, the *Right-Aligned* button, or the *Decimal* button (see Figure 5.2)

- Point at the desired tab-stop position in the ruler (directly under the tick marks) and click the mouse button

Figure 5.2   **Ribbon tab buttons**

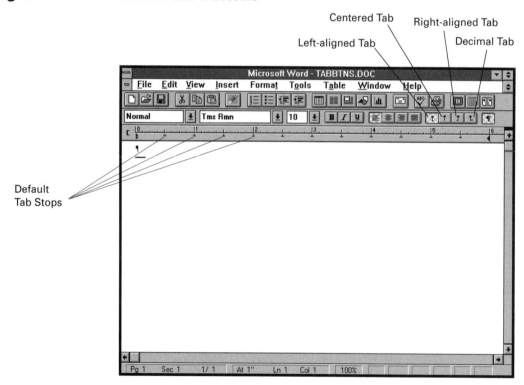

Your custom tab stop is set and all default tab stops to the left of your custom stop are automatically cleared.

If you are not running Word, please start it now.

Note: The further you progress in this book, the more succinct our activity instructions tend to be. For example, instead of saying "Click on the Open button, select the WRKFILES directory, and then double-click on CHAP5.DOC to open it," we now simply say "Open CHAP5.DOC from your WRKFILES directory." If you are unsure of how to perform a certain Word task, use the Index, the end-of-chapter quick reference guides, or Word Help to jog your memory.

Let's open a new document and begin our exploration of tabs by adding text to a tabbed table.

1. Open **chap5.doc** from your WRKFILES directory.

2. Move to the top of page 2.

3. Scroll down and examine the tabbed table following the heading *Discounts*. Note that the Paris and Sydney savings percentages (20% and 10%) are misaligned. We will fix this in the next activity.

4. Place the insertion point in the first blank line after the tabbed table.

5. Press **Tab** to move the insertion point to the first tab stop (.5" to the right) and then type **Hong Kong**.

6. Press **Tab** to move to the second tab stop (1" to the right) and then type 25%.

7. Press **Enter** to create a new blank line. Compare your screen to Figure 5.3.

Now let's set some new left-aligned tab stops to fix the Paris and Sydney savings-percentage misalignments. First we need to select the entire table (all five lines). Let's use our multiple paragraph selection shortcut to do this:

1. Select all the text from *Savings* (in the first line) up to and including *Hong* (in the last line). Even though the first and last lines of the table are only partially highlighted, they are fully selected. Any paragraph formatting changes you now make will apply equally to all five lines.

2. Observe the ruler. Note that Word's default tab stops are set every half inch (.5").

3. Observe that the Left-Aligned tab button is selected. (This button shows an arrow whose shaft extends to the *right*, because text flows to the right of a left-aligned tab stop.) As indicated

earlier in this section, the ribbon tab buttons determine the alignment of the *next* tab stop that you set; a left-aligned tab stop is the default.

Figure 5.3　　**Adding text to the Discounts tabbed table**

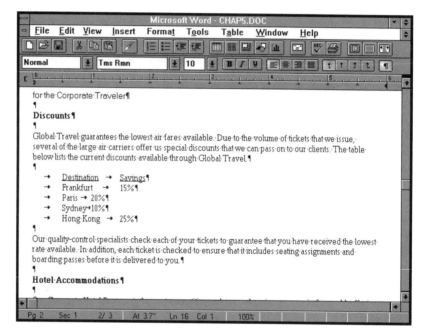

4. Point directly beneath the 1" tick mark in the ruler. Click the mouse button to set a left-aligned tab stop at 1". Note that the default tab stops to the left of 1" have automatically been cleared.

5. Observe the text. The first column in the tabbed table is now 1" from the left margin.

PRACTICE YOUR SKILLS

1. Set a second left-aligned tab stop at 2.5". The second column in the table is now properly aligned.

2. Deselect and compare your screen to Figure 5.4.

Figure 5.4   **Setting tab stops for the Discounts tabbed table**

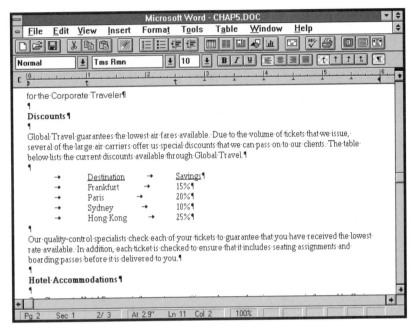

 SETTING DIFFERENT TYPES OF TABS

As mentioned in the previous section, Word provides four types of tab stops: left-aligned, centered, right-aligned, and decimal. Let's use the ruler and the tab buttons to experiment with these:

1. Scroll down to the tabbed table following the heading *Hotel Accommodations*, near the middle of page 2.

2. Use the multiple paragraph selection shortcut to select the body (lower four lines) of the tabbed table.

3. Click on the **Right-Aligned** tab button to right-align the next tab stop you set. (This button shows an arrow whose shaft extends to the *left*, because text flows to the left of a right-aligned tab stop.)

4. Set a right-aligned tab stop at 3.5".

5. Click the **Decimal** tab button to decimal-align the next tab stop you set. (This button shows an arrow with a decimal point to the right of its shaft.) Decimal tabs are used to align numbers containing decimals.

6. Set a decimal tab stop at 5".

PRACTICE YOUR SKILLS

1. Prepare to set tab stops for the heading (top line) of the tabbed table. (**Hint:** Use the single paragraph selection shortcut— place the insertion point anywhere within the heading.)

2. Set a centered tab stop at 2.5".

3. Set a right-aligned tab stop at 5".

4. Note that the heading and body columns are misaligned (see Figure 5.5). We will fix this in the next activity.

Figure 5.5   **The Hotel Accommodations table, misaligned**

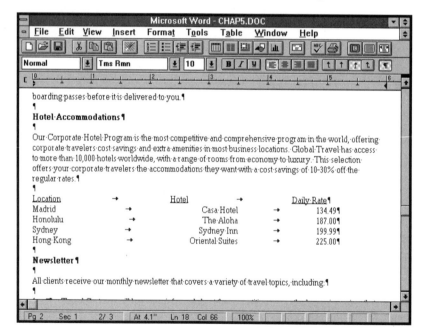

 CHANGING THE POSITIONS OF CUSTOM TAB STOPS

Word allows you to quickly and easily change the positions of your custom tab stops. To do this

• Select the desired paragraph(s)

• In the ruler, drag the custom tab stop to a new position

CLEARING CUSTOM TAB STOPS

Word also allows you to quickly clear (delete) your custom tab stops. To do this

- Select the desired paragraph(s)

- Drag the custom tab stop down into the text area

Now let's fix the Hotel Accommodations table's misalignment by changing and clearing tabs:

1. Select the body (four lines) of the tabbed table.

2. Drag the decimal tab stop at 5" to 4.75" to adjust the position of the table's numbers.

3. Place a centered tab stop at 2.5". Note that this causes a severe misalignment. Why? Because there is now an undesired tab stop in the ruler (the right-aligned tab stop at 3.5"), which prevents the final column of text (*Daily Rate*) from moving to its intended decimal tab-stop location at 4.75".

4. Drag the undesired right-aligned tab stop at 3.5" down off the ruler into the text area, then release the mouse button to clear this tab stop. Note that the misalignment problem has been fixed.

5. Deselect and compare your screen to Figure 5.6.

6. Save the disk file as **mychap5** (use File, Save As).

USING THE TABS DIALOG BOX TO MANAGE YOUR CUSTOM TAB STOPS

We've shown you how to use the ribbon and ruler to manage your custom tab stops. This is generally the preferred method of tab management because it is quick, easy, and provides immediate visual feedback. You can, however, perform all of the tab-management tasks already presented in this chapter (setting, changing, and clearing tab stops) by using the Tabs dialog box (see Figure 5.7).

The advantage of using the Tabs dialog box is that you can specify exact tab-stop positions that you couldn't choose by using the mouse and ruler (for example, 3.12" or 6.78"). The disadvantages are that you must type in your tab-stop positions and that you only see how your tab-stop settings affect the selected paragraph(s) when you exit the Tabs dialog box.

Figure 5.6   **The Hotel Accommodations table, properly aligned**

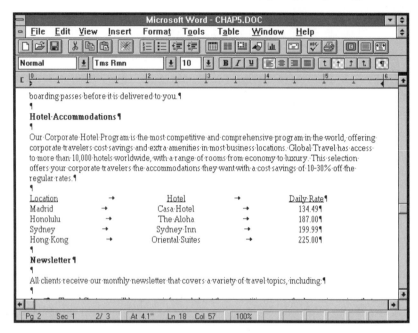

Figure 5.7   **The Tabs dialog box**

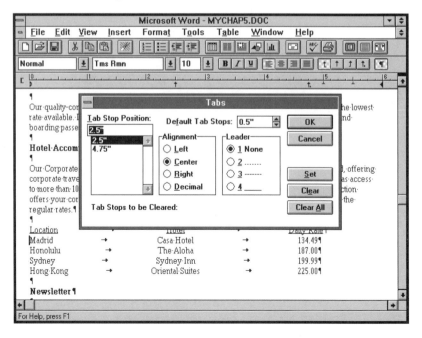

To use the Tabs dialog box for managing your custom tab stops

- Select the desired paragraph(s)

- Choose *Format, Tabs* to open the Tabs dialog box

Note: The Tabs dialog box in Figure 5.7 reflects the settings for the tabbed table line beginning with *Madrid*.

- Enter your desired settings to change or clear tab stops

- Click on *OK* (or press *Enter*)

Note: We recommend that you use the ribbon and ruler for managing your custom tab stops, except in those rare instances when you need to set an exact tab-stop position that you cannot choose with the mouse and the ruler.

SETTING INDENTS AND LINE BREAKS

Margins define the upper, lower, left, and right page boundaries of an entire document (see "Setting Margins" in Chapter 6 for details on this Word feature). *Indents* define the left and right boundaries of selected paragraphs within a document.

By default, a paragraph's left and right indents are set equal to the document's left and right margins. However, you can modify a paragraph's left and/or right indents, without changing the document's margins. Figure 5.8 illustrates the relationship between margins and indents.

 INDENT MARKERS

The ruler provides *indent markers* (displayed as black triangles; see Figure 5.8) that you can use to control the positions of a selected paragraph's indents. There are three types of indent markers:

Indent Marker Type	Location and Function
First-line Indent	Upper-left triangle in the ruler; controls the left boundary for the first line of a paragraph
Left Indent	Lower-left triangle in the ruler; controls the left boundary of every line in a paragraph but the first

Indent Marker Type	Location and Function
Right Indent	Triangle on the right end of the ruler; controls the right boundary for every line in a paragraph

Figure 5.8   **Margins and indents**

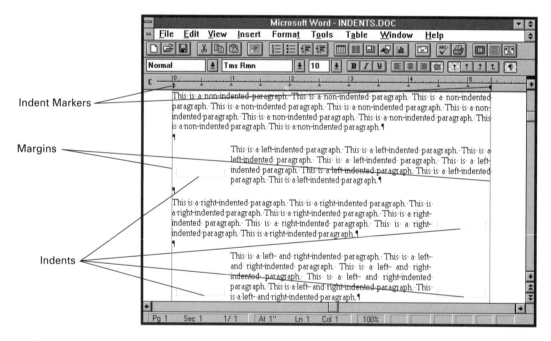

 SETTING INDENTS

Word allows you to quickly and easily set indents. To do this

- Select the paragraph(s) you wish to indent

- Drag the appropriate indent marker to your desired new position in the ruler

By default, if you drag the Left indent marker, the First-line indent marker moves along with it. To drag the Left indent marker by itself, hold down the Shift key as you drag.

REPEATING PARAGRAPH FORMATTING

In the last chapter, you learned how to repeat character formatting. Word also allows you to repeat paragraph formatting. To do this

- Format a paragraph
- Select a new paragraph
- Choose *Edit, Repeat Formatting* (or press *F4*)

Let's set some indents and then repeat them:

1. Move to the top of page 3.

2. Place the insertion point in the *Personal Vacations* heading. This heading is indented .5" from the left margin.

3. Observe the ruler. The Left indent marker and the First-line indent marker (the lower and upper triangles near the left end of the ruler, respectively) are both at .5".

4. Place the insertion point in the paragraph beginning with *Our corporate clients*. This paragraph is not indented. Observe the ruler. The indent markers are set even with the margins.

5. Drag the **Right** indent marker—the triangle at the right end of the ruler—to 5.5". (Align the marker's flat side with the 5.5" tick mark.) A right indent creates a different right-hand boundary for the selected paragraph.

6. Point the tip of the mouse pointer at the **Left** indent marker (the lower-left triangle).

7. Drag the **Left** indent and **First-line** indent markers together to .5" to change the left-hand boundary of the selected paragraph. As long as you point to the Left indent marker, both indent markers move together.

Now let's repeat our indent formatting:

1. Place the insertion point in the paragraph beginning with *We will supply all clients* (the next multiple-line paragraph on page 3).

2. Choose *Edit, Repeat Formatting* (or press *F4*) to repeat your indent formatting. Observe the new indents.

PRACTICE YOUR SKILLS

1. Format the paragraph beginning with *Telex service is available* with left and first-line indents at .5" and a right indent at 5.5". (**Hint:** Use F4.)

2. Compare your screen to Figure 5.9.

Figure 5.9   **CHAP5.DOC, after indent formatting**

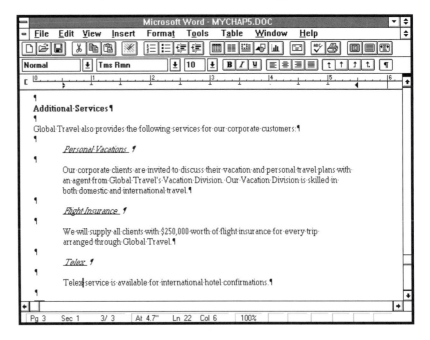

 SETTING HANGING INDENTS

The term *hanging indent* is used to describe a format in which a paragraph's first line is left-indented less than all of its subsequent lines. In effect, the first line *hangs* over the rest. Hanging indents are commonly used for the paragraphs in bulleted or numbered lists, such as the list of bulleted instructions that appears next or the lists of numbered instructions in the activities throughout this book.

To create a hanging indent

• Select the desired paragraph(s)

- If necessary, drag the First-line indent marker (the upper-left triangle) to the desired position

- Press and hold *Shift*, then drag only the Left indent marker (the lower-left triangle) to the desired position (to the right of the First-line indent marker)

Now let's set some hanging indents and then repeat them:

1. Scroll up to the heading *Newsletter* (near the bottom of page 2).

2. Place the insertion point in the paragraph beginning with *1. Travel Costs*.

3. Press and hold **Shift** and then drag the **Left** indent marker (the lower-left triangle in the ruler) marker to .5". Release **Shift**. Pressing the Shift key while dragging the Left indent marker leaves the First-line indent marker in position.

4. Observe your hanging indent. The second line is indented to .5", while the first line remains at the left margin—that is, unindented.

PRACTICE YOUR SKILLS

1. Repeat a .5" hanging indent for the paragraphs beginning with *2. Special Fares* and *3. Travel Basics*. (**Hint**: Use F4.)

2. Deselect and compare your screen to Figure 5.10.

USING THE PARAGRAPH DIALOG BOX TO MANAGE YOUR INDENTS

As you've learned in previous sections of this chapter, you can manage custom tab stops by using the ribbon and the ruler or the Tabs dialog box. Similarly, you can manage indents by using the ruler or the Paragraph dialog box. The same advantages and disadvantages apply to both situations (you may want to review the section on the Tabs dialog box, earlier in this chapter). Again, we recommend that you use the ruler for managing your indents, except in those instances when you need to set an exact indent position that you cannot choose with the mouse and the ruler.

To use the Paragraph dialog box to manage your indents

- Select the desired paragraph(s)

- Choose *Format, Paragraph* to open the Paragraph dialog box

Figure 5.10   **Setting hanging indents**

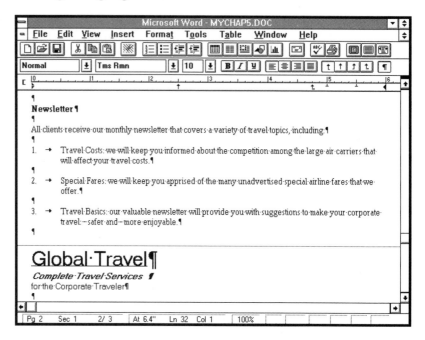

- Enter your desired indent settings
- Click on *OK* (or press *Enter*)

USING SHIFT+ENTER TO CREATE A NEW LINE

When you press Enter to create a new line in a document, you also create a new paragraph. At times, this may be undesirable. For example, let's say that you wanted to insert a new line in the middle of a list within a hanging-indent paragraph. If you pressed Enter to create the new line, you would lose your indent. (Remember, pressing Enter creates a new first-line paragraph, and the first line of a hanging-indent paragraph is not indented.) To remedy this problem, Word allows you to use Shift+Enter to create a new line without creating a new paragraph. To do so

- Place the insertion point where you want to end the current line and create a new line

- Press *Shift+Enter*; Word inserts a *newline character* (↵) and creates a new line (without creating a new paragraph)

Let's take a moment to observe the difference between new paragraphs and new lines:

1. In the paragraph beginning with *3. Travel Basics*, place the insertion point to the left of the hyphen (-) in *- safer and*.

2. Press **Enter** to create a new paragraph. All text to the right of the insertion point is moved onto the next line. Because you've created a new paragraph, the first (and in this case, the only) line loses its hanging indent and moves back flush with the left margin.

3. Press **Backspace** to delete the paragraph mark and return the text to its original position.

4. Now press **Shift+Enter** to create a new line without creating a new paragraph. Your hanging indent is maintained. Note that pressing Shift+Enter ends the line with a newline character (↵) instead of with the usual paragraph mark (see Figure 5.11).

Figure 5.11   **Inserting a newline character**

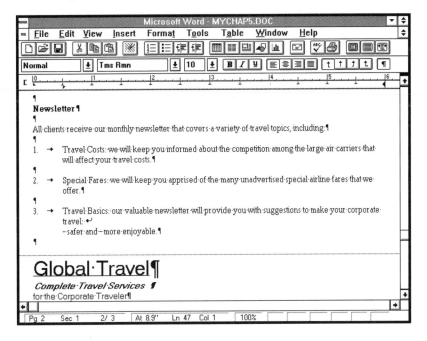

5. Press **Shift+Enter** to insert a blank line while maintaining the hanging indent.

6. Place the insertion point to the left of the second hyphen (-) in the same paragraph, - *more enjoyable*.

7. Press **Shift+Enter** twice to create two new lines.

SETTING PARAGRAPH ALIGNMENT

Paragraph alignment determines how text is positioned between the left and right indents. Word provides four types of paragraph alignment. Figure 5.12 illustrates how paragraph alignment appears on your computer screen, and Table 5.2 defines each type of paragraph alignment.

Figure 5.12   **Paragraph alignment types**

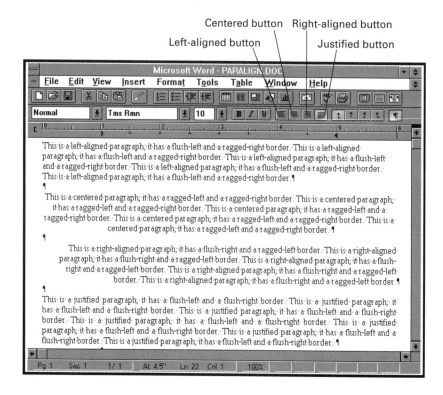

Table 5.2   **The Four Paragraph Alignment Types**

Type	Alignment
Left-aligned	Lines of text are *flush-left* (aligned evenly along the left indent) and *ragged-right* (aligned unevenly along the right indent); left-aligned is the default paragraph-alignment setting
Centered	Lines of text are centered between the indents; both the left and right sides of a centered paragraph are ragged
Right-aligned	Lines of text are flush-right and ragged-left, the opposite of left-aligned
Justified	Lines of text are both flush-left and flush-right; in a justified paragraph, Word adjusts the spacing between words so that they stretch from the left indent to the right indent

To set paragraph alignment

- Select the desired paragraph(s)

- Click on the appropriate alignment button in the ribbon (see Figure 5.12)

Note: You can also use the Paragraph dialog box to align paragraphs; but, once again, we recommend using the ribbon.

Let's begin our paragraph-alignment activities by centering some paragraphs:

1. Place the insertion point anywhere within the first line of the document, *Global Travel*. Observe the text alignment buttons (the four buttons to the left of the tab buttons in the ribbon). The Left-Aligned text button (the one with the flush-left lines) is selected.

2. Click on the **Centered** text button (the one with the centered short and long lines) to center each line of the selected paragraph between the left and right indents. In this example, the paragraph contains only one line.

3. Select lines 2 and 3 of the heading.

4. Click on the **Centered** text button to center both paragraphs.

5. Deselect and compare your screen with Figure 5.13.

Figure 5.13   **Centering paragraphs**

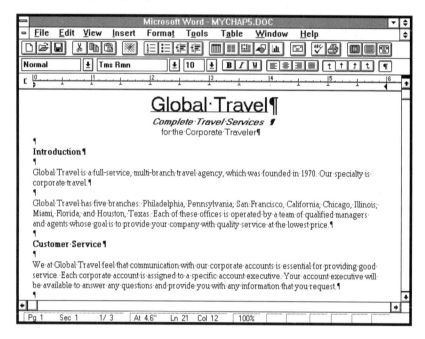

Now let's try out the other paragraph alignments:

1. Move to the top of the document.

2. Place the insertion point in the paragraph beginning with *Global Travel has five branches* (the second multiple-line paragraph on page 1).

3. Observe the last word in each line of the selected paragraph. Because the paragraph is left-aligned, text does not always reach the right indent before wrapping to the next line.

4. Click on the **Justified** text button (the one with the flush-right and flush-left lines).

5. Observe the last word in each line. Word increases the spacing between words in the selected paragraph to fill each line (except the last) so that the text is even with both the left and right indents.

6. Click on the **Right-Aligned** text button (the one with the flush-right lines). Observe the text. Text in the current paragraph now aligns only with the Right Indent marker.

7. Click on the **Left-Aligned** text button to return the paragraph to its original alignment.

PRACTICE YOUR SKILLS

1. Center all three lines of the heading on the top of page 2.

2. Repeat step 1 for the three-line heading on the top of page 3. (**Hint**: Use F4.)

3. Update the disk file (use File, Save).

SETTING LINE SPACING

Line spacing is the vertical distance between lines of text. Word provides six line-spacing options:

- *Auto* (the default and most commonly used setting) automatically adjusts the line spacing to accommodate the largest font in each line

- *Single* sets the line spacing to one single line; Single always maintains a minimum of 12-point (1/6") spacing

- *1.5 lines* sets the line spacing to a line-and-a-half

- *Double* sets the line spacing to two lines

- *At Least* allows you to specify a custom minimum line spacing

- *Exactly* allows you to specify exact line spacing that will not adjust according to font size

To set line spacing

- Select the desired paragraph(s)

- Choose *Format, Paragraph* to open the Paragraph dialog box; you cannot set line spacing by using the toolbar, ribbon, or ruler

- Select your desired line-spacing setting from the *Line Spacing* list box

- Click on *OK* (or press *Enter*)

Let's use the above procedure to change the line spacing of MYCHAP5.DOC:

1. Move to the top of the document.

2. Select the entire document (choose **Edit, Select All**).

3. Choose **Format, Paragraph**. Examine the Paragraph dialog box. Unlike the ribbon and ruler, the Paragraph dialog box provides access to *all* paragraph-formatting options and allows you to type in exact measurements.

4. Click on the **down arrow** of the **Line Spacing** list box to open the box and display the line-spacing choices.

5. Select **1.5 Lines** and then click on **OK** (or press **Enter**). Observe the text. The line spacing has changed from 1 to 1.5 lines (see Figure 5.14).

6. Choose **Format, Paragraph** and then open the **Line Spacing** list box (click on the **down arrow**).

Figure 5.14   **Changing the line spacing to 1.5 lines**

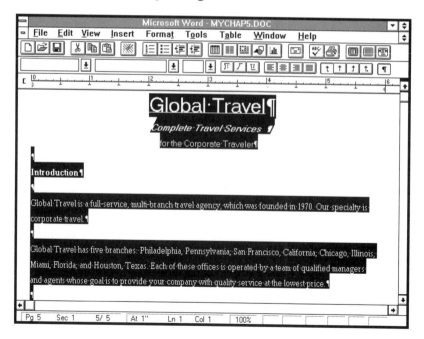

7. Select **Double** and then click on **OK** (or press **Enter**). Observe the text. The line spacing has changed to 2 lines from the original value of 1 line.

8. Choose **Format, Paragraph** and then open the **Line Spacing** list box.

9. Select **Auto** and then click on **OK** (or press **Enter**). Observe the text. The line spacing has returned to its original value of 1 line.

10. Deselect the text to avoid inadvertently deleting the entire document.

Up to now, you've always saved the changes you made to your active document before closing it. However, you can close a document without saving the changes. Let's see how:

1. Choose **File, Close**. Word prompts:

   `Do you want to save changes to MYCHAP5.DOC?`

2. Click on **No** to save the document without saving the changes.

PRACTICE YOUR SKILLS

In Chapters 4 and 5, you learned the basics of character and paragraph formatting. The following two Practice Your Skills activities give you the opportunity to apply these formatting techniques to realistic word-processing situations.

Follow these steps to produce the final document shown in Figures 5.15 and 5.16 from the original document PRAC5A.DOC:

1. Open **prac5a.doc** (Chapter 2).

2. Select the entire document and remove all of its character formats (Chapters 3 and 4). (**Hint:** Use the Ctrl+Spacebar shortcut.)

3. Bold the following headings (Chapter 4):

   1. Introduction

   2. Computer Study

   3. Regional Updates

   4. Quarterly Meeting

   5. Conclusion

Figure 5.15   **Page 1 of the completed document MYPRAC5A.DOC**

Macco Plastics Inc.
Quarterly Sales Report
First Quarter

1. Introduction

Congratulations to all of you! An initial review of the sales figures for the nation reveals a surge in sales in all of Macco's sales regions. Major new clients have been added and many new products are on the way.

As we expected when we entered the field, computer-related products, such as keyboard housings and protective carrying cases, are accounting for a major portion of this upswing.

2. Computer Study

A companywide study will begin in March, under the direction of Cathy Donaldson and Bill Schuster in data processing, to determine how to most effectively implement automation in our firm. We will be making a large commitment to productivity gains via computerization sometime late this year.

3. Regional Updates

Midwestern Region

After several years of falling sales due to the slump in the auto industry, Blair Williams and his folks have something to celebrate. The recent boom in auto manufacturing has led to renewed demand of Macco products in Detroit.

Northeastern Region

John Martinson and his group are doing a great job in Nashua. They have secured major contracts for a wide range of new and existing products. Much of this business is coming from Computer Equipment Corporation, a major client of Macco's.

Southern Region

Mark Daley and his group have done a fine job of maintaining relations with Becker's Product Development Division in Boca Raton. They have been working closely with Becker to decrease manufacturing costs.

Figure 5.16   **Page 2 of the completed document MYPRAC5A.DOC**

Macco Plastics Inc.
Quarterly Sales Report
First Quarter

4. Quarterly Meeting

The quarterly meeting will take place in Memphis this time. You will find the agenda attached to this report.

5. Conclusion

The following items will be discussed at the next managers' meeting:

A.   Marketing and sales strategies for the introduction of the new System 400 and System 500 product lines.

B.   Current available positions resulting from the early retirement program and normal attrition of personnel.

C.   Development of the new expense form to facilitate the prompt payment of -travel reimbursements - other out-of-pocket expenses and - commissions.

If the recovery continues at the current pace, this year should be a banner year for all of us at Macco. We want to thank all of you for the outstanding jobs you have done and, most important, for standing by Macco in hard times. Keep up the good work!

John Smith
Regional Coordinator
Macco Plastics Inc.

4. Using the Character dialog box, change the font and point size of the three-line heading on the top of page 2 to **12-point Helv** (Chapter 4).

5. Repeat the formatting in step 4 for the three-line heading on the top of page 1 (Chapter 4).

6. Scroll to the bottom of page 1 (Chapter 2).

7. In the paragraph beginning with *After several years* set left and first-line indents at .5" and a right indent at 5.5" (this chapter).

8. Repeat the indents in step 7 for the paragraphs beginning with *John Martinson* and *Mark Daley* (this chapter).

9. Center the three-line heading on the top of pages 1 and 2 (this chapter).

10. Save the disk file as **myprac5a** (Chapter 2).

11. Print the document and compare it to Figures 5.15 and 5.16 (Chapter 1).

12. Close the document (Chapter 1).

Follow these steps to produce the final document shown in Figures 5.17 and 5.18 from the original document PRAC5B.DOC:

1. Open **prac5b.doc** (Chapter 2).

2. Using the Character dialog box, italicize the first line on page 1, *Macco Plastics Inc.*, and change the point size to 24-point (Chapter 4).

3. Repeat the formatting in step 2 for the first line on page 2 (Chapter 4).

4. Single-underline the following subheadings (near the bottom of page 1) (Chapter 4):

Midwestern Region

Northeastern Region

Southern Region

5. Clear (delete) the 2" left-aligned tab stop from the paragraph that begins with *B. Current available positions* (near the top of page 2) (this chapter).

Figure 5.17   **Page 1 of the completed document MYPRAC5B.DOC**

Macco Plastics Inc.
Quarterly Sales Report
First Quarter

1. Introduction

Congratulations to all of you! An initial review of the sales figures for the nation reveals a surge in sales in all of Macco's sales regions. Major new clients have been added and many new products are on the way.

As we expected when we entered the field, computer-related products, such as keyboard housings and protective carrying cases, are accounting for a major portion of this upswing.

2. Computer Study

A companywide study will begin in March, under the direction of Cathy Donaldson and Bill Schuster in data processing, to determine how to most effectively implement automation in our firm. We will be making a large commitment to productivity gains via computerization sometime late this year.

3. Regional Updates

Midwestern Region

After several years of falling sales due to the slump in the auto industry, Blair Williams and his folks have something to celebrate. The recent boom in auto manufacturing has led to renewed demand of Macco products in Detroit.

Northeastern Region

John Martinson and his group are doing a great job in Nashua. They have secured major contracts for a wide range of new and existing products. Much of this business is coming from Computer Equipment Corporation, a major client of Macco's.

Southern Region

Mark Daley and his group have done a fine job of maintaining relations with Becker's Product Development Division in Boca Raton. They have been working closely with Becker to decrease manufacturing costs.

Figure 5.18   **Page 2 of the completed document MYPRAC5B.DOC**

Macco Plastics Inc.
Quarterly Sales Report
First Quarter

4. Quarterly Meeting

The quarterly meeting will take place in Memphis this time. You will find the agenda attached to this report.

5. Conclusion

The following items will be discussed at the next managers' meeting:

A.   Marketing and sales strategies for the introduction of the new System 400 and System 500 product lines.

B.   Current available positions resulting from the early retirement program and normal attrition of personnel.

C.   Development of the new expense form to facilitate the prompt payment of
-travel reimbursements
-other out-of-pocket expenses and
-commissions.

If the recovery continues at the current pace, this year should be a banner year for all of us at Macco. We want to thank all of you for the outstanding jobs you have done and, most important, for standing by Macco in hard times. Keep up the good work!

John Smith
Regional Coordinator
Macco Plastics Inc.

6. Set a .5" hanging indent for the paragraph beginning with *A. Marketing and sales* (this chapter).

7. Repeat the .5" hanging indent for the paragraphs beginning with *B. Current available positions* and *C. Development of the* (this chapter).

8. In the paragraph beginning with *C. Development of the*, create new lines (this chapter) for:

   - **travel reimbursements**

   - **other out-of-pocket expenses and**

   - **commissions**

9. Save the disk file as **myprac5b** (Chapter 1).

10. Print the document and compare it to Figures 5.17 and 5.18 (Chapter 1).

11. Close the document (Chapter 1).

SUMMARY

In this chapter, you learned the basics of paragraph formatting. You now know how to set, change, and clear tab stops, how to set and repeat paragraph indents, how to create new lines within a paragraph, how to align paragraphs, and how to set line spacing.

Here's a quick reference guide to the Word features introduced in this chapter:

Desired Result	How to Do It
Select a single paragraph for paragraph formatting	Place the insertion point anywhere in the paragraph
Select multiple paragraphs for paragraph formatting	Select (highlight) at least a portion of each paragraph

Desired Result	How to Do It
Create a custom tab stop	Select the desired paragraph(s); select the desired type of tab stop by clicking on the appropriate tab button in the ribbon; point at the desired tab-stop position in the ruler directly under the tick marks; click the mouse button
Change the position of a custom tab stop	Select the desired paragraph(s); drag the custom tab stop (in the ruler) to a new position
Clear (delete) a custom tab stop	Select the desired paragraph(s); drag the custom tab stop down into the text area
Use the Tabs dialog box to manage custom tab stops	Select the desired paragraph(s); choose **Format, Tabs** to open the Tabs dialog box; enter your desired settings to set, change, or clear tab stops; click on **OK** (or press **Enter**)
Set indents	Select the paragraph(s) you wish to indent; drag the appropriate indent marker to your desired new position in the ruler
Repeat paragraph formatting	Format a paragraph(s); select a new paragraph(s); choose **Edit, Repeat Formatting** or press **F4**
Create a hanging indent	Select the desired paragraph(s); if necessary drag the First-line indent marker to the desired position; press and hold **Shift**; drag only the **Left** indent marker to the desired position; release **Shift**
Use the Paragraph dialog box to manage your indents	Select the desired paragraph(s); choose **Format, Paragraph** to open the Paragraph dialog box; enter your desired indent settings; click on **OK** (or press **Enter**)
Create a new line without creating a new paragraph	Place the insertion point where you want to end the current line and create a new line; press **Shift+Enter**

Desired Result	How to Do It
Set paragraph alignment	Select the desired paragraph(s); click on the appropriate alignment button in the ribbon
Set line spacing	Select the desired paragraph(s); choose **Format**, **Paragraph** to open the Paragraph dialog box; select your desired line-spacing setting; click on **OK** (or press **Enter**)

In the next chapter, you will learn the basics of page formatting. You'll find out how to work with headers and footers, how to use Print Preview to preview a printed document, how to set margins, how to use page breaks to paginate a document, how to work in Page Layout view, how to hyphenate text, and how to control the printing of your documents.

IF YOU'RE STOPPING HERE

If you need to break off here, please exit Word. If you want to proceed directly to the next chapter, please do so now.

CHAPTER SIX:
PAGE FORMATTING

In Chapters 4 and 5, you learned how to format your documents at the character and paragraph levels. In this chapter, we'll introduce Word's final level of formatting—page formatting. Many powerful formatting features are controlled at the page level, including headers and footers, margins, page breaks, hyphenation, and advanced printing options.

We'll also present two new methods for displaying your documents—Print Preview and Page Layout view—both of which are well-suited for page-level formatting tasks.

When you're done working through this chapter, you will know

- How to create, edit, and view headers and footers
- How to use Print Preview to preview a printed document
- How to set margins
- How to use page breaks to paginate a document
- How to work in Page Layout view
- How to hyphenate text
- How to control the printing of your documents

CREATING HEADERS AND FOOTERS

A *header* is text that is automatically printed at the top of every page in a document, and a *footer* is text that is automatically printed at the bottom of every page. Headers and footers are used extensively in word processing to do such things as number each page in a document, place the current date on each page, print the document title and/or author name on each page, and so on.

To create a header or footer

- Choose *View, Header/Footer*
- Select *Header* or *Footer* and click on *OK* (or press *Enter*); this opens a *header* or *footer pane*
- In the header or footer pane, type your desired header or footer text, using the option bar buttons as desired (these buttons are discussed in the next section)
- Click on *Close* to accept the header or footer and to close the pane

To delete a header or footer

- Follow the previous procedure to open the header or footer pane
- Choose *Edit, Select All* to select the entire contents of the pane
- Press *Del* to delete these contents
- Click on *Close* to close the pane

HEADER/FOOTER OPTION BAR BUTTONS

You can use the buttons in the header or footer pane *option bar* to insert the page number, the current date, or the current time into your header or footer (see Figure 6.1). When using the Date and Time buttons, keep in mind that your printout will reflect the date and time when you *print* the document, rather than the date and time when you first *created* the document.

Figure 6.1　**The Header pane**

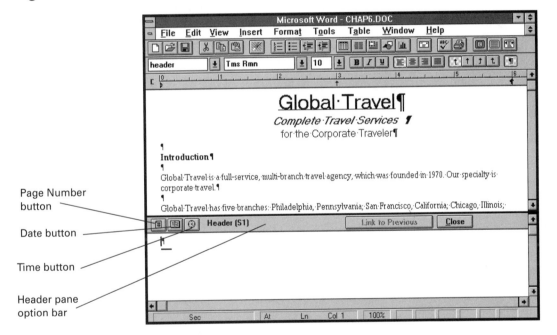

Page Number button

Date button

Time button

Header pane option bar

VIEWING HEADERS AND FOOTERS

Word provides three different *views* (screen representations) for your documents: Normal, Page Layout, and Print Preview. When you are working in Normal view (the view we've always used up to now), your headers and footers are not shown on-screen, though they will appear if you print the document. In order to see your headers and footers on-screen, you must be in Print Preview or Page Layout view. These views will be discussed later in this chapter.

If you are not running Word, please start it now. Let's begin this chapter's activities by opening a new document and creating a header for it:

1. Open **chap6.doc** from your WRKFILES directory.

2. Choose **View, Header/Footer**. Verify that Header is selected. Click on **OK** (or press **Enter**) to open the header pane.

3. Observe the header pane. Text entered here will automatically appear at the top of every page of your document. The buttons to the left of the header pane option bar can be used to insert the page number, the date, and the time into the header (see Figure 6.1).

4. Type **Global Travel**. Press **Tab** twice and then type **Travel Services**.

5. Observe the header text. Note that *Travel Services* is right-aligned. Observe the ruler. As long as the header pane is open, the ruler refers to the header, not to the document. Word has automatically set a centered tab stop at 3" (halfway between the left and right margins) and a right-aligned tab stop at 6" (at the right margin). These preset tab stops enable you to quickly and easily use tabs to center your header text or to align it with the right margin. (To align it with the left margin, you would simply begin typing without pressing Tab, as you did with *Global Travel*).

6. Click on **Close** to accept your header and close the header pane. Note that the ruler now refers to the document, not to the header. Note also that the header you just created is not displayed on the screen. As mentioned earlier in this section, headers and footers are only visible in Print Preview and Page Layout views.

Now let's create a footer:

1. Choose **View, Header/Footer**. Select **Footer** and then click on **OK** (or press **Enter**) to open the footer pane.

2. Examine the footer pane. It is identical to the header pane. However, the text you type here will be displayed at the *bottom* of every page, instead of at the top.

3. Click on the **Date** button (second from the left in the footer pane option bar, it shows a desk calendar) to insert the current date.

4. Press **Tab** twice to move to the right margin.

5. Type **Page** and then press the **spacebar**.

6. Click on the **Page Number** button (leftmost in the footer pane option bar, it shows a page with a number sign character (#) to number each page).

7. Close the footer pane to accept your footer and return to the document.

USING PRINT PREVIEW TO PREVIEW A PRINTED DOCUMENT

Print Preview provides a miniature view of how a document will look when it is printed out. You can use Print Preview to examine and adjust the layout of a document before you actually print it.

You cannot edit text in Print Preview. You can, however, control the placement of text on the page by changing the margins. You also can print the active document and view two pages at one time.

To use the Print Preview option

• Choose *File, Print Preview* to open the Print Preview window

• To change the margins, click on the *Margins* button in the Print Preview option bar (see Figure 6.2), and then select the desired margin boundary line and drag it to a new position; this technique is discussed in the next section

• To print the document, click on the *Print* button in the Print Preview option bar

• To view two pages at once, click on the *Two Pages* button in the Print Preview option bar; to return to single-page view, click on the *One Page* button

• To close the window, click on the *Close* button in the Print Preview option bar

Let's use Print Preview to examine our header and footer:

1. Choose **File, Print Preview** to open the Print Preview window (see Figure 6.1). Print Preview provides a miniature display of your document as it will print, including headers and footers. Remember, you cannot edit text in this view.

2. Click on the **Two Pages** button (in the *Print Preview option bar,* underneath the menu bar) to view two pages of the document

at one time (see Figure 6.3). Note that when two pages are displayed, the button changes to *One Page*.

Figure 6.2   **The Print Preview window**

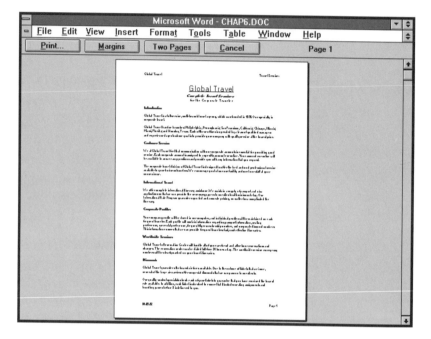

3. Click on the **down scroll arrow** to display pages 2 and 3 of the document (as shown in the page indicator on the right-hand side of the Print Preview option bar). In Print Preview, each click scrolls one full page.

4. Observe the headers and footers. They appear on every page.

5. Click again on the **down scroll arrow** to display page 3 (on the left) and a blank page (on the right). CHAP6.DOC is a three-page document. Click once again on the **down scroll arrow** to verify this; your computer beeps, but the screen display does not change, since there are no more pages to scroll to.

6. Click on the **up scroll arrow** twice to return to the top of the document.

Figure 6.3　　　**Print Preview in Two Pages view**

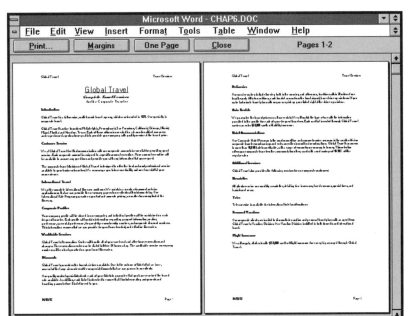

SETTING MARGINS

Margins determine the space between the four edges of the page and the text of the document. Figure 6.4 shows a Print Preview of a sample document with Word's default margin settings—the top and bottom margins are set to 1"; the left and right margins are set to 1.25". Figure 6.5 shows the same document with custom margins set to twice the default values—the top and bottom are set to 2"; the left and right are set to 2.5".

You can set a document's margins either from the Print Preview window (by using the Margins button) or in Normal or Page Layout views (by using the Page Setup dialog box).

To set margins in Print Preview

• Click on the *Margins* button to display the current margin boundary lines

Figure 6.4   **Sample document with default margins**

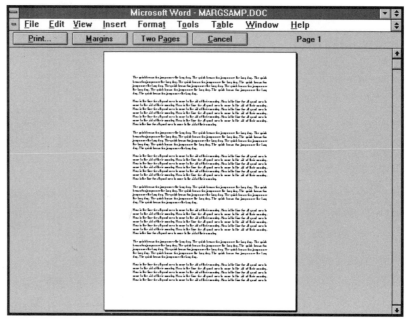

Figure 6.5   **Sample document with custom margins**

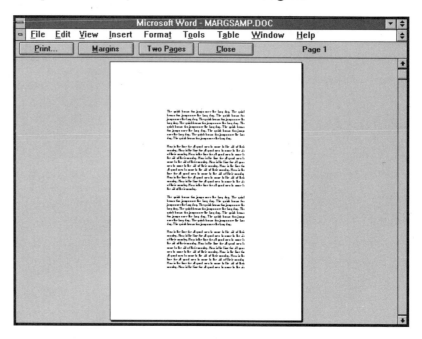

- Select the desired *margin handle* (the black box at one end of the margin boundary line) and drag it to your desired margin position

- Repeat the previous step until all margin boundary lines are set as desired

- Click on the *Margins* button to reformat the text to the new margins and to remove the margin boundary lines from the screen

To set margins by using the Page Setup dialog box

- Choose *Format, Page Setup* to open the Page Setup dialog box

- Enter the new margin settings in the appropriate margin text boxes

- Click on *OK* (or press *Enter*)

Let's practice changing margins from the Print Preview window:

1. Click on the **Margins** button in the Print Preview option bar. Observe the *margin boundary lines* (the page-length horizontal and vertical lines) and *margin handles* (the black boxes at one end of each margin boundary line).

2. Position the mouse pointer over the top margin handle (the black box at the top left of the Print Preview screen). The arrow changes to a crosshair.

3. Press and hold the mouse button, then begin to drag the top margin handle downward. Observe the page indicator in the Print Preview option bar; it reports the current position of the margin handle (and the attached margin boundary line). Drag the handle down to **1.5"**, then release the mouse button. Note that the new margin boundary line is displayed, but that the page is not reformatted to reflect this new top margin. As mentioned earlier in this section, you must click on the Margins button to reformat the text.

4. Click on the **Margins** button to view the results of your margin change. Note that both pages 1 and 2 reflect the new top margin. Margin settings apply to the whole document, not only the selected page.

5. Click on the **Margins** button to display the margin boundary lines and handles. Drag the bottom margin boundary line upward until the page indicator reads 1.5". Click on the **Margins** button to view the results (see Figure 6.6).

Figure 6.6   **Changing the margins in Print Preview**

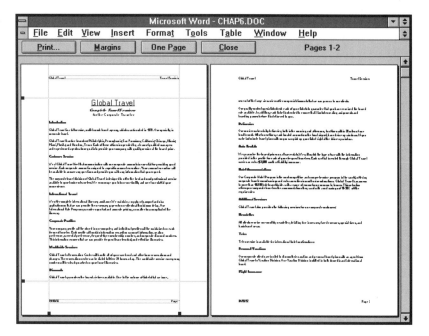

6. Scroll through the remaining pages of the document. The margins have changed on every page, leaving very little text on pages 3 and 4.

7. Click on **Close** to close the Print Preview window.

Now let's change margins by using the Page Setup command:

1. Move the insertion point to the top of the document.

2. Choose **Format, Page Setup** to open the Page Setup dialog box (see Figure 6.7). Verify that the Margins option is selected.

3. Verify that the top and bottom margins are set to 1.5".

4. Double-click in the Left text box to select the current left margin setting (1.25"). Type **1** to change the left margin to 1". Note that you do not have to type the inch symbol (").

5. Press **Tab** to select the current right margin setting (1.25"). Type **1** to change the right margin to 1".

6. Press **Enter** (or click on **OK**) to accept your margin changes. Due to the extra .5" of text width that you gained (by decreasing the left and right margins by .25" each), your text lines now run off the right end of the screen (see Figure 6.8). Note that the screen representation of the left margin has not changed. When you are working in Normal view (as opposed to Print Preview or Page Layout view), Word always displays your left margin in the same place (approximately one-quarter inch to the right of the document window edge), no matter how large or small the margin actually is.

Figure 6.7   **The Page Setup dialog box**

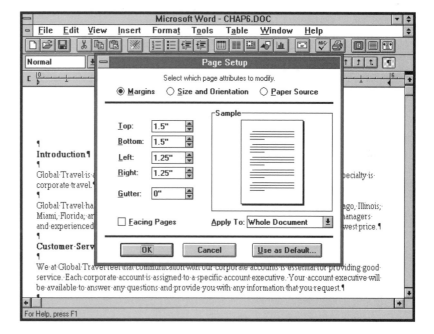

7. Save the disk file as **mychap6**.

Let's use the Zoom Page Width feature (covered in Chapter 2) to shrink the display, so that the text lines no longer run off the screen:

1. Observe the status bar. The magnification level is 100%.

2. Click on the **Zoom Page Width** button (right-most in the tool-bar, it shows a page with outward-pointing arrows on the left and right edges).

Figure 6.8   **Overwide text lines**

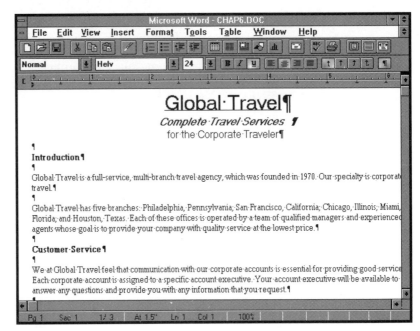

3. Observe the text and the status bar (see Figure 6.9). The magnification level automatically adjusts to fit the entire width (but not the length) of the page on the screen.

USING PAGE BREAKS TO PAGINATE A DOCUMENT

Pagination is the process of separating a document's text into pages. The separations between pages are called *page breaks*.

There are two types of page breaks in Word:

- *Automatic* page breaks, which Word automatically inserts into a document. Automatic page breaks appear as loosely spaced dotted lines across the text area.

- *Manual* page breaks, which you insert into the document. Manual page breaks appear as tightly spaced dotted lines.

To insert a manual page break

- Place the insertion point immediately to the left of the first character that you want on the new page

Figure 6.9   **Using the Zoom Page Width button**

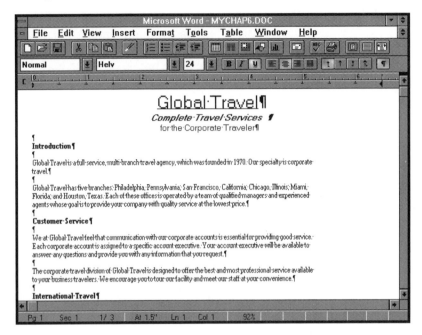

- Choose *Insert, Break*, verify that *Page Break* is selected, and then click on *OK*; or, simply press *Ctrl+Enter*

To delete a manual page break

- Move the mouse pointer into the selection bar

- Select the page break

- Press *Del*

You cannot delete automatic page breaks. However, if you insert a manual page break above an automatic page break, Word will remove the automatic page break.

Let's use the above procedure to insert some manual page breaks in MYCHAP6.DOC:

1. Move to the top of page 2. Observe the automatic page break before the paragraph beginning with *Our quality control specialists*. It is displayed as a loosely spaced dotted line.

2. Place the insertion point before the *D* in the heading *Discounts*, near the bottom of page 1.

3. Choose **Insert, Break** to open the Break dialog box. Verify that Page Break is selected. Point to **OK** and, while observing the automatic page break between pages 1 and 2, click on **OK**. Word inserts a manual page break (tightly spaced dotted line) at your insertion point and then, shortly afterward, deletes the automatic page break. Because you changed the beginning of page 2 to *Discounts*, Word no longer needed to break pages automatically at *Our quality control specialists*.

4. Move to the bottom of page 2. Place the insertion point before the *F* in the heading *Flight Insurance*.

5. Press **Ctrl+Enter** to insert a manual page break. As mentioned earlier in this section, pressing Ctrl+Enter is the keyboard shortcut for using the Insert, Break command.

6. Note that the automatic page break after *Flight Insurance* disappears, but that the manual page break before *Fax* does not disappear (Figure 6.10). Automatic page breaks are deleted or repositioned automatically, as necessitated by changes you make to the document (resetting margins, changing font size, inserting new page breaks, and so on). Undesired manual page breaks, however, must be deleted manually.

7. In the selection bar, point to the manual page break before *Fax*. Click the mouse button to select the page break.

8. Press **Del** to delete the manual page break.

WORKING IN PAGE LAYOUT VIEW

Word's Page Layout view allows you to view all page areas, including headers, footers, and margins. Page Layout view is like a cross between Normal view (where you can edit and format body text, but cannot view headers and footers) and Print Preview (where you can see headers and footers but cannot edit text).

Note: Page Layout view can be useful for applying the finishing touches to your documents. However, you might find that this view significantly slows the operating speed of Word and makes it awkward to move around in the document. For these reasons, it is recommended that you do most of your work in Normal view.

To enter Page Layout view

• Choose *View, Page Layout*

Figure 6.10   **Inserting a manual page break**

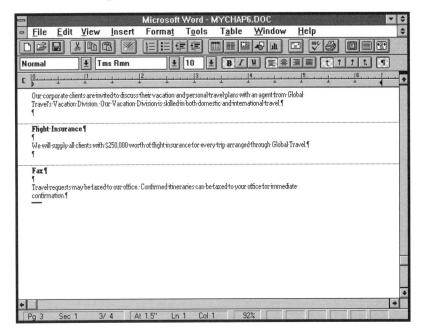

• To return to Normal view, choose *View, Normal*

Let's edit your header and footer in Page Layout view. But first we'll open the Print Preview window to observe a page-positioning problem with the header and footer:

1. Move to the top of the document.

2. Choose **File, Print Preview** to open the Print Preview window.

3. Click on **Margins** to display the margin boundary lines. Note that the header and footer text no longer aligns with the right margin. Why? Because you changed the document's margins in a previous activity, but did not adjust the position of the right-aligned tab stop in the header and footer. This tab stop does not reach the new right margin. Click on **Cancel** to close the Print Preview window.

4. Choose **View, Page Layout** to switch to Page Layout view.

5. Observe the screen (see Figure 6.11). In Page Layout view, you can both view and edit headers and footers.

Figure 6.11   **Page Layout view**

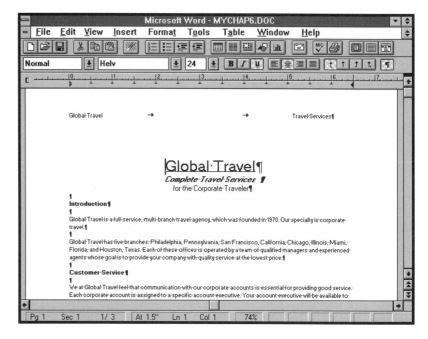

6. Place the insertion point in the header before the *T* in *Travel Services*. Type **Complete** and then press the **spacebar**.

7. Observe the ruler. The right-aligned tab stop at 6" did not automatically adjust when you changed the margins.

8. Drag the right-aligned tab stop at 6" to **6.5"** to set it even with the right margin.

9. Press **Pg Dn** three times to view the footer.

10. Place the insertion point anywhere within the footer. Drag the right-aligned tab stop at 6" to **6.5"**.

11. Open the Print Preview window. Click on **Margins**. Scroll through the document to verify that the headers and footers now align with the right margin on every page. Click on **Cancel** to close the Print Preview window.

12. Choose **View, Normal** to return to Normal view.

13. Click on the **Zoom 100 Percent** button (second from the right in the toolbar, it shows a full-sized page) to return to 100% magnification.

14. Update the disk file (use File, Save).

HYPHENATING TEXT

Up to now, we have worked exclusively with unhyphenated text: Each of our documents' lines has ended with a whole word, rather than a *hyphenated* word—a word broken into two parts by a hyphen. You may, at times, wish to hyphenate a document to reduce the raggedness of its right margin (with left-aligned text) or to tighten things up by minimizing the blank space between words (with justified text). Word provides two methods for doing this: *manual hyphenation*, in which you use the keyboard; and *automatic hyphenation*, in which you use the Tools, Hyphenate command.

 ### MANUAL HYPHENATION

To hyphenate text manually

- Place the insertion point between the desired letters of the word you wish to hyphenate

- Insert your desired hyphen, choosing from the three types shown in the following table:

Type of Hyphen	How and When to Use
Regular	Press the Hyphen key (-); use when you always want the hyphen to appear, such as in compound words (left-aligned, right-aligned, and so on)
Optional	Press Ctrl+Hyphen; use when you only want the hyphen to appear if the word is broken at the end of a line (such as auto-matic)
Hard	Press Ctrl+Shift+Hyphen; use when you always want the hyphen to appear, but you never want the word to be broken at the end of a line, such as with names (Ann-Marie, for instance)

Let's use the Ctrl+Hyphen technique to insert an optional hyphen into a word:

1. Move to the top of the document.

2. Use **Format, Page Setup** to change the left and right margins to 1.5".

3. Click on the **Show/Hide** button (rightmost in the ribbon, it shows a paragraph mark (¶) character) to hide nonprinting characters.

4. In the paragraph beginning with *We at Global Travel* (under the heading *Customer Service*), place the insertion point between the *o* and the *v* of *providing*. Press **Ctrl+Hyphen** to insert an optional hyphen at the insertion point.

5. Observe the result. The word *providing* is broken into two parts, *pro-* and *viding* (see Figure 6.12).

Figure 6.12   **Inserting an optional hyphen into *providing***

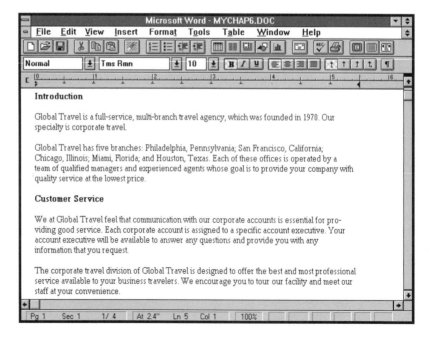

6. Place the insertion point before *essential* (in the same sentence). Type **absolutely** and then press the **spacebar** to force the entire word *providing* to move to the next line. Note that the optional hyphen disappears when it is not needed.

7. Click on **Show/Hide** to show nonprinting characters. Note that the optional hyphen now appears on-screen as a horizontal line with a slightly downturned right end. (Optional hyphens do not appear when you print a document.)

8. Delete **absolutely** (and the trailing space) from the text.

AUTOMATIC HYPHENATION

To hyphenate a document automatically

- Move the insertion point to the top of the document.

- Choose *Tools, Hyphenation* to open the Hyphenation dialog box.

- Check or uncheck the *Confirm* option. When Confirm is checked, Word hyphenates semiautomatically—it asks you to accept, change, or reject each of its hyphenation decisions. When Confirm is unchecked, Word hyphenates automatically—it makes all of its hyphenation decisions without asking for your confirmation.

- Click on *OK* (or press *Enter*) to begin the hyphenation procedure. If Confirm is checked, accept, change, or reject each of the hyphenation decisions Word makes for the document. If Confirm is unchecked, sit back and wait for Word to perform the hyphenation automatically.

- Word displays a message box informing you that the entire document is hyphenated. Click on *Yes* (or press *Enter*) to remove this box and return to your document.

Now let's use the Tools, Hyphenate command to semiautomatically hyphenate the entire document:

1. Move to the top of the document.

2. Choose **Tools, Hyphenation** to open the Hyphenation dialog box (see Figure 6.13). Verify that the Confirm option is checked in preparation for semiautomatic hyphenation.

Figure 6.13   **The Hyphenation dialog box**

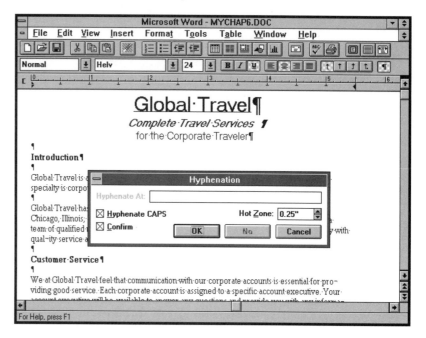

3. Click on **OK** (or press **Enter**) to begin the hyphenation procedure. After a moment, the first suggested hyphenation appears in the Hyphenate At text box: *Chi-cago*. Let's say we do not want to hyphenate city names.

4. Click on **No** to reject the suggested hyphenation. Word leaves *Chicago* intact (unhyphenated) and moves on to its next candidate for hyphenation, *in-for-ma-tion*. Observe the blinking highlight between *ma* and *tion*. This marks Word's suggested point of hyphenation. This time, let's accept Word's suggestion.

5. Click on **Yes** to accept the suggested hyphenation and move on to the next hyphenation candidate, *ef-fec-tive*. Normally we would accept Word's suggested hyphenation. However, because *effective* is preceded by *cost-*, we would end up with a doubly hyphenated word fragment at the end of the line (*cost-ef-*).

6. Click on **No** to reject the suggested hyphenation and move on to the next candidate, *serv-ice*.

7. Click on **Yes** to accept the suggested hyphenation and move on to the next candidate, *is-sue*.

8. Click on **Yes** to accept the suggested hyphenation and move on to the next candidate, *as-sign-ments*. Note the blinking rectangle suggesting that you hyphenate between *as* and *sign*. Let's say we want Word to fit *assign-* (instead of *as-*, as suggested) on the upper line.

9. Click on the hyphen between *sign* and *ments* to move the hyphenation point, then click on **Yes** to accept your modified hyphenation and move on to the next candidate, *in-for-ma-tion*.

10. Click on **Yes** to accept the suggested hyphenation. A message box appears, informing you that the hyphenation procedure has been completed.

11. Click on **Yes** to remove this message box and return to the document.

12. Take a few moments to scroll through the document and examine the words you hyphenated (*informa-tion, serv-ice, is-sue, assign-ments*, and *infor-mation*) and chose not to hyphenate (*Chicago* and *cost-effective*).

13. Choose **Edit, Undo Hyphenation** to return the document to its prehyphenated state in preparation for the following Practice Your Skills activity.

PRACTICE YOUR SKILLS

1. Use the Tools, Hyphenate command to automatically hyphen-ate your entire document. (**Hint:** Uncheck the Confirm option before beginning to hyphenate.)

2. Scroll through the document to examine the results. Note the different end-of-line word breaks produced by automatic and semiautomatic hyphenation.

CONTROLLING THE PRINTING OF YOUR DOCUMENTS

Several times in this book, you've used the File, Print command to print your active document. Let's revisit this very powerful com-mand and learn how to use some of its more advanced features. In addition to printing a single copy of your entire document, File,

Print allows you to print the current page, multiple pages, multiple copies, selected text, or nondocument items such as Summary Info.

To use the Print dialog box to control how your documents print

- If you wish to print selected text, select that text
- Choose *File, Print* to open the Print dialog box
- Choose the desired Print options (see Table 6.1)
- Click on *OK* (or press *Enter*)

 PRINT DIALOG BOX OPTIONS

The Print dialog box provides the options shown in Table 6.1:

Table 6.1   **Print Dialog Box Options**

Option	Description
Print	In this drop-down list box, you choose what you wish to print. The default choice is the current document, but you can also print summary information (covered later in this section), styles, and glossaries (printing glossaries will be discussed in Chapter 9).
Copies	In this text box, you enter the number of copies that you wish to print. The default is 1 copy.
Range	In this area of the dialog box, you specify the portion of the document that you wish to print. Choose *All* to print the entire document. Choose *Current Page* to print the page where the insertion point is located. (If you selected text in your document before issuing the File, Print command, this button changes to *Selection*; choose it to print the selected text.) Choose *Pages* to print a range of pages; use the *Pages From* and *To* boxes to specify the starting and ending pages.

Let's practice using the print options in the Print dialog box. (If you do not have a printer, please skip this activity.)

1. Move the insertion point to the top of the document.

2. Choose **File, Print** to open the Print dialog box (see Figure 6.14).

Figure 6.14   **The Print dialog box**

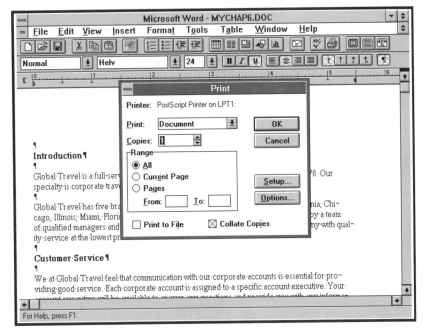

3. In the Range area of the box, choose the **Current Page** option (click on the circle to the left of the option). Click on **OK** to print only the current page (the page on which the insertion point is located), which in this case is page 1. After the page has been sent to the printer, the Print dialog box is automatically closed.

4. Choose **File, Print** to reopen the Print dialog box. Note that Range has been reset to its default (All). Each time you open the Print dialog box, all of its settings are reset to their default values.

5. In the Range area of the box, select the **Pages** option. Type **1** in the From text box and type **2** in the To text box; this informs Word to print only from page 1 through page 2 of the document. Click on **OK** to print these pages.

6. Choose **File, Print** to reopen the Print dialog box.

7. In the Range area of the box, select the **Current Page** option. Double-click in the Copies text box to select the current value (1); type **2** to tell Word to print two copies of the current page. Click on **OK** to print these copies.

8. Select all text from the heading *Customer Service* up to and including the empty paragraph before *International Travel*.

9. Choose **File, Print** to reopen the Print dialog box. Note that the Copies and Range options have been reset to their default values of 1 and All, respectively. Note also that the second Range option is *Selection* (see Figure 6.15) instead of *Current Page* (see Figure 6.14). Whenever you select text in the active document, the Print dialog box provides a Selection option that lets you print only the selected text.

Figure 6.15   **The Selection option**

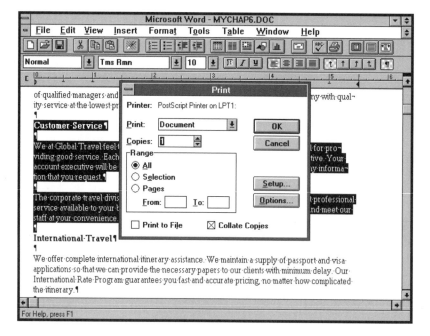

10. Choose the **Selection** option and then click on **OK** to print only your selected text.

11. Press **Ctrl+Home** to deselect and move to the top of the document. Choose **File, Print** to reopen the Print dialog box. Note that the second Range option has returned to *Current Page* (because there is no text selected).

12. Click on the **down arrow** to the right of the Print list box to display the Print options. Select **Summary Info** to tell Word to

print the Summary Info sheet of the current document. Click on **OK** to print this sheet.

USING THE PRINT BUTTON TO PRINT A DOCUMENT

In addition to the File, Print command, Word provides a Print button that you can use to print a single copy of an entire document. To do this, click on the Print button (the fourth from the right in the toolbar, it shows a printer).

Let's end this chapter's activities by using the Print button to print your entire document. (If you do not have a printer, please skip this activity.)

1. Click on the Print button (the one showing a printer) to print a single copy of your entire document.

2. Save the disk file and close the document.

SUMMARY

In this chapter, you learned the basics of page formatting. You now know how to create, edit, and view headers and footers, how to use Print Preview to preview a printed document, how to set margins, how to use page breaks to paginate a document, how to work in Page Layout view, how to hyphenate text, and how to control the printing of your documents.

Congratulations on completing your foundation of Word formatting techniques! You now know how to format your documents at the character, paragraph, and page levels. These skills will allow you to create highly professional-looking documents.

Here's a quick reference guide to the Word features introduced in this chapter:

Desired Result	How to Do It
Create a header or footer	Choose **View, Header/Footer**; select **Header** or **Footer** and click on **OK** (or press **Enter**) to open the header or footer pane; type your desired header or footer text; click on **Close** to accept the header or footer and to close the pane

Desired Result	How to Do It
Delete a header or footer	Follow the previous procedure to open the header or footer pane; choose **Edit, Select All** to select the entire contents of the pane; press **Del** to delete these contents; click on **Close** to close the pane
Use Print Preview to preview a printed document	Choose **File, Print Preview** to open the Print Preview window
Set margins in Print Preview	Click on the **Margins** button to display the current margin boundary lines; select the desired margin handle and drag it to your desired margin position; repeat the previous step until all margin boundary lines are set as desired; click on the **Margins** button to reformat the text to the new margins and to remove the margin boundary lines from the screen
Set margins by using the Page Setup dialog box	Choose **Format, Page Setup** to open the Page Setup dialog box; enter the new margin settings in the appropriate margin text boxes; click on **OK** (or press **Enter**)
Insert a manual page break	Place the insertion point immediately to the left of the first character that you want on the new page; choose **Insert, Break**; verify that **Page Break** is selected; click on **OK**; or place the insertion point and press **Ctrl+Enter**
Delete a manual page break	Move the mouse pointer into the selection bar; select the page break; press **Del**
Enter Page Layout view	Choose **View, Page Layout**
Return to Normal view	Choose **View, Normal**
Hyphenate text manually	Place the insertion point between the desired letters of the word you wish to hyphenate; insert your desired hyphen (regular, optional, or hard)

Desired Result	How to Do It
Hyphenate a document semiautomatically	Move the insertion point to the top of the document; choose **Tools, Hyphenation** to open the Hyphenation dialog box; check or uncheck the **Confirm** option; click on **OK** (or press **Enter**) to begin the hyphenation procedure; if Confirm is checked, accept, change, or reject each of the hyphenation decisions Word makes for the document; if Confirm is unchecked, sit back and wait for Word to perform the hyphenation automatically
Use the Print dialog box to control the printing of your documents	If you wish to print selected text, select this text; choose **File, Print** to open the Print dialog box; choose your desired Print options; click on **OK** (or press **Enter**)
Use the Print button to print a single copy of a document	Click on the toolbar **Print** button

In the next chapter, we'll explore ways in which Word can help you improve your writing. You'll learn how to check your documents' spelling, how to use the thesaurus to find alternative words, and how to check the grammar, style, and readability of your documents.

IF YOU'RE STOPPING HERE

If you need to break off here, please exit Word. If you want to proceed to the next chapter, please do so now.

CHAPTER SEVEN: PROOFING YOUR DOCUMENTS

Checking the
Spelling of Your
Documents

Using the
Thesaurus to Find
Alternative Words

Checking the
Grammar and
Style of Your
Documents

Misspellings and grammatical mistakes can severely undermine the credibility of your documents. In this chapter, we'll introduce you to tools that allow you to *proof* (check) your documents for potential spelling, grammar, and style errors. Wording is also a critical factor in determining the effectiveness of a document; using inappropriate words may alienate or confuse your readers. We'll explore Word's electronic thesaurus and see how easy it is to find vocabulary alternatives in your documents.

When you're done working through this chapter, you will know

- How to check the spelling of your documents

- How to use the thesaurus to find alternative words

- How to check the grammar, style, and readability of your documents

CHECKING THE SPELLING OF YOUR DOCUMENTS

Word provides a spelling checker that you can use to proof the spelling of your documents. The spelling checker checks each word in a document against the words in its own internal dictionary and highlights the words it does not recognize. The spelling checker also checks for such common typing mistakes as repeated words (such as *the the*) and irregular capitalization (such as *tHe*).

Here are Word's options for spell-checking documents:

- To spell-check an entire document, press *Ctrl+Home* to move the insertion point to the top of the document; to spell-check a portion of a document, select the text that you wish to check; to check a single word, select that word

- Choose *Tools, Spelling* or click on the *Spelling* button (the fifth from the right in the toolbar, it shows a check beneath the letters ABC) to open the Spelling dialog box and begin the spelling check

- Follow the dialog box prompts to spell-check the document or selected text

Figure 7.1 illustrates the Spelling dialog box.

When the spelling checker finds a potential spelling error (a word not included in the checker's internal dictionary), this word appears in the Not in Dictionary text box (see Figure 7.1), and a list of suggested spelling corrections appears in the Suggestions list box. The first of these suggested spellings is placed in the Change To text box. At this point, you can choose from the following options:

Option	Action Required
Leave the word unchanged	If you want to leave the word as it is and continue the spelling check, click on *Ignore*. To ignore all further occurrences of the word, click on *Ignore All*.

Figure 7.1   **The Spelling dialog box**

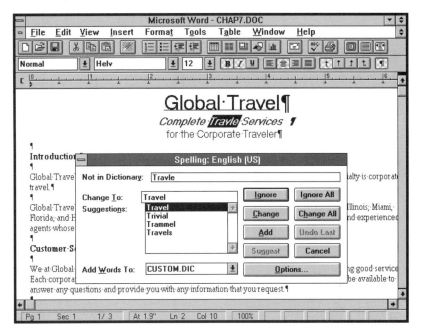

Option	Action Required
Correct the spelling	If the correction that you want is in the Change To text box, click on *Change*. If the correction that you want is in the Suggestions list box, click on that correction and then click on Change. (Or, as a shortcut, simply double-click on the desired correction.) If the correction that you want is not suggested, type the correction in the Change To text box and then click on Change. To change all the occurrences of the word throughout the document, click on *Change All*.
Add the word to a dictionary	Word allows you to build a custom dictionary that contains words not found in the spelling checker's dictionary. This is particularly useful for proper names (such as *Alexa*), abbreviations (such as *ACCTDEPT*), and acronyms (such as *UNICEF*) that you use frequently in your documents. If you want to add the word to a custom dictionary, click on *Add*.

Option	Action Required
Delete the word	If you want to delete the highlighted word from the document, delete the word in the Change To text box and then click on the *Delete* button (this button appears in place of the Change button when you delete the contents of the Change To text box). To delete all further occurrences of the word, delete the word in the Change To text box and then click on *Delete All* (this button appears in place of the Change All button when you delete the contents of the Change To text box).
Undo the last correction	If you want to undo the last correction, click on *Undo Last*. Word allows you to undo your last five corrections.
Stop the spelling check	If you want to cancel the spelling check procedure at any point, click on *Cancel* (for close). All changes made up to that point will be preserved. If you used the *Change All* or *Delete All* options, instances of these words that appear after the point where you cancel will not be changed or deleted.

If the error is repeated words (such as *the the*), you can

- Click on *Delete* to delete the second instance of the word

- Click on *Ignore* to ignore the repeated words and continue the spelling check

If you are not running Word, please start it now. Let's begin by opening a document and spell-checking a selected portion of it:

1. Open **chap7.doc** from your WRKFILES directory.

2. Select the heading of the document (the first 3 lines).

3. Choose **Tools, Spelling** to open the Spelling dialog box (see Figure 7.1). Note the dialog box title, *Spelling: English (US)*. By default, United States English is the language against which the words in your document are checked. Word allows you to specify a different language (for example, UK English, French, German, Italian, and so on) by using the *Format, Language* command.

4. Observe the dialog box. In the Not in Dictionary text box, Word displays the first word it found that was not in its internal dictionary (*Travle*, which appears in the second line of the heading). In the Suggestions list box, Word displays a list of suggested spelling corrections (*Travel*, *Trivial*, and so on). The first of these suggestions (*Travel*) is also placed in the Change To box.

5. Click on **Change** to change *Travle* to *Travel* and search for the next potential spelling error in your text selection. In this case, no further errors are found. Word prompts

   ```
   Word finished checking the selection. Do you
   want to continue checking the remainder of
   the document?
   ```

6. Click on **No** to end the spelling check and return to the document. Note that *Travle* has been corrected to *Travel* (see Figure 7.2).

Figure 7.2   **A corrected spelling error**

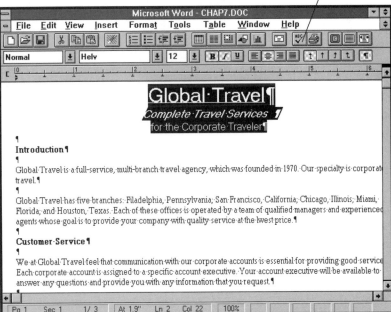

Now let's check the spelling of the entire document:

1. Press **Ctrl+Home** to deselect and move the insertion point to the top of the document.

2. Click on the toolbar **Spelling** button (the one with the check beneath the letters ABC) to open the Spelling dialog box and initiate the spelling check. Word displays the first word it finds that is not in its dictionary (*multi*). Here's a good example of a word that is correct as it appears in the document, but is not included in Word's dictionary.

3. Click on **Ignore** to leave *multi* unchanged and search for the next potential spelling error. Word finds *Filadelphia*.

4. Click on **Change** to replace *Filadelphia* with *Philadelphia* (the entry in the Change To box) and to search for the next potential spelling error. Word displays *lwest*. Note that *lowest* is listed as a suggestion, but is not displayed in the Change To text box (see Figure 7.3).

Figure 7.3   **Using the Change To text box**

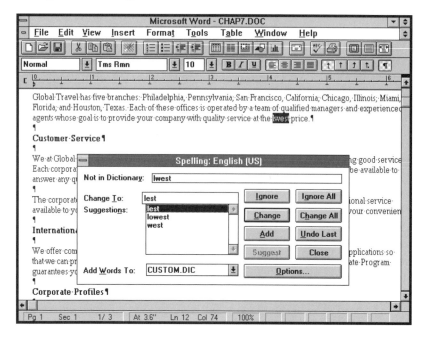

5. Select (click on) **lowest** to place it in the Change To text box. Click on **Change** to change *lwest* to *lowest* and to search for the next potential spelling error. Word displays *the* in the uppermost text box, which is now entitled *Repeated Word* (instead of *Not in Dictionary*). Although *the* is not misspelled, it appears twice in a row (*the the*) in your document.

6. Click on **Delete** to delete the second *the*. Word prompts

```
The spelling check is complete.
```

7. Click on **OK** (or press **Enter**) to close the message box.

8. Save the disk file as **mychap7**.

USING THE THESAURUS TO FIND ALTERNATIVE WORDS

You can use Word's internal thesaurus to look up vocabulary alternatives in your documents. The thesaurus provides both *synonyms* (words with similar meanings) and *antonyms* (words with opposite meanings). Having a powerful and lightning-fast electronic thesaurus at your fingertips can greatly enhance the quality of the writing in your documents.

To use the thesaurus to find alternative words

* Select the desired word in your document, or simply place the insertion point anywhere within the word

* Choose *Tools, Thesaurus* (or press *Shift+F7*) to open the Thesaurus dialog box; a list of synonyms appears

Note: If antonyms are available, an Antonyms option appears in the Meanings list box. If you click on *Antonyms*, a list of antonyms will replace the list of synonyms.

* To replace the selected word, select the desired synonym or antonym and click on *Replace*

Let's practice using the thesaurus to find synonyms:

1. Select the word **specialty** (located in the first line of the paragraph beginning with *Global Travel is a full-service*).

2. Choose **Tools, Thesaurus** to open the Thesaurus dialog box and display a list of synonyms for *specialty* (see Figure 7.4). Note the dialog box title, *Thesaurus: English (US)*. As with the spelling checker, you can use the Format, Language command to change your thesaurus language.

Figure 7.4 **The Thesaurus dialog box**

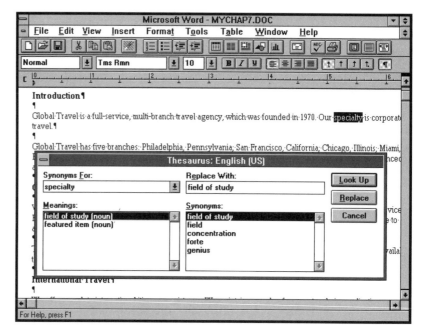

3. In the Synonyms list box, select **forte** to place it in the Replace With text box.

4. Click on **Replace** to replace *specialty* with *forte*.

Now let's use the thesaurus to find antonyms:

1. Place the insertion point anywhere in the word *qualified* (located in the paragraph beginning with *Global Travel has five branches*).

2. Press **Shift+F7** to use the shortcut keyboard method for opening the Thesaurus dialog box.

3. In the Meanings list box, select **Antonyms** to display a list of antonyms (opposites) for *qualified*.

4. Observe that the Synonyms list now displays antonyms (see Figure 7.5).

Figure 7.5   **Displaying a list of antonyms**

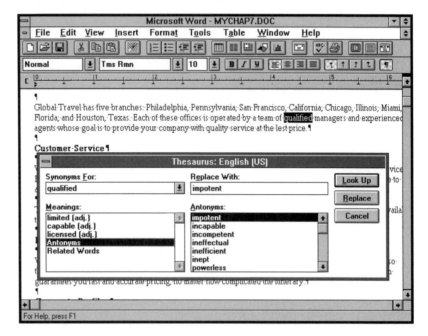

Let's say that you found none of these antonyms appealing and decided to cancel the thesaurus look-up procedure.

5. Click on **Cancel** to close the Thesaurus dialog box and return to your document.

CHECKING THE GRAMMAR AND STYLE OF YOUR DOCUMENTS

You can use Word's grammar checker to identify and correct sentences in your document that contain grammatical errors and weak writing style.

To check the grammar and style of a document

• To check an entire document, press *Ctrl+Home* to move the insertion point to the top of the document; to check a portion of a document, select the text that you wish to check

- Choose *Tools, Grammar* to open the Grammar dialog box and begin the grammar check (see Figure 7.6)

Figure 7.6 **The Grammar dialog box**

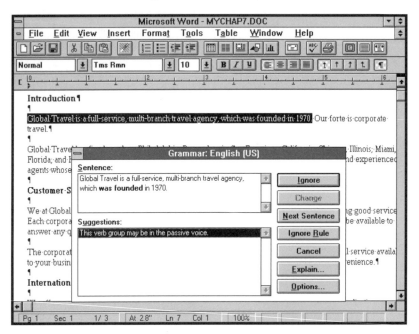

When a potential grammar or style error is found, the dialog box displays the questionable sentence in the Sentence box, with words that are related to the potential error displayed in bold letters. It might also provide one or more suggested corrections in the Suggestions list box. At this point, you can choose from the following options:

Option	Action Required
Accept a suggested correction	Select the desired correction in the Suggestions list box and click on *Change*; or, as a shortcut, simply double-click on the desired suggestion

Option	Action Required
Leave the sentence as it is and continue the grammar check	Click on *Next Sentence*
Leave the sentence as it is and ignore similar potential grammar or style errors	Click on *Ignore Rule*
Get more information about the potential error	Click on *Explain*
Stop the grammar check	Click on *Cancel* (or *Close*); all corrections made up to that point will be preserved

CUSTOMIZING THE GRAMMAR CHECKER

You may disagree with certain rules that the grammar checker uses in assessing the correctness of a sentence. For example, you may find it perfectly acceptable to use the passive voice—a practice that the grammar checker considers to be a potential error. In recognition of the varying grammatical and style preferences of its users, Word allows you to customize the grammar checker to fit your own specific needs. To do this

- Click on *Options* in the Grammar dialog box
- Click on *Customize Settings* in the Options dialog box
- Set (check or uncheck) your desired grammar and style rules
- Click on *OK* (or press *Enter*) to return to the Options dialog box, then click on *OK* (or press *Enter*) to accept your customized settings and return to the Grammar dialog box

The changes you made to Word's grammar and style rules will apply to all your grammar checks from this point on.

SPELL-CHECKING WITH THE GRAMMAR CHECKER

By default, Word checks your document for spelling when you run a grammar check. When it finds a spelling error, it opens the Spelling dialog box, allows you to make any necessary changes, and then continues checking for grammar and spelling. For this reason, if you intend to perform both a spelling and grammar check for a document, simply choose Tools, Grammar.

READABILITY STATISTICS

When you complete a grammar check, Word provides character, word, paragraph, and sentence counts for your document. It also provides *readability statistics*—the average number of sentences per paragraph, words per sentence, and characters per word. These readability statistics are calculated into standard *readability indexes* such as the Flesch Reading Ease and Gunning Fog indexes. (You'll learn how to access these indexes in the following activity.)

Let's use the grammar checker to check the grammar and writing style of MYCHAP7.DOC:

1. Press **Ctrl+Home** to move the insertion point to the top of the document.

2. Choose **Tools**, **Grammar** to open the Grammar dialog box and search for the first potential grammar or style error (see Figure 7.6). Word finds *was founded* and informs you that this verb group may be in the passive voice. (By default, Word considers passive voice verbs to be potential errors.) Let's say we disagree and find passive verbs to be appropriate in this document's context.

3. Click on **Ignore** to leave the sentence unchanged and search for the next potential grammar or style error. Word finds *is operated*, another passive voice verb. It's clear that Word is going to call our attention to every passive verb group that it finds. Let's stop it from doing this for the remainder of the proofing session.

4. Click on **Ignore Rule** to leave all passive voice verb groups unchanged (throughout the entire document) and search for the next potential error. Word finds *You're* and suggests changing it to *Your*. In this case, we'll agree.

5. Click on **Change** to accept the suggested correction (to change *You're* to *Your*) and search for the next potential error. Word finds .. (a double period), but does not offer a specific suggestion for how to correct it. When Word makes a specific suggestion, the Change option is *available*—it is displayed in bold letters. When Word makes a general suggestion (as it does

here), the Change option is *not* available—it is dimmed. Since Word offers no specific change suggestion, we'll have to fix things manually.

6. Position the mouse pointer between the two highlighted periods in the document. Click the mouse button to select the document window (and deselect the Grammar dialog box). Click again to place the insertion point between the periods.

7. Press **Backspace** to delete the first period. You should now have a single period at the end of the sentence.

8. Click on **Start** in the Grammar dialog box to restart the grammar-checking procedure. Word accepts the change you made to the sentence and searches for the next potential error. It finds *provide* and suggests the alternative, *provides*.

9. Click on **Change** to accept the suggested correction and search for the next potential error. Word finds *client* and suggests the alternative *clients*.

10. Click on **Change** to accept the suggested correction and search for the next potential error. Word finds *travel* and suggests that you change it to *travels*. In this case, we'll disagree; *travel* is what we want.

11. Click on **Ignore** to leave *travel* unchanged and search for the next potential error. Word prompts

   ```
   Do you want to continue checking at the
   beginning of the document?
   ```

12. Click on **No**. We started our grammar check at the beginning of the document; it would be redundant to return there now.

Note: When you clicked on *Start* in step 8 to restart the proofing procedure after manually editing the document, you "fooled" Word into thinking that the current proofing session began at this point in the document. That is why Word asked if you would like to return to the beginning.

13. A *Readability Statistics* box appears, summarizing the grammar checker's findings for your document (see Figure 7.7).

14. Press **F1** to display Word Help on readability statistics. Read through this topic to learn more about what each of these statistics means, particularly the Flesch Reading Ease and Gunning Fog indexes.

Figure 7.7   **The Readability Statistics box**

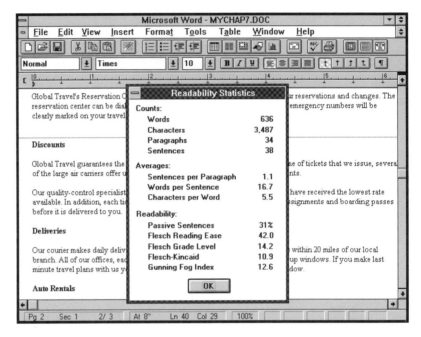

15. Close the Help window. Take a moment to reexamine the Readability Statistics box in light of your new knowledge. When you are finished, click on **OK** (or press **Enter**) to close the box.

16. Save the disk file and close the document.

SUMMARY

In this chapter, you learned how to proof your documents and improve their quality. You now know how to check the spelling of your documents, how to use the thesaurus to find alternative words, and how to check the grammar, style, and readability of your documents.

Here's a quick reference guide to the Word features introduced in this chapter:

Desired Result	How to Do It
Spell-check a document	Press **Ctrl+Home** to move the insertion point to the top (to spell-check an entire document) or select the desired text (to spell-check part of a document); choose **Tools**, **Spelling** or click on the toolbar **Spelling** button; follow the Spelling dialog box prompts
Use the thesaurus to find alternative words	Select the desired word or place the insertion point anywhere within the word; choose **Tools**, **Thesaurus** or press **Shift+F7**; follow the Thesaurus dialog box prompts
Check the grammar and style of a document	Press **Ctrl+Home** to move the insertion point to the top (to check an entire document) or select the desired text (to check part of a document); choose **Tools**, **Grammar**; follow the Grammar dialog box prompts
Customize the grammar checker	Click on **Options** in the Grammar dialog box; click on **Customize Settings** in the Options dialog box; set (check or uncheck) your desired grammar and style rules; click on **OK** (or press **Enter**) to return to the Options dialog box; click on **OK** (or press **Enter**) to accept your customized rule settings and return to the Grammar dialog box

In the next chapter, you will build on the basic formatting and editing skills that you have already acquired. You'll learn advanced techniques for moving and copying text, and we'll show you how to copy character formats using the mouse. You'll also learn how to disable the Summary Info dialog box, add numbers and bullets to selected text, as well as how to replace and revise character formats.

IF YOU'RE STOPPING HERE

If you need to break off here, please exit Word. If you want to proceed directly to the next chapter, please do so now.

CHAPTER EIGHT: ADVANCED FORMATTING AND EDITING TECHNIQUES

To help you distinguish between steps presented for your general knowledge and steps you should carry out at your computer as you read, we have adopted the following system:

- A bulleted step, like this, is provided for your information and reference only.

1. A numbered step, like this, indicates one in a series of steps that you should carry out in sequence at your computer.

In Chapters 3 and 4, you learned basic techniques for editing and changing character formats of text. In this chapter, you will build on this information by learning more advanced methods of editing and formatting text. For example, you will learn how to copy text from one document to another and how to enhance the readability and visual appeal of your documents by turning selected text into a numbered or bulleted list.

When you're done working through this chapter, you will know

- How to move and copy text using the mouse and the toolbar

- How to copy text from one document to another

- How to add bullets and numbers to selected paragraphs

- How to copy character formats

- How to replace character formats using the *Edit, Replace* command

DISABLING THE SUMMARY INFO DIALOG BOX

When you start Word, certain defaults are already set. Summary Info, introduced in Chapter 1, is one such default. However, there are ways to customize the program so that it can best suit your specific needs. In this section, you'll learn how to *disable*, or reset, the Summary Info dialog box.

You can modify defaults using the Tools, Options command. From the Options dialog box, shown in Figure 8.1, you can, for instance

- Change the design of the toolbar

- Change the way that menus are displayed

- Modify settings for saving disk files so that you can save them in fewer steps

Here's how the Options dialog box works: You simply click on an icon in the Category list box. (You can view all of the available categories by clicking on the scroll bar.) When you select a category, options pertaining to that category are displayed in the Options panel, the area in the center of the dialog box. Then you may easily change any settings that you wish in the Options panel. After you've finished making your changes, click on OK.

For example, to disable the Summary Info dialog box, which displays when you first save a disk file

- Choose *Tools, Options*

- In the Category list box, select *Save*

- In the Save Options box, uncheck *Prompt for Summary Info*

- Click on *OK*

Figure 8.1   **Setting save options in the Options dialog box**

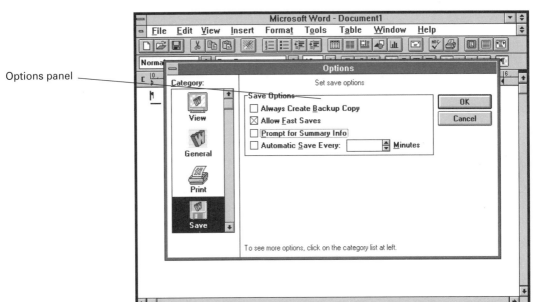

Options panel

Now let's open the Options dialog box and disable the Summary Info dialog box:

1. Choose **Tools, Options** to open the Options dialog box.

2. In the Category list box, select **Save** to display the Save Options box.

3. In the Save Options box, uncheck **Prompt for Summary Info** to disable the Summary Info dialog box so that it does not display when you save a disk file for the first time. Compare your screen to Figure 8.1.

4. Click on **OK**. The Summary Info dialog box is now disabled.

ALTERNATIVES FOR COPYING AND MOVING TEXT

In Chapter 3, you learned how to copy and move text by using the Edit menu. You can also copy text by using the Copy button on the toolbar. In addition to using the Edit menu to move text, you can also use either the Cut and Paste buttons in the toolbar or the mouse.

To copy text (within the same document) using the toolbar

- Select the text you wish to copy
- Click on the *Copy* button
- Move the insertion point to where you want to place the text
- Click on the *Paste* button

To move text (within the same document) using the toolbar

- Select the text you wish to move
- Click on the *Cut* button
- Move the insertion point to where you want to place the text
- Click on the *Paste* button

To move text (within the same document) using the mouse

- Select the text you wish to move
- Point to the selected text
- Press and hold the mouse button (a small dotted box and dotted insertion point appear attached to the mouse pointer)
- Drag the dotted insertion point to where you want to place the text
- Release the mouse button

Let's use the toolbar to copy text, then use the mouse to move text:

1. Open **chap8a.doc**.

2. Select the two lines of the *Global Travel* heading and the blank line below it.

3. Click on the **Copy** button (the fifth button from the left in the toolbar). A copy of the selected text is now placed on the Clipboard.

4. Go to the top of page 2.

5. Click on the **Paste** button (the one showing a clipboard). The contents of the Clipboard are now placed at the insertion point.

6. Go to the top of page 3.

7. Click on the **Paste** button to paste the contents of the Clipboard at the insertion point (see Figure 8.2). Remember, the
contents of the Clipboard will remain there until another selection is cut or copied.

Figure 8.2   **Copied heading (using the Copy button)**

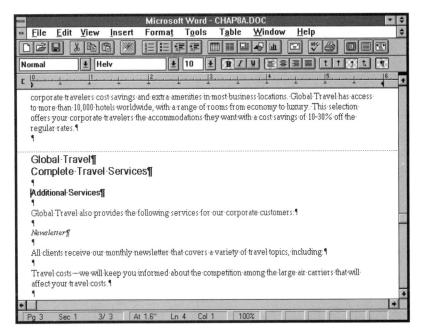

8. Move the insertion point to the top of the document.

9. Scroll to view the Introduction section of the document.

10. Drag to select the entire section, from the *Introduction* heading through the blank line above the *International Travel* heading (see Figure 8.3).

11. Point to the selected text. The mouse pointer becomes an
arrow.

12. Press and hold the mouse button. A small, dotted box and a
dotted insertion point appear.

Figure 8.3   **Selected text to be moved (using the mouse)**

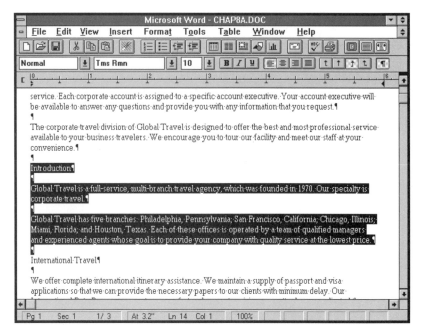

13. Drag the dotted insertion point to the left of the *C* in *Customer Service* (toward the top of page 1) to place the Introduction section above the Customer Service section.

14. Release the mouse button. The selected text is now displayed in its new location.

15. Save the disk file as **mychap8a** and compare your screen to Figure 8.4.

COPYING TEXT FROM ANOTHER DOCUMENT

The first document you open appears in the document window. If you create or open a second document without closing the first one, Word will open the second document on top of the first document, so that both documents are open at the same time. The second document then becomes the active document. You can open up to nine documents at one time, but only one document can be active.

Figure 8.4   **Moved text (using the mouse)**

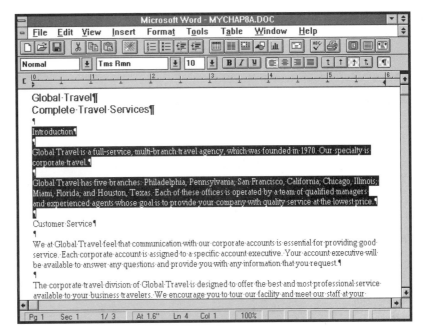

The names of the documents appear in the title bars and under the Window menu. To make a document active, either click on the document window, if it is visible, or select the document name from the Window menu.

Tiling is the arrangement of open windows in an equally spaced layout on the screen. To view more than one document window at a time, you can tile the open windows by choosing Window, Tile. However, the more windows you have open, the smaller each window will be when it is tiled. You also can use the document Maximize/Restore button to enlarge or reduce the size of each window.

Once you have placed text on the Clipboard, you can move or copy the text from one document to another, in the same way that you would within a document.

Let's open a second document window, then copy and paste between the two documents:

1. Place the I-beam to the left of the *H* in *Hotel Accommodations*, near the bottom of page 2.

2. Open **chap8b.doc**. The document consists of a single paragraph, followed by a blank line.

3. Select the paragraph and the blank line below it.

4. Click on the **Copy** button to place a copy of the selected text on the Clipboard.

5. Choose **Window, 2 MYCHAP8A.DOC** (see Figure 8.5) to move to the MYCHAP8A.DOC document window.

Figure 8.5   **Switching between documents**

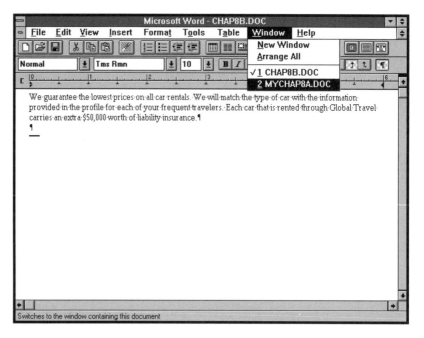

6. Click on the **Paste** button. The paragraph and blank line are now displayed below the *Auto Rentals* heading.

7. Click on the **Save** button (the third button from the left in the toolbar) to update the disk file.

8. Choose **Window, 1 CHAP8B.DOC** to move to the CHAP8B.DOC document window.

9. Choose **File, Close** to close CHAP8B.DOC.

ADDING HEADINGS, NUMBERS, AND BULLETS

The longer your document, the more important it is for you to clearly define its major sections and subsections. In order to achieve this, you can use headings, which you can format differently from the surrounding text. In fact, you've already seen several examples of headings in exercises throughout the course of this book. Furthermore, when your document contains lists of items that you would like to call attention to, such items can be numbered or bulleted. This section focuses on using numbers and bullets to improve your document's organization and appearance.

ADDING NUMBERS AND BULLETS

To add numbers to specific paragraphs, select the desired paragraphs and click on the Numbered List button. To add bullets to specific paragraphs, select the desired paragraphs and click on the Bulleted List button. When you add bullets or numbers to paragraphs, Word automatically formats the paragraphs with hanging indents. (See "Setting Hanging Indents" in Chapter 5 for details on this feature.)

If you apply numbers to a series of paragraphs and then want to change them to bullets, or vice versa

- Select the desired paragraphs

- Click on the *Bulleted List* or *Numbered List* button; a message box displays, asking if you want to replace the existing numbers or bullets

- Click on *Yes*

Let's select a list of items, then add numbers and bullets to the list:

1. Scroll to place the *Newsletter* heading, on page 3, at the top of the screen.

2. Drag to select the paragraphs that begin *Travel costs...*, *Special fares...*, and *Travel basics....*

3. Click on the **Numbered List** button (the eighth button from the left in the toolbar). Numbers appear to the left of the selected paragraphs.

4. Deselect the text to view the numbers. Compare your screen to Figure 8.6.

Figure 8.6   **Numbered list**

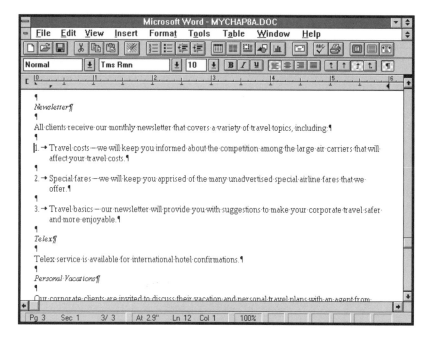

5. Drag to select the numbered list. Be sure to select all the numbers and paragraph marks.

6. Click on the **Bulleted List** button, immediately to the right of the Numbered List button. A message box opens, asking you if you want to replace the existing numbers with bullets.

7. Click on **Yes**. Bullets now appear to the left of the selected paragraphs.

8. Deselect the text and compare your screen to Figure 8.7.

REMOVING NUMBERS AND BULLETS

You can remove bullets or numbers from a series of paragraphs. To do so

• Select the numbered or bulleted list

• Choose *Tools, Bullets and Numbering*

• Click on *Remove* in the *Bullets and Numbering* dialog box

Figure 8.7   **Bulleted list**

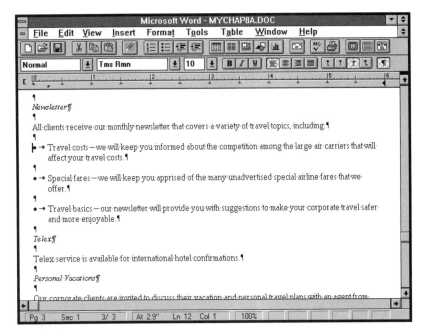

You can also use the Undo command to remove bullets or numbers, provided that you select the command immediately after applying the bullets or numbers, or before you perform any other editing in your document.

Let's remove the bullets from our list:

1. Drag to select the bulleted list. Be sure to select all of the bullets and paragraphs.

2. Choose **Tools, Bullets and Numbering** to open the Bullets and Numbering dialog box (see Figure 8.8).

3. Click on **Remove** to remove the bullets from the selected text.

Note: In the Bullets and Numbering dialog box, you can set various options for the type of bullet character you want to use, the size of the bullet, and the distance of the hanging indent.

Figure 8.8   **Bullets and Numbering dialog box**

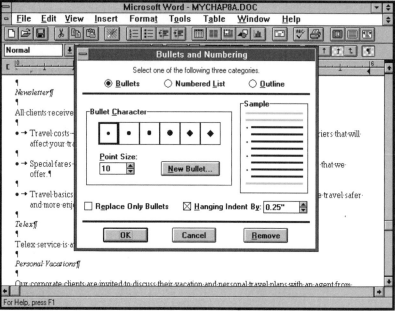

PRACTICE YOUR SKILLS

Replace the bullets in the *Travel costs...*, *Special fares...*, and *Travel basics...* paragraphs.

USING THE MOUSE TO COPY CHARACTER FORMATS

In Chapter 4, you learned how to apply multiple character styles using the Format menu. In the same chapter you also learned that you could use the F4 (Repeat) key or choose Edit, Repeat Formatting to repeat the formatting on other text. Remember, however, that when you use either of these methods, only the *last* format applied will be repeated. For example, if you select text and apply first the bold and then the italic formats from the ribbon, then select different text and press F4, only the italic formatting will be applied.

To copy *all of* the character formatting from one block of text to another, you can use the mouse. To do so

• Select the text you want to format

- Place the I-beam on the text that has the formatting you want to copy
- Press (and hold) Ctrl+Shift and click the mouse button

Let's apply and copy some character formats:

1. Select the *Introduction* heading, near the top of the document.

2. Open the **Font** drop-down list box and select **Helv.**

3. On the ribbon, click on the **Bold, Italic,** and **Underline** buttons to apply those character styles to the selected text.

4. Select the *Customer Service* heading, below the introduction section.

5. Press **F4** (or choose **Edit, Repeat Formatting**). Only the under-lining was applied to the selected text.

6. Choose **Edit, Undo Formatting** to remove the underlining from *Customer Service.*

7. Verify that *Customer Service* is still selected.

8. Without clicking the mouse button, place the I-beam any-where within the *Introduction* heading to point to the charac-ter formats that will be copied.

9. Press **Ctrl+Shift** and click the mouse button to copy the char-acter formatting from *Introduction* to *Customer Service.*

10. Select the *International Travel* heading, below the Customer Service section.

11. Place the I-beam on the *Customer Service* heading, to point to the character formats that you will copy.

12. Press **Ctrl+Shift** and click the mouse button to copy the char-acter formatting to *International Travel.*

PRACTICE YOUR SKILLS

1. Apply bold, italic, and underline styles to the *Corporate Pro-files* and *Worldwide Services* headings.

2. Deselect the text.

3. Save the disk file and compare your screen to Figure 8.9.

Figure 8.9   **Copied character formats**

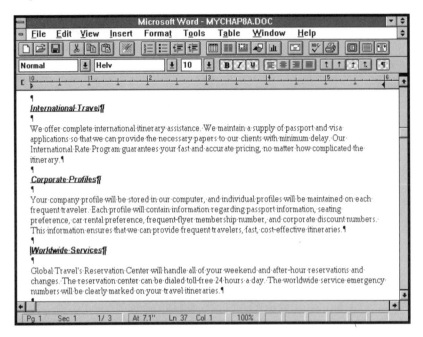

REPLACING CHARACTER FORMATS

You can use the Replace dialog box to search for and replace character formats in a manner that is similar to the way you find and replace text.

To replace character formats

- Choose *Edit, Replace*
- Click on *Character*
- Select the character formats you want to find
- Click on *OK*
- Press *Tab* to move to the *Replace With* text box
- Click on *Character*
- Select the character formats that you want to change to
- Click on *OK*

- Click on *Find Next*

- Click on *Replace* to replace the character formatting, or click on *Find Next* to leave the existing formatting

- Click on *Close* to close the Replace dialog box when you are finished

In the Style list box, grayed or unchecked formats will not change. Clicking in the check box selects the format; clicking twice clears the check box, indicating that you want to remove the format.

Let's replace character formats:

1. Move the I-beam to the top of the document.

2. Choose **Edit, Replace** to open the Replace dialog box (see Figure 8.10). The insertion point is placed in the Find What text box.

3. Click on **Character** to open the Find Character dialog box.

Figure 8.10   **Replace dialog box**

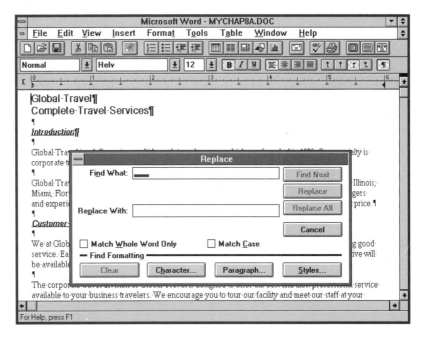

4. Open the **Font** drop-down list box. Then select **Helv** to search for text with the Helvetica font.

5. In the Style list box, check **Bold** and **Italic** to search for text that is both bold and italic.

6. Open the **Underline** drop-down list box. Then select **Single** to search for text with a single underline. Compare your screen to Figure 8.11.

Figure 8.11   **Searching for specified character formats**

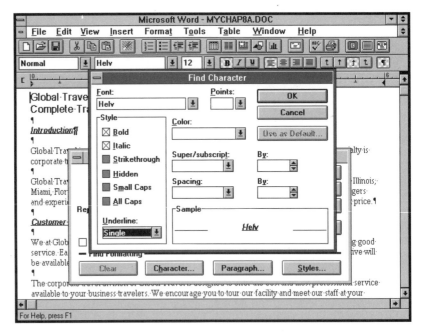

7. Click on **OK** to return to the Replace dialog box.

8. Press **Tab** to move the insertion point to the Replace With text box.

9. Click on **Character** to open the Replace Character dialog box.

10. In the Style list box, check **Italic** to apply the italic character style to selected text. Compare your screen to Figure 8.12.

Figure 8.12   **Specified replacement character format**

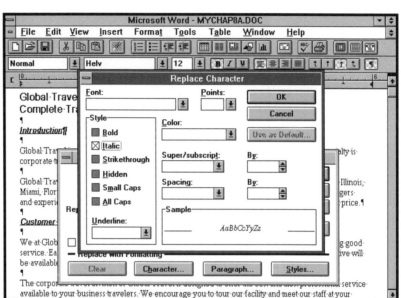

11. Click on **OK** to return to the Replace dialog box. Notice the character formats listed under the Find What and Replace With boxes, as shown in Figure 8.13.

12. Click on **Find Next** to begin the search and replace. The *Introduction* heading is selected.

13. Click on **Replace** to replace the current format with the italic character style. The *Customer Service* heading is now selected.

PRACTICE YOUR SKILLS

1. Continue replacing character formats until you have found and replaced all of them.

2. Close the Replace dialog box.

3. Save the disk file.

Figure 8.13   **Specified formats**

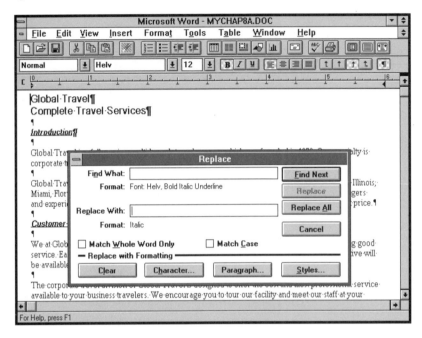

REVISING CHARACTER FORMATS IN THE REPLACE DIALOG BOX

When you select the character formatting you want to find and replace, the formats you choose appear below the Find What and Replace With text boxes. These formats will remain selected until you exit Word or clear them. To clear the selected formats so that you can specify different formats in the Replace dialog box, click on the Clear button.

Let's revise character formats in the Replace dialog box, changing the Helvetica italic text to Helvetica bold:

1. Choose **Edit, Replace** to open the Replace dialog box. The insertion point is placed in the Find What text box.

2. Observe the text below the Find What text box (see Figure 8.13); the character formats you previously specified remain selected.

3. Click on **Clear** to clear the Format selections displayed below the Find What text box.

4. Click on **Character** to open the Find Character dialog box.

5. Open the **Font** drop-down list box. Then select **Helv** to search for Helvetica text.

6. In the Style list box, check **Italic** to search for italic text.

7. Click on **OK** to return to the Replace dialog box.

8. Press **Tab** to move the insertion point to the Replace With text box.

9. Click on **Clear** to clear the Format selections displayed below the Replace With text box.

10. Click on **Character** to open the Replace Character dialog box.

11. In the Style list box, select **Bold** to apply the bold character style to selected text.

12. Click on **OK**. Compare your screen to Figure 8.14.

13. Click on **Find Next** to begin to search and replace.

Note: If you know in advance that you want to replace all occurrences of a format, instead of clicking on Find Next, you can click on Replace All.

PRACTICE YOUR SKILLS

1. Use the Replace button in the Replace dialog box to make the selected text bold.

2. Close the Replace dialog box.

3. Save the disk file.

4. Print the disk file and compare your printout to Figure 8.15.

5. Close the document.

PRACTICE YOUR SKILLS

The following instructions lead you through the steps necessary to edit the file PRAC8A.DOC to produce the document shown in Figure 8.16.

Follow these steps at your computer:

1. Open **prac8a.doc**.

Figure 8.14   **Revised character format**

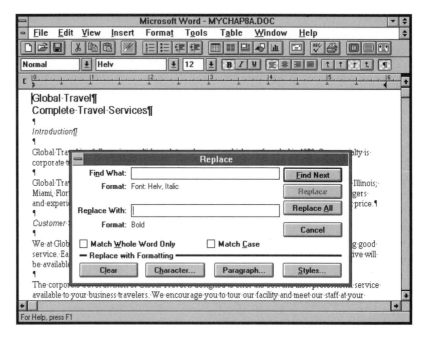

2. Use the mouse to highlight the International Travel section, which is below the Corporate Profiles section. Be sure to select the entire section and the blank line following it.

3. Use the toolbar to copy the heading and the blank line below it to the top of pages 2 and 3.

4. Open **prac8b.doc**.

5. Use the toolbar to copy all of PRAC8B.DOC to the Clipboard.

6. Move to the PRAC8A.DOC window.

7. Paste the contents of the Clipboard below the *Deliveries* heading.

8. In the Newsletter section, select the paragraphs that begin *Travel costs...*, *Special fares...*, and *Travel basics....*

9. Add bullets to the selected paragraphs.

10. Change the bulleted list to a numbered list.

Figure 8.15   **Completed MYCHAP8A.DOC document**

Global Travel
Complete Travel Services

Introduction

Global Travel is a full-service, multi-branch travel agency, which was founded in 1970. Our specialty is corporate travel.

Global Travel has five branches: Philadelphia, Pennsylvania; San Francisco, California; Chicago, Illinois; Miami, Florida; and Houston, Texas. Each of these offices is operated by a team of qualified managers and experienced agents whose goal is to provide your company with quality service at the lowest price.

Customer Service

We at Global Travel feel that communication with our corporate accounts is essential for providing good service. Each corporate account is assigned to a specific account executive. Your account executive will be available to answer any questions and provide you with any information that you request.

The corporate travel division of Global Travel is designed to offer the best and most professional service available to your business travelers. We encourage you to tour our facility and meet our staff at your convenience.

International Travel

We offer complete international itinerary assistance. We maintain a supply of passport and visa applications so that we can provide the necessary papers to our clients with minimum delay. Our International Rate Program guarantees you fast and accurate pricing, no matter how complicated the itinerary.

Corporate Profiles

Your company profile will be stored in our computer, and individual profiles will be maintained on each frequent traveler. Each profile will contain information regarding passport information, seating preference, car rental preference, frequent-flyer membership number, and corporate discount numbers. This information ensures that we can provide frequent travelers fast, cost-effective itineraries.

Worldwide Services

Global Travel's Reservation Center will handle all of your weekend and after-hour reservations and changes. The reservation center can be dialed toll-free 24 hours a day. The worldwide service emergency numbers will be clearly marked on your travel itineraries.

Figure 8.15   **(Continued)**

Global Travel
Complete Travel Services

Discounts

Global Travel guarantees the lowest air fares available. Due to the volume of tickets that we issue, several of the large air carriers offer us special discounts that we can pass on to our clients.

Our quality-control specialists check each of your tickets to guarantee that you have received the lowest rate available. In addition, each ticket is checked to ensure that it includes seating assignments and boarding passes before it is delivered to you.

Deliveries

Our courier makes daily deliveries, both in the morning and afternoon, to offices within 20 miles of our local branch. All of our offices, each located across from the local airport, have drive-up windows. If you make last minute travel plans with us you can pick up your ticket right at the drive-up window.

Auto Rentals

We guarantee the lowest prices on all car rentals. We will match the type of car with the information provided in the profile for each of your frequent travelers. Each car that is rented through Global Travel carries an extra $50,000 worth of liability insurance.

Hotel Accommodations

Our Corporate Hotel Program is the most competitive and comprehensive program in the world, offering corporate travelers cost savings and extra amenities in most business locations. Global Travel has access to more than 10,000 hotels worldwide, with a range of rooms from economy to luxury. This selection offers your corporate travelers the accommodations they want with a cost savings of 10-30% off the regular rates.

Figure 8.15   **(Continued)**

Global Travel
Complete Travel Services

Additional Services

Global Travel also provides the following services for our corporate customers:

Newsletter

All clients receive our monthly newsletter that covers a variety of travel topics, including:

- Travel costs – we will keep you informed about the competition among the large air carriers that will affect your travel costs.

- Special fares – we will keep you apprised of the many unadvertised special airline fares that we offer.

- Travel basics – our newsletter will provide you with suggestions to make your corporate travel safer and more enjoyable.

Telex

Telex service is available for international hotel confirmations.

Personal Vacations

Our corporate clients are invited to discuss their vacation and personal travel plans with an agent from Global Travel's Vacation Division. Our Vacation Division is skilled in both domestic and international travel.

Flight Insurance

We will supply all clients with $250,000 worth of flight insurance for every trip arranged through Global Travel.

Fax

Travel requests may be faxed to our office. Confirmed itineraries can be faxed to your office for immediate confirmation.

Figure 8.16   Completed MYPRAC8A.DOC document

Global Travel
Complete Travel Services

Introduction

Global Travel is a full-service, multi-branch travel agency, which was founded in 1970. Our specialty is corporate travel.

Global Travel has five branches: Philadelphia, Pennsylvania; San Francisco, California; Chicago, Illinois; Miami, Florida; and Houston, Texas. Each of these offices is operated by a team of qualified managers and experienced agents whose goal is to provide your company with quality service at the lowest price.

Customer Service

We at Global Travel feel that communication with our corporate accounts is essential for providing good service. Each corporate account is assigned to a specific account executive. Your account executive will be available to answer any questions and provide you with any information that you request.

The corporate travel division of Global Travel is designed to offer the best and most professional service available to your business travelers. We encourage you to tour our facility and meet our staff at your convenience.

International Travel

We offer complete international itinerary assistance. We maintain a supply of passport and visa applications so that we can provide the necessary papers to our clients with minimum delay. Our International Rate Program guarantees you fast and accurate pricing, no matter how complicated the itinerary.

Corporate Profiles

Your company profile will be stored in our computer, and individual profiles will be maintained on each frequent traveler. Each profile will contain information regarding passport information, seating preference, car rental preference, frequent-flyer membership number, and corporate discount numbers. This information ensures that we can provide frequent travelers fast, cost-effective itineraries.

Worldwide Services

Global Travel's Reservation Center will handle all of your weekend and after-hour reservations and changes. The reservation center can be dialed toll-free 24 hours a day. The worldwide service emergency numbers will be clearly marked on your travel itineraries.

Figure 8.16   **(Continued)**

Global Travel
Complete Travel Services

Discounts

Global Travel guarantees the lowest air fares available. Due to the volume of tickets that we issue, several of the large air carriers offer us special discounts that we can pass on to our clients.

Our quality-control specialists check each of your tickets to guarantee that you have received the lowest rate available. In addition, each ticket is checked to ensure that it includes seating assignments and boarding passes before it is delivered to you.

Deliveries

Our courier makes daily deliveries, both in the morning and afternoon, to offices within 20 miles of our local branch. All of our offices, each located across from the local airport, have drive-up windows. If you make last minute travel plans with us you can pick up your ticket right at the drive-up window.

Auto Rentals

We guarantee the lowest prices on all car rentals. We will match the type of car with the information provided in the profile for each of your frequent travelers. Each car that is rented through Global Travel carries an extra $50,000 worth of liability insurance.

Hotel Accommodations

Our Corporate Hotel Program is the most competitive and comprehensive program in the world, offering corporate travelers cost savings and extra amenities in most business locations. Global Travel has access to more than 10,000 hotels worldwide, with a range of rooms from economy to luxury. This selection offers your corporate travelers the accommodations they want with a cost savings of 10-30% off the regular rates.

Figure 8.16   **(Continued)**

Global Travel
Complete Travel Services

<u>**Additional Services**</u>

Global Travel also provides the following services for our corporate customers:

Newsletter

All clients receive our monthly newsletter that covers a variety of travel topics, including:

1. Travel costs—we will keep you informed about the competition among the large air carriers that will affect your travel costs.

2. Special fares—we will keep you apprised of the many unadvertised special airline fares that we offer.

3. Travel basics—our newsletter will provide you with suggestions to make your corporate travel safer and more enjoyable.

Telex

Service is available for international hotel confirmations.

Personal Vacations

Our corporate clients are invited to discuss their vacation and personal travel plans with an agent from Global Travel's Vacation Division. Our Vacation Division is skilled in both domestic and international travel.

Flight Insurance

We will supply all clients with $250,000 worth of flight insurance for every trip arranged through Global Travel.

Fax

Travel requests may be faxed to our office. Confirmed itineraries can be faxed to your office for immediate confirmation.

11. Change the character formatting of the *Introduction* heading to **Helv**, **Bold**, and **Underline**.

12. Use the mouse to apply the character formats from the *Intro-duction* heading to the *Customer Service* heading.

13. Apply the character formats from the *Customer Service* heading to the following headings:

International Travel

Corporate Profiles

Worldwide Services

Discounts

Deliveries

Auto Rentals

Hotel Accommodations

Additional Services

14. Save the disk file as **myprac8a.doc**.

15. Print the document and compare your printout to Figure 8.16.

16. Close both document windows.

In the next activity you will edit PRAC8C.DOC to produce the final document shown in Figure 8.17. You will use the Replace dialog box to replace character formats. Be sure to clear the contents of the Find What and Replace With text boxes before selecting new find and replace criteria.

Follow these steps at your computer:

1. Open **prac8c.doc**.

2. Use the Replace dialog box to find text that is Helvetica, 24 point, bold, and replace these formats with Times Roman, 14 point, bold.

Figure 8.17   **Completed MYPRAC8C.DOC**

Global Travel
Complete Travel Services

Introduction

Global Travel is a full-service, multi-branch travel agency, which was founded in 1970. Our specialty is corporate travel.

Global Travel has five branches: Philadelphia, Pennsylvania; San Francisco, California; Chicago, Illinois; Miami, Florida; and Houston, Texas. Each of these offices is operated by a team of qualified managers and experienced agents whose goal is to provide your company with quality service at the lowest price.

Customer Service

We at Global Travel feel that communication with our corporate accounts is essential for providing good service. Each corporate account is assigned to a specific account executive. Your account executive will be available to answer any questions and provide you with any information that you request.

The corporate travel division of Global Travel is designed to offer the best and most professional service available to your business travelers. We encourage you to tour our facility and meet our staff at your convenience.

International Travel

We offer complete international itinerary assistance. We maintain a supply of passport and visa applications so that we can provide the necessary papers to our clients with minimum delay. Our International Rate Program guarantees you fast and accurate pricing, no matter how complicated the itinerary.

Corporate Profiles

Your company profile will be stored in our computer, and individual profiles will be maintained on each frequent traveler. Each profile will contain information regarding passport information, seating preference, car rental preference, frequent-flyer membership number, and corporate discount numbers. This information ensures that we can provide frequent travelers fast, cost-effective itineraries.

Worldwide Services

Global Travel's Reservation Center will handle all of your weekend and after-hour reservations and changes. The reservation center can be dialed toll-free 24 hours a day. The worldwide service emergency numbers will be clearly marked on your travel itineraries.

Figure 8.17   **(Continued)**

Global Travel
Complete Travel Services

Discounts

Global Travel guarantees the lowest air fares available. Due to the volume of tickets that we issue, several of the large air carriers offer us special discounts that we can pass on to our clients.

Our quality-control specialists check each of your tickets to guarantee that you have received the lowest rate available. In addition, each ticket is checked to ensure that it includes seating assignments and boarding passes before it is delivered to you.

Deliveries

Our courier makes daily deliveries, both in the morning and afternoon, to offices within 20 miles of our local branch. All of our offices, each located across from the local airport, have drive-up windows. If you make last minute travel plans with us you can pick up your ticket right at the drive-up window.

Auto Rentals

We guarantee the lowest prices on all car rentals. We will match the type of car with the information provided in the profile for each of your frequent travelers. Each car that is rented through Global Travel carries an extra $50,000 worth of liability insurance.

Hotel Accommodations

Our Corporate Hotel Program is the most competitive and comprehensive program in the world, offering corporate travelers cost savings and extra amenities in most business locations. Global Travel has access to more than 10,000 hotels worldwide, with a range of rooms from economy to luxury. This selection offers your corporate travelers the accommodations they want with a cost savings of 10-30% off the regular rates.

Figure 8.17   **(Continued)**

Global Travel
Complete Travel Services

Additional Services

Global Travel also provides the following services for our corporate customers:

Newsletter

All clients receive our monthly newsletter that covers a variety of travel topics, including:

Travel costs – we will keep you informed about the competition among the large air carriers that will affect your travel costs.

Special fares – we will keep you apprised of the many unadvertised special airline fares that we offer.

Travel basics – our newsletter will provide you with suggestions to make your corporate travel safer and more enjoyable.

Telex

Telex service is available for international hotel confirmations.

Personal Vacations

Our corporate clients are invited to discuss their vacation and personal travel plans with an agent from Global Travel's Vacation Division. Our Vacation Division is skilled in both domestic and international travel.

Flight Insurance

We will supply all clients with $250,000 worth of flight insurance for every trip arranged through Global Travel.

Fax

Travel requests may be faxed to our office. Confirmed itineraries can be faxed to your office for immediate confirmation.

3. Clear the contents of the Find What and Replace With text boxes.

4. Use the Replace dialog box to find text that is formatted as Times Roman, 12 point, bold and italic, and change it to Helvetica, 10 point, bold.

5. Clear the contents of the Find What and Replace With text boxes.

6. Use the Replace dialog box to find text that is formatted as Times Roman, 14 point, with a single underline. Change the formatting to Helvetica, 10 point, bold.

7. Clear the contents of the Find What and Replace With text boxes.

8. Use the Replace dialog box to find text that is formatted as Helvetica, 14 point, italic. Replace these character formats with Times Roman, 10 point, italic.

9. Clear the contents of the Find What and Replace With text boxes.

10. Use the Replace dialog box to find text that is formatted as Helvetica, 12 point, with a single underline. Replace them with Times Roman, 10 point character formats.

11. Close the Replace dialog box.

12. Save the disk file as **myprac8c.doc**.

13. Print the document and compare your printout to Figure 8.17.

14. Close the document.

SUMMARY

In this chapter, you learned a number of advanced formatting and editing techniques that make use of the toolbar and mouse, including copying and moving text within a single document and between documents. You learned how to create numbered lists and bulleted lists by adding numbers or bullets to a contiguous string of paragraphs. You also learned how to change a numbered list to a bulleted list, and vice-versa. Finally, you learned how to copy and replace character formats.

Here is a quick reference guide to the Word features introduced in this chapter:

Desired Result	**How to Do It**
Disable the Summary Info dialog box	Choose **Tools, Options**; select **Save** in the Category list box; uncheck **Prompt for Summary Info** in the Save Options box; click on **OK**
Copy text using the toolbar	Select the desired text; click on the **Copy** button; place the insertion point in the desired destination; click on the **Paste** button
Move text using the mouse pointer	Select the desired text; point to the selected text; drag the selection to the desired destination; release the mouse button
Copy text from one document to another	Open the second document; select the desired text; click on the **Copy** button; choose **Window** and choose the file name of the destination document; place the insertion point where you wish to place the copied text; click on the **Paste** button
Save a document using the toolbar	Click on the **Save** button (if the disk file has not been previously named, the Save As dialog box will open and you should name the disk file)
Close an inactive document window	Choose **Window** and the name of the document you wish to close; choose **File, Close**
Add numbers or bullets to existing text	Select the desired paragraphs; click on the **Numbered List** button or the **Bulleted List** button
Change numbers to bullets or vice-versa	Select the numbered or bulleted list; click on the **Bulleted List** or **Numbered List** button, whichever you desire; click on **Yes**
Remove numbers or bullets	Select the desired text; choose **Tools, Bullets and Numbering**; click on **Remove**

Desired Result	How to Do It
Copy character formats	Select the text to which you wish to apply formatting; place the I-beam anywhere within the text that has the formatting that you wish to copy; press and hold **Ctrl+Shift**; click the mouse button
Replace character formats	Place the insertion point at the top of the document; choose **Edit, Replace**; click on **Character**; select the settings you want to find; click on **OK**; press **Tab**; click on **Character**; select the replacement settings; click on **OK**; click on **Find Next**; click on **Replace**; continue clicking on **Find Next**, then **Replace**, until you have finished replacing the formats
Revise character formats	Place the insertion point at the top of the document; choose **Edit, Replace**; click on **Clear**; click on **Character**; select the settings you wish to find; click on **OK**; press **Tab**; click on **Clear**; click on **Character**; select the new replacement settings; click on **OK**; click on **Find Next**; click on **Replace**; and so on

In the next chapter, you will learn how to create and use glossaries to store frequently used text and graphics.

IF YOU'RE STOPPING HERE

If you need to break off here, please exit Word. If you want to proceed directly to the next chapter, please do so now.

CHAPTER NINE: USING GLOSSARIES TO STORE FREQUENTLY USED TEXT

- Creating Glossary Entries

- Inserting Glossary Entries

- Modifying Glossary Entries

- Saving Global Glossary Entries

- Printing Glossary Entries

To help you distinguish between steps presented for your general knowledge and steps you should carry out at your computer as you read, we have adopted the following system:

- A bulleted step, like this, is provided for your information and reference only.

1. A numbered step, like this, indicates one in a series of steps that you should carry out in sequence at your computer.

Suppose you needed to send out a large number of letters, and that in each one the letterhead and closing were to be exactly the same. It would certainly save you a great deal of time to have to enter the letterhead and closing only once, and then simply paste them into each document, as needed. You could copy the information to the Clipboard and paste it into each letter. However, you already know that the Clipboard is only a temporary storage area; as soon as you cut or copied other text or exited Windows, the information would be lost.

Word enables you to save such information as a glossary entry. A *Glossary* is a kind of shorthand that allows you to save text or graphics, then retrieve it whenever you need it. You can insert glossaries anywhere in your documents.

When you're done working through this chapter, you will know

- How to create glossary entries
- How to modify and delete glossary entries
- How to print glossary entries

CREATING GLOSSARY ENTRIES

Glossary entries enable you to store frequently used text and graphics so that you can insert them into your documents quickly and easily. You can store glossaries so that they can be used *globally*, in all *templates.* A template is a kind of "model" that determines the general format of the document it is attached to. Templates allow you to custom-tailor your documents. You'll learn about templates in Chapter 13; saving global glossary entries is covered later in this chapter. If you do not wish to use glossaries globally, you can store them to be used with a specific template.

To create a glossary entry

- Select the text or graphics you want in the glossary entry
- Choose *Edit, Glossary*
- In the Glossary Name text box, type a name for the glossary entry
- Click on *Define*

Glossary entries can contain any type of formatting. Entry names can have up to 31 characters and can contain spaces. For ease of use, you might want to keep your glossary entry names brief.

Let's create glossary entries for a letterhead and closing:

1. Click on the **New** button (the first toolbar button on the left) to open a new document window.

2. Type **Global Travel** and press **Enter**.

3. Type **2345 Industrial Parkway** and press **Enter**.

4. Type **Chicago, Illinois 60603** and press **Enter** three times.

5. Select all of the text. Do *not* select the blank lines below the text.

6. Change the font to **Helv** (use the Font drop-down box).

7. Apply the **Bold** character style to the selected text.

8. Center the selected text and compare your screen to Figure 9.1.

Figure 9.1   **Completed letterhead**

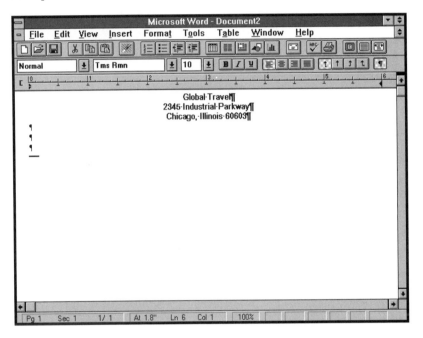

9. Deselect the text.

10. Select all of the text and the three blank lines. The heading and blank lines will be included in the glossary entry.

11. Choose **Edit, Glossary** (see Figure 9.2) to open the Glossary dialog box.

12. Observe the Selection line at the bottom of the Glossary dialog box. The Selection line can be used to verify the desired selection.

13. In the Glossary Name text box, type **letterhead** to name the glossary entry. Compare your screen to Figure 9.3.

Figure 9.2   **Choosing Edit, Glossary**

Figure 9.3   **Naming the letterhead glossary entry**

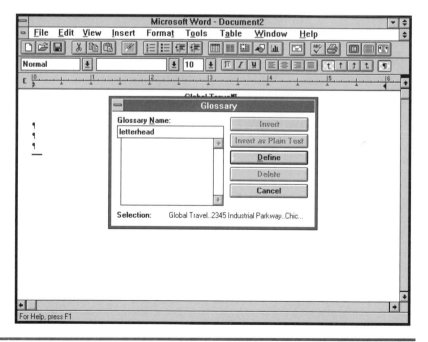

14. Click on **Define** to add the glossary entry to the list.

15. Close the document without saving it; saving is not necessary because the document's text has already been saved as a glossary entry.

16. Click on the **New** button (the first toolbar button on the left) to open a new document window.

17. Type **Cordially,**.

18. Press **Enter** four times.

19. Type your name and press **Enter**.

20. Type **Corporate Sales Coordinator** and press **Enter** twice.

21. Type **cc:** then press **Tab** to move to the first tab stop.

22. Type **R. Allen** and press **Enter**.

23. Press **Tab**, type **G. Berg** and compare your screen to Figure 9.4.

Figure 9.4   **Completed letter closing**

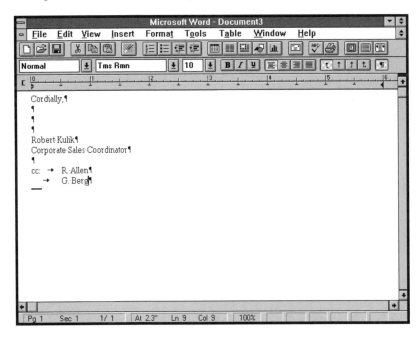

24. Select all of the text and paragraph marks. The selected text will be included in the glossary entry.

25. Choose **Edit, Glossary** to open the Glossary dialog box again.

26. In the Glossary Name text box, type **cordially** to name the glossary entry. Compare your screen to Figure 9.5. Notice that the letterhead entry, which you created earlier, is listed in the Glossary Name list box.

Figure 9.5 **Naming the letter closing glossary entry**

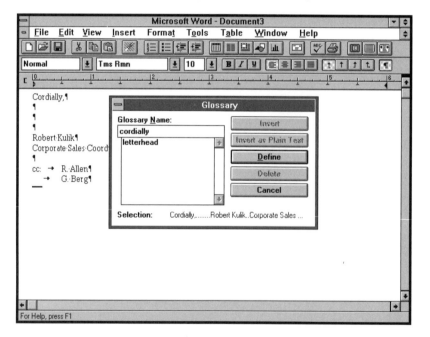

27. Click on **Define** to add the glossary entry to the list.

28. Close the document without saving it.

INSERTING GLOSSARY ENTRIES

To insert a glossary entry in a document

- Place the insertion point where you want to insert the glossary entry

- Choose *Edit, Glossary*
- Select the name of the glossary entry you want to insert
- Click on *Insert*

If you click on Insert as Plain Text, Word will apply the formatting of the surrounding text to the glossary entry.

To insert a glossary entry using the keyboard

- Place the I-beam where you want to insert the glossary entry
- Type the name of the glossary entry
- Press *F3*

Note: If you type the glossary entry name in front of text, be sure to type a space after the glossary name, otherwise the entry will run into the existing text. Also remember that the glossary name must be typed exactly the way you typed it when you named it.

Let's insert the glossary entries in our document:

1. Open **chap9.doc**.

2. Verify that the insertion point is at the top of the document.

3. Choose **Edit, Glossary** to open the Glossary dialog box.

4. In the Glossary Name list box, select **letterhead** (see Figure 9.6).

5. Click on **Insert** to insert the glossary entry in the document. Compare your screen to Figure 9.7.

6. Move the insertion point to the end of the document.

7. Choose **Edit, Glossary**.

8. In the Glossary Name list box, select **cordially**.

9. Click on **Insert** to insert the glossary entry in the document. Compare your screen to Figure 9.8.

10. Save the disk file as **mychap9.doc**.

Note: The "extra" paragraph mark (¶) after the closing in Figure 9.8 was produced by inserting the glossary entry before an existing paragraph mark.

Figure 9.6   **Inserting a glossary entry**

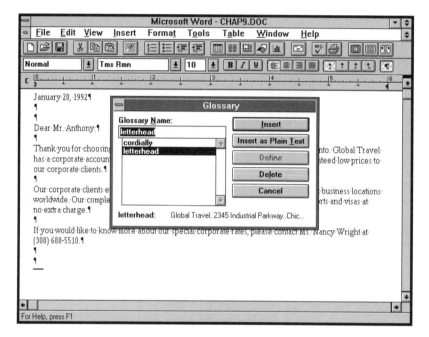

Figure 9.7   **Inserted letterhead glossary entry**

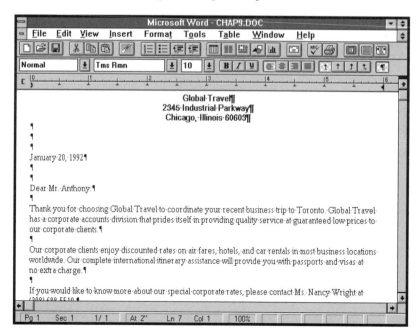

Figure 9.8   **Inserted closing glossary entry**

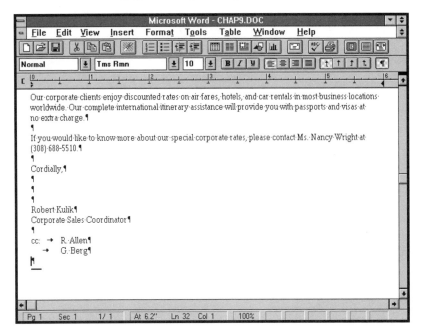

MODIFYING GLOSSARY ENTRIES

After you have created a glossary entry, you can go back and edit the text of the entry, in much the same way as you would a normal document.

 EDITING GLOSSARY ENTRIES

To edit a glossary entry

- Insert the glossary entry that you want to edit into your document

- Make the desired changes

- Select the text and/or graphics you want in the glossary entry

- Choose *Edit, Glossary*

- Select the original name of the glossary entry

- Click on *Define*; a message box displays, asking if you want to redefine the glossary entry

• Click on *Yes*

Let's edit one of our glossary entries:

1. Verify that the insertion point is at the end of the document.

2. Press **Tab**, then type **K. Donnelly** and press **Enter** (to add more names to the list).

3. Press **Tab**, then type **A. Hutton** and press **Enter**.

4. Select the entire closing, from *Cordially* through *A. Hutton*. Do *not* select the last paragraph mark.

5. Choose **Edit, Glossary**.

6. In the Glossary Name text box, select **cordially**.

7. Click on **Define**. A message box displays, asking if you wish to redefine the glossary entry (see Figure 9.9).

8. Click on **Yes** to redefine the *cordially* glossary entry with the same name.

Figure 9.9   **Editing a glossary entry**

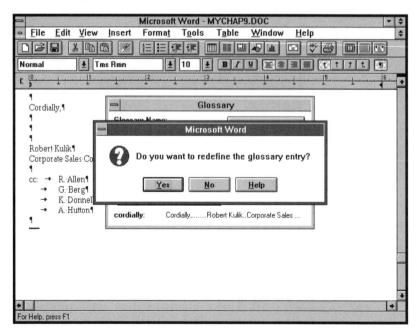

PRACTICE YOUR SKILLS

1. Delete the selected text. Do *not* move the insertion point.

2. Insert the new *cordially* glossary entry.

 DELETING GLOSSARY ENTRIES

To remove a glossary entry

- Choose *Edit, Glossary*
- Select the name of the glossary entry that you want to delete
- Click on *Delete*
- Click on *Close*

Let's edit the glossary entry, give it a new name, then delete the old entry:

1. Select **Cordially,** and type **Sincerely,**.

2. Select the entire closing, from *Sincerely* through *A. Hutton.* Do not select the last paragraph mark.

3. Choose **Edit, Glossary**.

4. In the Glossary Name text box, type **sincerely** to name the glossary entry.

5. Click on **Define** to add the glossary entry to the list.

6. Delete the selected text. Do *not* move the insertion point.

7. Type **sincerely**.

8. Press **F3** to insert the glossary entry using the keyboard. Notice that the glossary entry replaced the word *sincerely*.

9. Save the disk file and compare your screen to Figure 9.10.

10. Choose **Edit, Glossary**.

11. Select **cordially**.

12. Click on **Delete** to delete the selected glossary entry.

13. Click on **Close** to close the Glossary dialog box.

Figure 9.10 **New *sincerely* glossary entry**

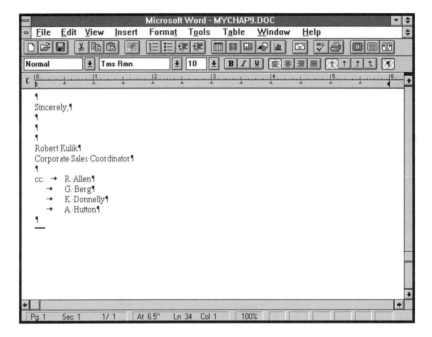

PRACTICE YOUR SKILLS

Delete the *letterhead* glossary entry.

SAVING GLOBAL GLOSSARY ENTRIES

As mentioned earlier in this chapter, you can save a glossary entry so that you can use it globally or with a specific template. (See Chapter 13 for more information on templates.)

To save a global glossary, choose File, Save All. A message box displays, asking if you want to save the global glossary and command changes. Click on Yes.

Note: The glossary entries that you save globally can be inserted in any document, regardless of which template you use.

Let's save our glossary entries globally so that they can later be used with any document:

1. Choose **File, Save All** to save the document and all glossary entries. A message box displays, asking if you want to save the global glossary and command changes (see Figure 9.11).

2. Click on **Yes**.

Figure 9.11 **Saving glossary entries globally**

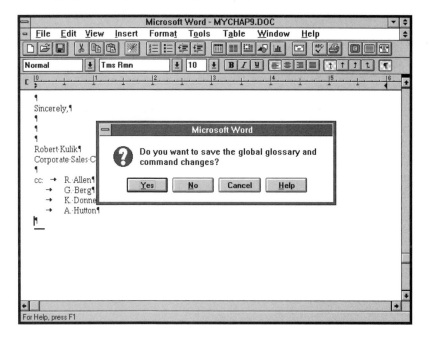

PRINTING GLOSSARY ENTRIES

You can print your glossary entries so that you can see the contents of each entry. To print glossary entries

- Choose *File, Print*

- In the Print drop-down list box, select *Glossary*

- Click on *OK*

All glossary entries available to the active document are printed, in alphabetical order. The formatting appears as it would if it were inserted in a document.

Let's print our glossary entries:

1. Choose **File, Print**.

2. In the Print drop-down list box, select **Glossary** to print only glossary entries (see Figure 9.12).

Figure 9.12   **Printing glossary entries**

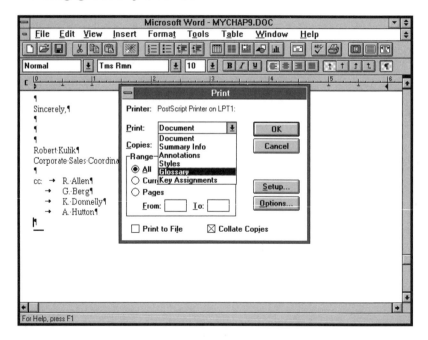

3. Click on **OK**.

4. Compare your printout with Figure 9.13. There is currently only one glossary entry available.

5. Close the document.

Figure 9.13   **Printed glossary file**

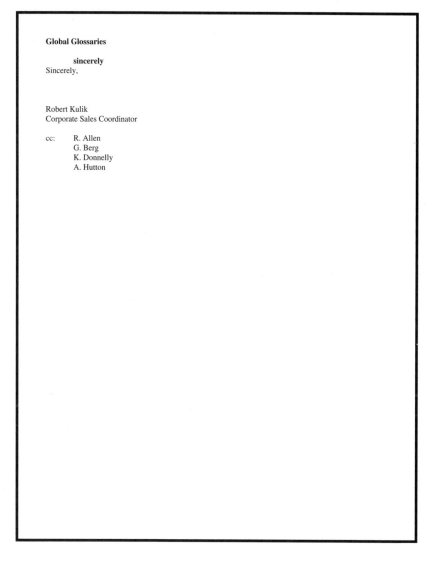

SUMMARY

In this chapter, you learned how to create glossary entries and insert them in your documents. You also learned how to edit, delete, save, and print your glossary entries.

Here is a quick reference guide to the Word features introduced in this chapter:

Desired Result	How to Do It
Create a glossary entry	Select the desired text and/or graphics to be placed in the entry; choose **Edit, Glossary**; name the entry in the Glossary Name text box; click on **Define**
Insert a glossary entry in a document using the mouse	Place the insertion point at the desired destination for the glossary entry; choose **Edit, Glossary**; select the name of the desired entry; click on **Insert**
Insert a glossary entry using the keyboard	Place the insertion point at the desired destination for the glossary entry; type the name of the entry; press **F3**
Edit a glossary entry	Insert the glossary entry to be edited in the document; make the desired changes; select the desired contents of the entry; choose **Edit, Glossary**; select the original name of the entry; click on **Define**; click on **Yes**
Delete a glossary entry	Choose **Edit, Glossary**; select the name of the glossary to be deleted; click on **Delete**; click on **Close**
Save a glossary entry globally	Choose **File, Save All**; click on **Yes**
Print glossary entries	Choose **File, Print**; in the Print box, select **Glossary**; click on **OK**

In the next chapter, you will learn how to create, modify, and enhance tables.

IF YOU'RE STOPPING HERE

If you need to break off here, please exit Word. If you want to proceed directly to the next chapter, please do so now.

CHAPTER TEN: WORKING WITH TABLES

Creating Tables

Modifying Tables

Enhancing Tables

Converting Tabbed
Text to a Table

If you want to arrange information in a table, you can do so by setting tabs. However, creating tabbed tables is a slow and tricky process; you must figure out exactly how the table should look, measure the width of each column, and then set tabs that correspond to each measurement. (You've already seen an example of a tabbed table in Chapter 5. See Figure 5.6 if you'd like to refer to the Hotel Accommodations tabbed table.) You can also run into problems if your text does not fit between your tabs.

The Word Table feature allows you to create rows and columns of information without having to set tabs. You can even convert tabbed text to a table. A table can be useful for enhancing the presentation of data in your document, for creating side-by-side paragraphs, and for organizing information used in form letters.

When you're done working through this chapter, you will know

- How to create a table

- How to modify a table

- How to enhance a table

- How to convert tabbed text to a table

CREATING TABLES

To insert a table into your document

- Place the insertion point where you want to insert the table

- Choose *Table, Insert Table* or click on the *Table* button in the toolbar

When you create tables by using the Menu command, you specify the number of columns and rows in the *Insert Table* dialog box. You can also specify the width of the columns. When you use the *Table* button to create tables, you drag on the Table button grid to specify the number of columns and rows. (You'll learn how to use the Table button grid later in this section.) Word creates a table that fills the area inside the margins. The width of the columns adjusts automatically according to the amount of space available between the left and right margins.

A table consists of vertical *columns* and horizontal *rows* (see Figure 10.1). The intersection of a column and a row is called a *cell*. Dotted lines called *gridlines* are displayed between the cells. You can hide the gridlines by choosing *Table, Gridlines.* Dotted lines called *column borders* are displayed between the columns. The gridlines and column borders are for visual reference only; they do not appear when you print the document.

If you display nonprinting characters, *end-of-cell* marks appear in each cell and *end-of-row* marks appear at the end of each row. Both of these types of marks are displayed as superscript double x's. You can use these marks to select and edit the table. Small T-shaped characters, called *column markers*, are displayed in the ruler when the insertion point is placed in the table. You can use column markers to adjust the width of the columns.

Figure 10.1 **Table components**

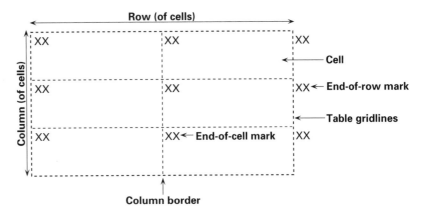

When you Print Preview the table, the gridlines, end-of-cell marks, and end-of-row marks are not displayed. To display these symbols in Print Preview, click on the Zoom button.

Let's create and examine a table:

1. Open **chap10.doc**.

2. Go to page 2 and scroll to place the paragraph that begins *Global Travel guarantees,* near the top of the document window. Place the insertion point in the blank line directly above the paragraph that begins *Our quality control.*

3. Choose **Table, Insert Table** to open the Insert Table dialog box, shown in Figure 10.2.

4. Observe the Number of Columns text box. You can change the number of columns by typing a number in the text box or by clicking on the increment indicators.

5. Observe the Number of Rows text box. You can change the number of rows by typing a number in the text box or by clicking on the increment indicators.

6. Click on **Cancel**.

7. Click on the toolbar **Table** button (the eleventh button from the right) to display the Table button grid.

8. Point to the upper-left corner of the Table button grid.

Figure 10.2   **Insert Table dialog box**

Table button

Increment
indicators

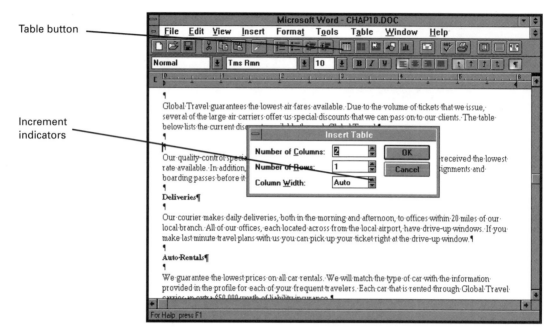

9. Press and hold the mouse button and drag down to select four rows of the grid. Then drag to the right to select two columns of the grid. The bottom of the grid displays *4x2 Table* (see Figure 10.3).

10. Release the mouse button to display the table at the insertion point.

11. Observe the columns, which are displayed vertically on the page (see Figure 10.1).

12. Observe the rows, which are displayed horizontally on the page.

13. Observe the cells, which are the intersections of columns and rows.

14. Observe the gridlines, the dotted lines between the cells.

15. Observe the column borders, the vertical dotted lines between the columns.

Figure 10.3   **Table button grid**

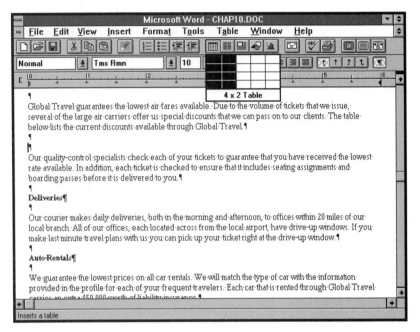

16. Observe the end-of-cell marks, the superscript double x's inside the cells.

17. Observe the end-of-row marks, the superscript double x's at the end of each row.

18. Observe the column markers in the ruler; these are small T-shaped characters.

 MOVING IN A TABLE

You can use the mouse to move to a table cell, or you can use the keyboard. To move to a specific cell using the mouse, simply place the I-beam on the end-of-cell mark in the desired cell, and click. Table 10.1 lists the keystrokes used for moving within a table.

Table 10.1   **Moving in a Table Using the Keyboard**

Desired Result	How to Do It
Move one cell to the right	Press *Tab*
Move one cell to the left	Press *Shift+Tab*
Move up one row	Press *up arrow*
Move down one row	Press *down arrow*

If the insertion point is in the last cell of a row when you press Tab, the insertion point will move to the first cell in the next row. Likewise, if the insertion point is in the first cell of a row when you press Shift+Tab, it will move to the last cell in the previous row.

Note: If you use the arrow keys on the numeric keypad, Num Lock must be off.

Let's practice moving in the table we've created:

1. Press **Tab** to move the insertion point to the second column of the first row.

2. Press **Tab** to move the insertion point to the first column in the second row.

3. Press **Shift+Tab** to move back to the second column of the first row.

4. Press **down arrow** to move down one row.

5. Press **up arrow** to move up one row.

6. Place the I-beam on the end-of-cell mark in the last cell of the table.

7. Click the mouse button to place the insertion point in the last cell.

PRACTICE YOUR SKILLS

Place the insertion point in the first cell of the table.

SELECTING TABLE COMPONENTS

You can select a cell, a row, a column, or the entire table. Table 10.2 lists the methods used for making these selections.

Table 10.2   **Selecting in a Table**

Desired Selection	How to Do It
Cell	Move the mouse pointer until it becomes an arrow and click on the end-of-cell mark within the desired cell
Row	Click the mouse button in the selection bar, to the left of the row; or place the insertion point anywhere within the desired row and choose *Table, Select Row*
Column	Click the right mouse button in any cell within the desired column; or place the insertion point in any cell within the desired column and choose *Table, Select Column*
Entire table	Place the insertion point anywhere within the table and choose *Table, Select Table*

Let's try various selection techniques within our table:

1. Point to the left of the end-of-cell mark in the first cell until the mouse pointer becomes an arrow. (Make sure that the mouse pointer is still located within the cell; the mouse pointer should appear as an arrowhead.)

2. Click to select the cell. Compare your screen to Figure 10.4.

3. In the selection bar, point to the left of the first row.

4. Click the mouse button to select the entire row (see Figure 10.5).

5. Point to any cell in the second column.

6. Click the *right* mouse button to select the entire column (see Figure 10.6).

Figure 10.4   **Selected cell**

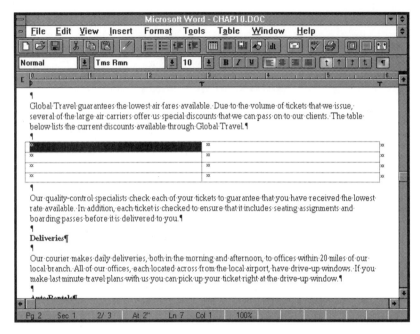

Figure 10.5   **Selected row**

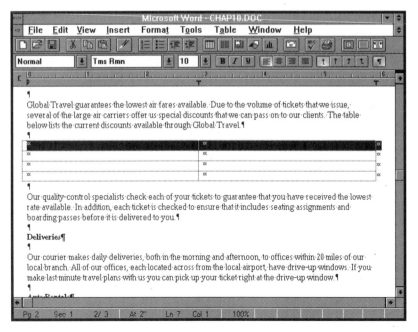

Figure 10.6   **Selected column**

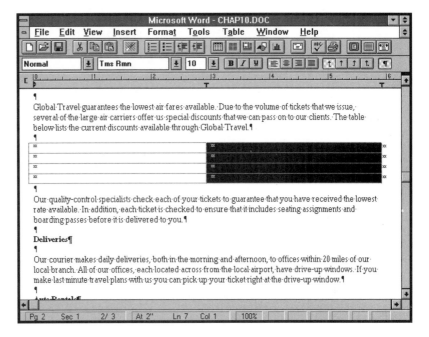

7. Choose **Table, Select Table** to select the entire table. Compare your screen to Figure 10.7.

8. Deselect the table (click outside the table).

9. Choose **Table**. Notice that when the insertion point is not in the table, only two Table menu commands are available.

10. Choose **Table** to close the Table menu.

ENTERING TEXT IN A TABLE

To enter text in a table, either select a cell or place the insertion point in the cell; then begin typing.

Let's enter text in our table:

1. Place the I-beam on the end-of-cell mark in the first cell and click.

2. Type **Destination**.

Figure 10.7   **Selected table**

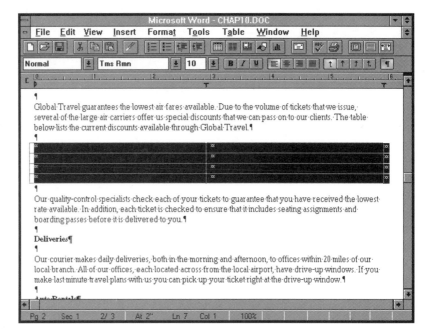

3. Press **Tab** to move to the next cell.

4. Type **Your Price** and press **Tab**.

PRACTICE YOUR SKILLS

1. Complete the table as shown in Figure 10.8.

2. Print Preview the completed document.

3. Save the disk file as **mychap10**.

MODIFYING TABLES

After you have created your table—even after you have entered all the desired data—you can still change its structure. You can insert rows and columns within the table, add rows to the bottom or columns to the right side of the table, change the width of the columns, and delete rows and columns.

Figure 10.8   **Completed table**

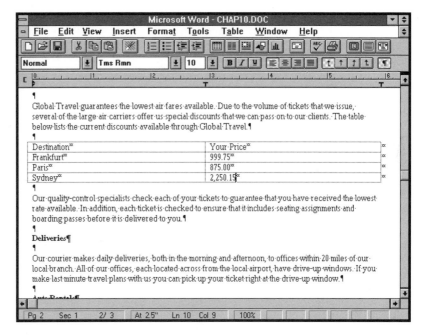

INSERTING ROWS AND COLUMNS

To insert a row at the end of a table, place the insertion point in the last cell of the table and press the Tab key. To insert a row *within* a table, select the row where you want to insert the new row (the new row will be inserted above the selected row) and choose *Table, Insert Rows*. To insert more than one row in a table, select as many rows as you want to insert (the new rows will be inserted above the selected rows) and choose Table, Insert Rows. The number of rows that you select is the number of rows that will be inserted.

To insert a column at the end of a table, select all of the end-of-row marks; then choose *Table, Insert Columns.* To insert a column within a table, select the column where you want to insert a new column (the new column will be inserted to the left of the selected column) and choose Table, Insert Columns. To insert more than one column within a table, select as many columns as you want to insert (the new columns will be inserted to the left of the selected columns) and choose Table, Insert Columns. The number of columns that you select is the number of columns that will be inserted.

Let's insert rows and columns in our table:

1. Verify that the insertion point is in the last cell of the table.

2. Press **Tab** to create a new row at the end of the table.

3. Type **Hong Kong** and press **Tab**.

4. Type **2,100.00**.

5. In the selection bar, point to the left of the second row.

6. Press and hold the mouse button. Next, drag to select the second and third rows (so that two rows that will be inserted). Then release the mouse button.

7. Choose **Table, Insert Rows** to insert two rows above the selected rows. Compare your screen to Figure 10.9.

8. Select the entire second column (point anywhere in the second column and click the right mouse button).

Figure 10.9   **Inserted rows**

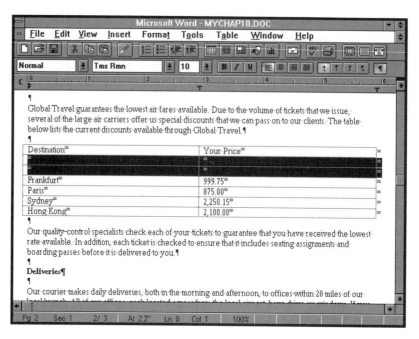

9. Choose **Table, Insert Columns** to insert a column between the two existing columns. Compare your screen to Figure 10.10.

10. Scroll right to view the end-of-row marks.

11. Place the I-beam on one of the end-of-row marks and click the right mouse button to select the entire column. Notice that all end-of-row marks are selected.

12. Choose **Table, Insert Columns** to insert a column at the end of the table.

13. Scroll right to view the entire inserted column, and compare your screen to Figure 10.11.

PRACTICE YOUR SKILLS

1. In the first row of the second column, enter the heading **Standard Price**.

2. Complete the second column as shown in Figure 10.12.

3. In the first row of the fourth column, enter the heading **Savings**.

Figure 10.10   Inserted column

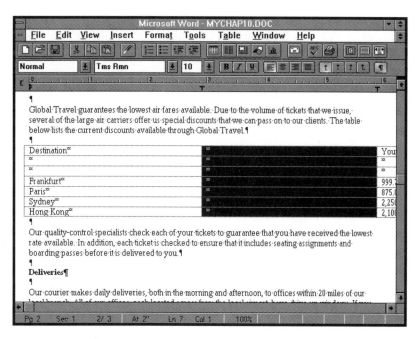

Figure 10.11   **Column added to the end of the table**

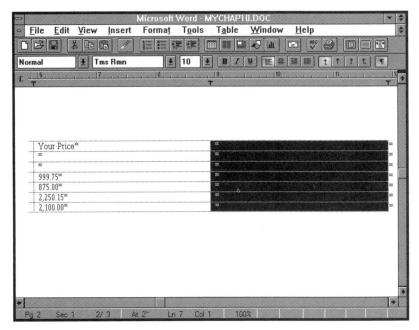

Figure 10.12   **Data entered in second column**

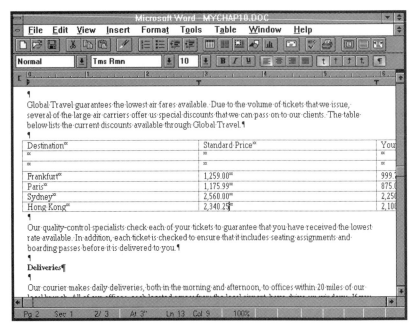

4. Complete the fourth column as shown in Figure 10.13.

5. Save the disk file.

Figure 10.13   **Data entered in fourth column**

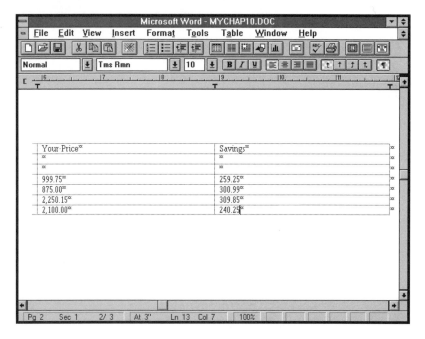

DELETING ROWS, COLUMNS, AND ENTIRE TABLES

To delete one or more contiguous rows in a table, select the row or rows that you want to delete; then choose *Table, Delete Rows.*

To delete one or more contiguous columns, select the column or columns that you want to delete; then choose *Table, Delete Columns.*

To delete an entire table, select the table; then choose Table, Delete Rows.

Let's delete a row in our table:

1. Select the second row (click in the selection bar, to the left of the second row).

2. Choose **Table, Delete Rows** to delete the selected row (see Figure 10.14).

Figure 10.14   **Table after deleting a row**

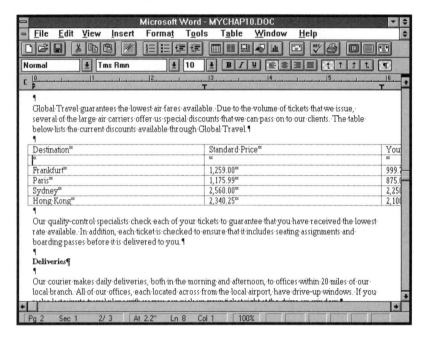

CHANGING COLUMN WIDTH

To change column width by dragging column borders

- Point to the column border that you want to move; the mouse pointer will become a horizontal, double-headed arrow

- Press and hold the mouse button

- Drag the column border to the desired location

- Release the mouse button

To change column width by using the ruler

- On the ruler, point to the column marker that you want to move

- Press and hold the mouse button

- Drag the column marker to the desired location

- Release the mouse button

To change column width by using the menu

- Select the desired column (or the entire table)

- Choose *Table, Column Width*
- Type the desired width in the *Width of Columns* text box
- Click on *OK*

When you change the column width using any of these techniques, the width of the entire table changes to accommodate the adjusted width of its columns. If you decrease the width of the columns, the width of the entire table decreases. If you increase the width of the columns, the width of the entire table increases.

Note: Before you print a document that contains a table, use Print Preview to make sure that the entire table fits on the page.

Let's try using all three methods to change the width of columns in our table:

1. Point to the column border between the *Destination* and *Standard Price* headings. The mouse becomes a double-headed arrow.

2. Press and hold the mouse button. Next, drag the column border to the left until it touches the end-of-cell mark in the *Hong Kong* cell; this decreases the width of the first column.

3. Release the mouse button. The width of the entire table has also decreased; more of it is now visible in the document window.

4. In the ruler, point to the column marker near the 3.75" mark.

5. Press and hold the mouse button. Next, drag the column marker to the 2.5" mark on the ruler to decrease the width of the second column.

6. Release the mouse button. Notice that the width of the entire table has again decreased.

7. Select the entire table (choose **Table, Select Table**).

8. Choose **Table, Column Width** to open the Column Width dialog box.

9. In the Width of Columns 1-4 text box, type 1.25 to set the width of all columns in the table to 1.25" (see Figure 10.15).

10. Click on **OK**.

11. Deselect the table. Notice that all four columns are now equal in width. Compare your screen to Figure 10.16.

Figure 10.15   Setting column width in the Column Width dialog box

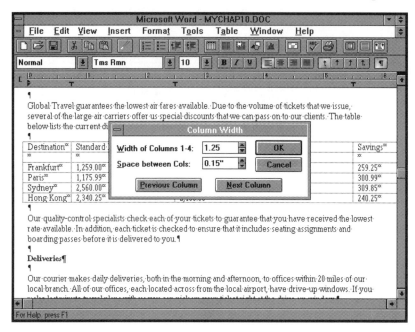

Figure 10.16   Table with columns of equal width

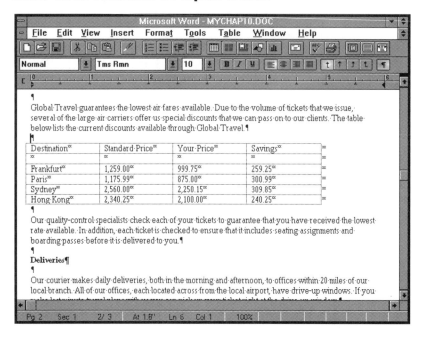

ENHANCING TABLES

You already know how to enhance text in your document; doing so can improve its appearance and often its readability. Accentuating important text helps the eye to locate these reference points. The same text enhancements that are available in standard document text are also available when working in tables, including, for example, bold and italic character styles, changes in font and font size, and text alignment within a cell. In addition, you can alter the alignment of the entire table relative to the margins you're using. You can apply any character formats to text within a table. You can also enhance a table by adding a border or a gridline that will appear when the document is printed.

ALIGNING A TABLE

To align a table between the left and right margins

- Select the entire table

- Choose *Table, Row Height*

- In the Alignment box, select the desired alignment

- Click on *OK*

Let's format and align text in our table, then center the table between the left and right margins:

1. Select the first row, which contains the column headings.

2. Make all of the text in the first row bold.

3. Place the I-beam on any cell in the second column.

4. Press and hold the right mouse button and drag to select the second through the fourth columns.

5. Right-align the selected text. All of the text in the selected columns is now right-aligned.

6. Click on the **Show/Hide** button to hide the end-of-cell marks. Now you can view the table without all the extraneous marks.

7. Click on the **Show/Hide** button to display the end-of-cell marks.

8. Print Preview **page 2**. The table is currently aligned along the left margin.

9. Close Print Preview.

10. Click inside the table.

11. Select the entire table.

12. Choose **Table, Row Height** to open the Row Height dialog box.

13. In the Alignment box, select **Center** to center the table between the margins (see Figure 10.17).

14. Click on **OK**.

15. Deselect the table.

16. Print Preview the document. The table is centered between the left and right margins.

17. Close Print Preview.

18. Save the disk file and compare your screen to Figure 10.18.

Figure 10.17   Centering the table from the Row Height dialog box

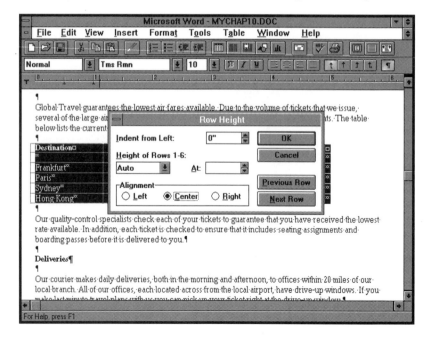

Figure 10.18   Centered table

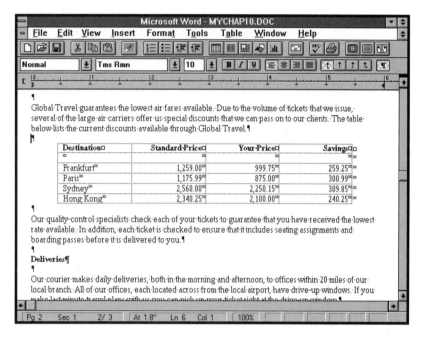

ADDING BORDERS

To add a border to a table

- Select the table, column, row, or cell around which you want to add a border

- Choose *Format, Border*

- In the *Preset* box, select a border type

- In the *Line* box, select the style of line that you want the border to consist of

- Click on *OK*

Before closing the dialog box, you can observe the sample diagram in the Border box to see the effect of the border and line type that you selected.

Let's add borders to our table:

1. Select the entire table.

2. Choose **Format Border** to open the Border Table dialog box.

3. In the Preset box (in the bottom-left corner of the dialog box), select **Box**.

4. In the Line box, select the second box from the top in the first column (the one containing the thin double lines, directly below the *None* selection). Compare your screen to Figure 10.19.

5. Observe the Border box. The double line is displayed around the sample diagram.

6. Click on **OK**.

7. Deselect the table.

8. Observe the table. Double lines are displayed around the table.

9. Click inside the table.

10. Select the entire table.

11. Choose **Format, Border** to open the Border Table dialog box.

Figure 10.19   Selecting a border in the Border Table dialog box

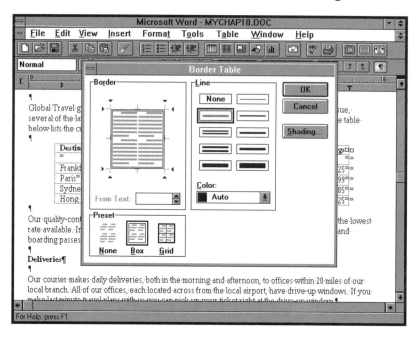

12. In the Preset box, select **Grid** to place a grid around the cells. Unlike the gridlines, this grid will appear when the document is printed.

13. Click on **OK**.

14. Deselect the table.

15. Observe the change in the table. The dotted gridlines are replaced with solid ones (see Figure 10.20).

Figure 10.20   **Completed table with border and gridlines**

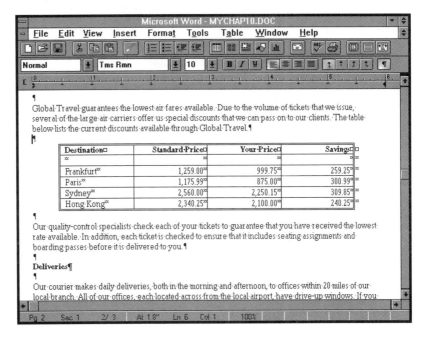

CONVERTING TABBED TEXT TO A TABLE

Word enables you to convert a tabbed table created by inserting tabs between columns of text into an actual table consisting of cells, rows, and columns. To convert tabbed text to a table

- Select the text that you want to convert to a table

- Choose *Table, Convert Text to Table*

You can also convert table text into ordinary text.

Note: Occasionally, tables that have been created from tabbed text will require some modifications. For example, you can convert text that is separated by paragraph marks, tabs, and commas. If Word cannot determine how to convert the text, it will display a dialog box asking you what type of character to use to separate the text.

Let's convert tabbed text to a table:

1. Scroll to place the *Hotel Accommodations* heading, near the bottom of page 2, at the top of the screen.

2. Observe the tabbed text at the bottom of page 2.

3. Select all of the lines in the tabbed table, from *Location* to *Hong Kong*, that will be placed in the table.

4. Choose **Table, Convert Text to Table**. The selected text appears in a table.

5. Verify that the entire table is selected.

6. Choose **Table, Column Width** to open the Column Width dialog box.

7. In the Width of Columns 1-3 text box, type **1.5** to set the width of all of the columns to 1.5".

8. Click on **OK**. The table now consists of three equally spaced columns.

PRACTICE YOUR SKILLS

1. Place a grid border around the table.

2. Center all the information in column 2.

3. Right-align all the information in column 3.

4. Center the table between the left and right margins.

5. Deselect the table.

6. Save the disk file and compare your screen to Figure 10.21.

7. Close the document.

Figure 10.21 **Converted table**

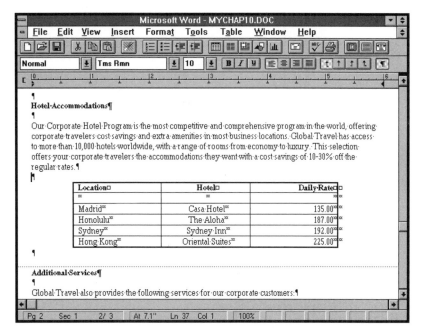

PRACTICE YOUR SKILLS

This exercise gives you the opportunity to practice the skills you just learned. The following instructions lead you through the steps necessary to edit the disk file PRAC10A.DOC to produce the document in Figure 10.22.

Follow these steps at your computer:

1. Open **prac10a.doc** (Chapter 2).

2. Type the following information into your table:

Row 3:	Trader Tom's	2300	1.49
Row 4:	Aunt Emily's Market	4900	1.29
Row 5:	Hamlet Farms	6500	1.29

Figure 10.22   **Completed MYPR10A.DOC document**

The Garden Patch
Product Line Announcement

Introduction

The Garden Patch is pleased to announce the unveiling of a new food line in the Garden Patch series: the Fruit Patch. The Fruit Patch product line was developed after two years of intense work through the cooperation and dedication of Dr. Faye Shad and her staff. The FDA recently approved the food and it will be released for public sale in three weeks.

The Fruit Patch includes a variety of organically-grown fruit: berries (cherries, strawberries, raspberries, blackberries, and blueberries), apricots, peaches, grapes, and plums.

Projected Quarterly Sales

Our finance department has been hard at work, determining sales projections for the next quarter. the results are shown in the following table.

Projected Quarterly Sales Table

Vendors	Boxes Sold	Profit (per box)
Trader Tom's	2300	1.49
Aunt Emily's Market	4900	1.29
Hamlet Farms	6500	1.29
B and J's	10000	.79
Hout and Wallace Inc.	11500	.79

3. Delete the row that contains information for *Price Farms*.

4. Right-align the second and third columns (this chapter).

5. Change the column width for the *Boxes Sold* column to 1" (this chapter).

6. Change the column width for *Profit (per box)* to 1.25" (this chapter).

7. Center the table on the page (this chapter).

8. Save the disk file as **mypr10a** (Chapter 1).

9. Print the document and compare it to Figure 10.22 (Chapter 1).

10. Close the document (Chapter 1).

If you have finished the activity, you might like to try a more challenging one requiring similar skills. In the next activity you will edit PRAC10B.DOC to create the document shown in Figure 10.23.

Follow these steps at your computer:

1. Open **prac10b.doc** (Chapter 2).

2. Below the *Projected Quarterly Sales Table* heading, create a table that contains three columns and five rows (this chapter).

3. Enter the data as shown in Figure 10.23 (this chapter).

4. Right-align the second and third columns (this chapter).

5. Decrease the column width for the second and third columns to 1.5" (this chapter).

6. Center the table on the page (this chapter).

7. Place a grid border on the table (this chapter).

8. Save the disk file as **mypr10b** (Chapter 2).

9. Print the document and compare it to Figure 10.23 (Chapter 1).

10. Close the document (Chapter 1).

Figure 10.23   **Completed MYPR10B.DOC**

The Garden Patch
Product Line Announcement

Introduction

The Garden Patch is pleased to announce the unveiling of a new food line in the Garden Patch series: the Fruit Patch. The Fruit Patch product line was developed after two years of intense work through the cooperation and dedication of Dr. Faye Shad and her staff. The FDA recently approved the food and it will be released for public sale in three weeks.

The Fruit Patch includes a variety of organically-grown fruit: berries (cherries, strawberries, raspberries, blackberries, and blueberries), apricots, peaches, grapes, and plums.

Projected Quarterly Sales
Our finance department has been hard at work, determining sales projections for the next quarter. the results are shown in the following table.

Projected Quarterly Sales Table

Vendors	Boxes Sold	Total Profit
Trader Tom's	2,300	3,427.37
Aunt Emily's Market	4,900	6,321.25
Hamlet Farms	6,500	7,085.98

SUMMARY

In this chapter, you learned how to create tables using the Table button in the toolbar or the Table, Insert Table command from the menu. You learned how to move within a table, how to select cells, rows, columns, and the entire table, and how to enter data in a table. You also learned how to insert and delete rows and columns, how to change column width, how to change the alignment of a table between the left and right margins, and how to enhance the appearance of a table by creating various types of borders. Finally, you learned how to convert tabbed text to a table.

Here is a quick reference guide to the Word features introduced in this chapter:

Desired Result	How to Do It
Create a table using the menu	Choose **Table, Insert Table**; type the desired number of columns in the Number of Columns text box; type the number of rows in the Number of Rows text box; click on **OK**
Create a table using the toolbar	Click on the Table button; drag to select the boxes of the grid corresponding to the desired number of rows and columns; release the mouse button
Move within the table using the mouse	Place the I-beam on the end-of-cell mark of the desired cell; **click**
Move within the table using the keyboard:	
Move one cell to the right	Press **Tab**
Move one cell to the left	Press **Shift+Tab**
Move up one row	Press **up arrow**
Move down one row	Press **down arrow**
Select a cell	Move the mouse pointer until it becomes an arrow; click on the end-of-cell mark within the desired cell

Desired Result	How to Do It
Select a row	Click the mouse button in the selection bar, to the left of the row, or place the insertion point anywhere within the desired row; choose **Table, Select Row**
Select a column	Click the right mouse button in any cell within the desired column, or place the insertion point in any cell within the desired column; choose **Table, Select Column**
Select an entire table	Place the insertion point anywhere within the table; choose **Table, Select Table**
Add a row at the end of a table	Place the insertion point in the last cell of the table; press **Tab**
Insert a row within a table	Select the row where you want to insert the new row; choose **Table, Insert Rows**
Insert more than one row in a table	Select as many rows as you want to insert; choose **Table, Insert Rows**
Add a column to the right side of a table	Select all the end-of-row marks; choose **Table, Insert Columns**
Insert a column within a table	Select the column to the left of which you want to insert a new column; choose **Table, Insert Columns**
Insert more than one column within a table	Select as many columns as you want to insert; choose **Table, Insert Columns**
Delete one or more rows	Select the row or rows that you want to delete; choose **Table, Delete Rows**
Delete one or more columns	Select the column or columns that you want to delete; choose **Table, Delete Columns**
Delete an entire table	Select the table; choose **Table, Delete Rows**

Desired Result	How to Do It
Change column width by dragging column borders	Point to the column border that you want to move until the mouse pointer becomes a horizontal, double-headed arrow; drag the column border to the desired location; release the mouse button
Change column width by using the ruler	On the ruler, point to the column marker that you want to move; drag the column marker to the desired location; release the mouse button
Change column width by using the menu	Select the desired column (or the entire table); choose **Table, Column Width**; type the desired width in the Width of Columns text box; click on **OK**
Align a table between the left and right margins	Select the entire table; choose **Table, Row Height**; in the Alignment box, select the desired alignment; click on **OK**
Create a table border	Select the table, column, row, or cell around which you want to add a border; choose **Format, Border**; in the Preset box, select a border type; in the Line box, select the style of line that you want the border to consist of; click on **OK**
Convert tabbed text to a table	Select the tabbed text that you want to convert to a table; choose **Table, Convert Text to Table**

In the next chapter, you will learn how to create newspaper-style columns and add graphics to your documents.

IF YOU'RE STOPPING HERE

If you need to break off here, please exit Word. If you want to proceed directly to the next chapter, please do so now.

CHAPTER ELEVEN: NEWSPAPER-STYLE COLUMNS AND GRAPHICS

Creating
Multicolumn Text

Modifying
Multicolumn Text
Formats

Using Graphics

> To help you distinguish between steps presented for your general knowledge and steps you should carry out at your computer as you read, we have adopted the following system:
>
> - A bulleted step, like this, is provided for your information and reference only.
>
> **1.** A numbered step, like this, indicates one in a series of steps that you should carry out in sequence at your computer.

This chapter introduces ways to format text into newspaper-style columns. *Newspaper-style columns* are useful in creating documents such as newsletters, brochures, and reports. In newspaper columns, the document text "snakes," or flows, down the length of one column, then continues at the top of the next column, and so on. If all of the columns on the page become filled, any additional text continues onto the first column of the next page.

Word also provides you with a powerful tool for incorporating graphic images, or *graphics,* into your documents.

When you're done working through this chapter, you will know

- How to format text into newspaper-style columns
- How to insert a graphic into your document
- How to size and move a graphic
- How to create a border around a graphic

CREATING MULTICOLUMN TEXT

You can define your columns before typing the text, or you can reformat existing text into newspaper-style columns.

To create newspaper-style columns

- Place the insertion point where you want the columns to begin
- Choose *Format, Columns*, or click on the *Columns* button in the toolbar
- Specify the desired number of columns in the *Number of Columns* text box of the Columns dialog box
- In the *Apply To* drop-down list box, select *This Point Forward*
- Click on *OK*

Note: There is a limit to the number of columns you can specify. This limit is based on your document's margins and the default tab stops. Each column must be at least as wide as the distance between the default tab stops, or the program will display the following error message:

```
The margins, column spacing, or paragraph
indents are too large for some sections.
```

When you select This Point Forward, the multicolumn format is set from the insertion point to the end of the document. The program then inserts a *section break*, which is displayed in the document as a double dotted line that runs horizontally across the page. Compare this to a page break, which is displayed as a single horizontal line. Dividing a document into sections allows you to apply different page-formatting options to each section of a document. A section can consist of one or more pages. The status bar displays the section number in which the insertion point is placed.

To create a multicolumn format for an entire document, select Whole Document in the Apply To drop-down list box. This formats the entire document in columns, regardless of the location of the insertion point. You can also click on the Text Columns button in the toolbar and drag to select the number of columns you want. When you use this button, all of the text in the document is formatted, regardless of the location of the insertion point.

Columns will not appear in the document window in Normal view. To display the text in columns, you must either Print Preview the document or change to Page Layout view.

Let's open a new document and create a newspaper-style column format:

1. Open **chap11.doc**.

2. Click on the **Zoom Whole Page** button (the third toolbar button from the right). Notice that all of the text is currently in a standard, single-column format.

3. Click on the **Zoom 100 Percent** button (the second toolbar button from the right).

4. Place the insertion point to the left of the *I* in the *Introduction* heading, near the top of the page.

5. Choose **Format, Columns** to open the Columns dialog box.

6. In the Number of Columns box, click once on the up increment indicator to change the number to **2**. The Sample box displays a sample of the two-column format.

7. Open the **Apply To** drop-down list box. Select **This Point Forward** to format the text as two columns from the insertion point to the end of the document. Compare your screen to Figure 11.1.

8. Click on **OK**.

9. Observe the section break, the double line below the heading. All of the text from the section break to the end of the document is formatted as two columns. *Sec 2* appears in the status bar. Notice that the side-by-side columns are not visible in Normal view.

10. Choose **View, Page Layout**. The side-by-side columns are now visible.

11. Scroll to view the document.

Figure 11.1   Changing to two-column format

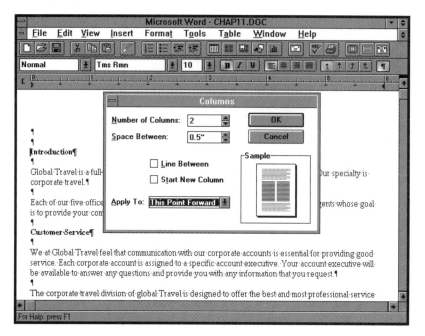

MODIFYING MULTICOLUMN TEXT FORMATS

When you create multiple columns, Word automatically apportions even amounts of space within each column and between columns, based on your document's margins. However, you can modify these values. For example, by default, Word places one-half inch of space between each column. Depending on the effect you desire, as well as how many columns appear on the page, you might want to increase or reduce this amount.

To change the space between columns

- Place the insertion point in the section containing the columns

- Choose *Format, Columns* or click on the *Columns* button in the toolbar

- In the *Space Between* box, specify the desired width

- Click on *OK*

You can also insert a vertical dividing line between adjacent columns, which can produce a visually pleasing effect and further help the eye separate the columns. This is particularly true of columns that are by necessity spaced closely together.

To add a vertical line between columns

- Place the insertion point in the section containing the columns

- Choose *Format, Columns* or click on the *Columns* button in the toolbar

- Check the *Line Between* box

- Click on *OK*

Let's change the space between our columns, then add a vertical line between them:

1. Check the status bar to verify that the insertion point is in the second section of the document.

2. Observe the space between the columns. It is large enough to be reduced slightly to make more room within the columns for text. Notice also that a few lines of text have wrapped up to the second column, above the *Worldwide Services* heading.

3. Click on the **Columns** button (the tenth button from the right) to open the Columns dialog box.

4. Click twice on the Space Between down increment indicator, to decrease the amount of space between the columns of text to 0.3" or as close to this value as your configuration will allow.

5. Click on **OK**. The text columns now appear closer together. Notice that the text that earlier wrapped to the second column has now moved to the bottom of the first column, placing the *Worldwide Services* heading neatly at the top of the second column.

6. Delete the paragraph mark above *Worldwide Services* to move the heading to the top of the column.

7. Verify that the insertion point is in the second section.

8. Click on the **Columns** button.

9. Check **Line Between**. Compare your screen to Figure 11.2.

10. Click on **OK**. Notice that the line is not visible in Page Layout view.

Figure 11.2   **Inserting a vertical line between columns**

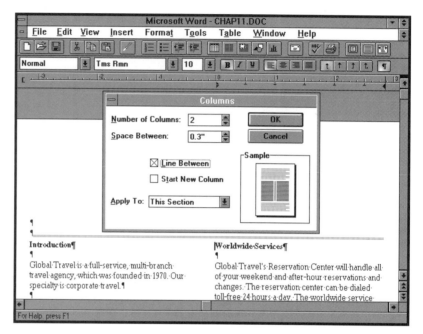

11. Print Preview the document. You can now see the line between the columns of text (see Figure 11.3).

12. Close Print Preview.

13. Save the disk file as **mychap11**.

Note: Remember that, if you prefer, you may use the Format, Columns menu option to add a vertical line rather than clicking on the Columns button.

USING GRAPHICS

You can place graphics in any Word document, as well as in headers and footers. Images can be imported into a document from many draw or paint software programs or from *clip art* (sources of digitized images). Word also comes with a number of graphics files, which you can use in your documents and even edit.

To insert a graphic in your document

• Place the insertion point where you want to insert the graphic

Figure 11.3   **Completed column modifications**

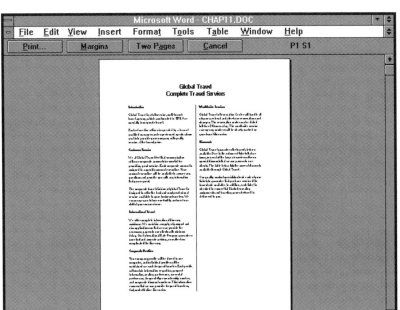

- Choose *Insert, Picture*
- Select the drive and directory where the graphic is stored
- Select the file name of the desired graphic
- Click on *OK*

If you click on the Preview button in the Picture dialog box after you have selected a file, you can preview the graphic before inserting it in your document.

Let's insert a graphic in our document:

1. Place the insertion point to the left of the *W* in the *Worldwide Services* heading at the top of the second column. Doing so will place the graphic above the heading.

2. Choose **Insert, Picture** to open the Picture dialog box.

3. From your WRKFILES directory, move to the CLIPART directory (in the Directories list box, double-click on the **winword** directory, then double-click on the **clipart** directory).

4. In the File Name list box, select **yacht.wmf**.

5. Click on the **Preview** button. The graphic is displayed in the Preview Picture box so that you can view it before placing it in your document (see Figure 11.4).

Figure 11.4   **Previewed graphic**

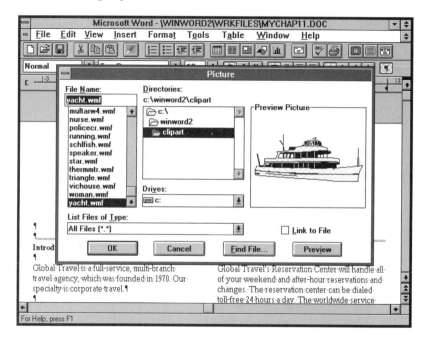

6. Click on **OK** to place the graphic in your document.

7. Observe the graphic. It is inserted above the *Worldwide Services* heading. You might need to scroll to see the entire second column.

INSERTING A FRAME AROUND A GRAPHIC

When you insert a graphic in a document, if the graphic is not wide enough to fill the column of text, the text will "flow" around the graphic. However, it will flow around the graphic unevenly, following the graphic's shape. You can make the text flow evenly around the graphic by placing a frame around the graphic.

Before you can place a frame around a graphic, you must select the graphic by clicking on it with the mouse. When the graphic is selected, you will notice small black *handles* on each side and in each corner of the graphic.

To place a frame around the graphic, you can either use the Insert, Frame command, or select the graphic and click on the Frame button.

Let's insert a frame around the graphic:

1. Point to the middle of the graphic and click the mouse button to select it.

2. Observe the handles around the graphic.

3. Click on the **Frame** button (the ninth toolbar button from the right) to insert a frame around the graphic.

4. Observe the frame. The frame enables you to move and size the graphic; however, it will not print. Compare your screen to Figure 11.5.

Figure 11.5   **Framed graphic**

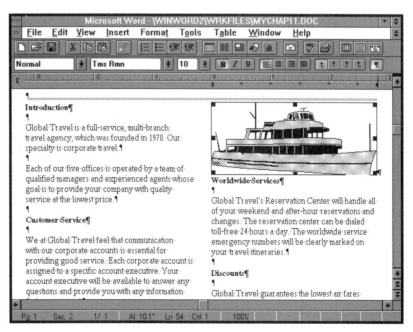

SIZING A GRAPHIC

The simplest way to size a graphic is by using the mouse to drag the handles. When you drag a handle on the side of the graphic, only the width of the graphic changes. When you drag a handle on the top or bottom of the graphic, only the height of the graphic changes. When you drag a corner handle, the width *and* height of the graphic change proportionately.

If you have sized the graphic and it appears distorted, you can restore it to its original size by choosing Format, Picture, clicking on Reset, and then clicking on OK.

Let's experiment with sizing the graphic:

1. Place the mouse pointer on the handle in the middle of the right side of the graphic. The mouse pointer becomes a horizontal, two-headed arrow.

2. Press and hold the mouse button. Drag the handle out into the right margin. A dotted frame is displayed as you drag the handle.

3. Release the mouse button. The graphic is now wider.

4. Place the mouse pointer on the handle in the middle of the bottom of the graphic. The pointer becomes a vertical, two-headed arrow.

5. Drag the handle to the top of the *Discounts* heading. A *dotted frame* appears as you drag the handle.

6. Release the mouse button. The height of the graphic is increased (see Figure 11.6).

7. Verify that the graphic is selected (the handles are displayed on the frame).

8. Choose **Format, Picture** to open the Picture dialog box.

9. Observe the *Scaling* box. The percentages of Width and Height are not equal. Once you've used the mouse to size the graphic, its width and height may no longer be proportionate.

10. Click on **Reset** to restore the graphic to its original size.

11. Observe the Scaling box. The Width and Height are once again displayed as *100%*, meaning that the graphic's original size has been restored (see Figure 11.7).

12. Click on **OK**. The graphic is displayed at its original size.

Figure 11.6   **Graphic increased in size**

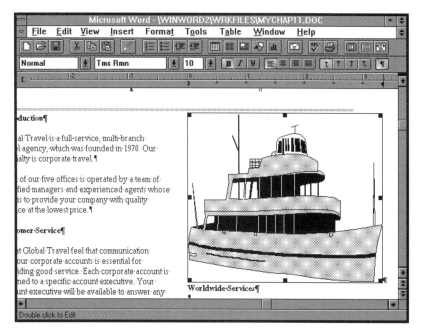

Figure 11.7   **Restoring the graphic to its original size**

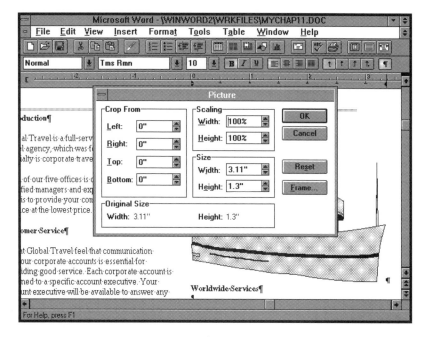

13. Verify that the graphic is selected.

14. Place the mouse pointer on the handle in the bottom-right corner of the graphic. The mouse pointer becomes a diagonal, two-headed arrow.

15. Drag the handle until the right border of the graphic is even with the right edge of the section break, which is located at the top of the document window.

16. Release the mouse button and compare your screen to Figure 11.8. The width and height of the graphic have changed proportionately.

Figure 11.8   **Proportionately sized graphic**

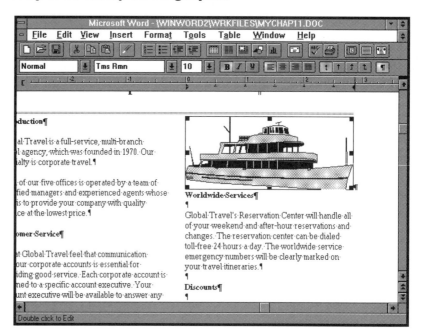

17. Choose **Format, Picture.**

18. Observe the Scaling box. The Width and Height percentages are similar (to within 1%).

19. Click on **Cancel.**

MOVING A GRAPHIC

Suppose that you insert a graphic, and perhaps even size it, and then decide that you don't like its placement in your document. After you have inserted a graphic in your document, you do have the option of moving it.

To move a graphic

- Select the graphic

- Press and hold the mouse button

- Drag the dotted frame to the desired location

- Release the mouse button

We have decided that our graphic would be more appropriate below the *Worldwide Services* heading. Let's move the graphic:

1. Verify that the graphic is selected.

2. Press and hold the mouse button and drag the graphic until the bottom of the dotted frame is positioned on the paragraph mark directly below *Worldwide Services*.

3. Release the mouse button. The mouse becomes a four-headed arrow. The graphic is now displayed below the *Worldwide Services* heading (see Figure 11.9; the message displayed in the status bar may vary according to your configuration).

 ADDING A BORDER TO A GRAPHIC

You can add a border around a graphic by using the Format, Border command. In the Border Picture dialog box, you can select the type of border you want.

To add a border to a graphic

- Select the graphic

- Choose *Format, Border*

- The Border box displays a representation of the graphic's boundaries; simply click on the top, bottom, left, or right boundary to select it

- In the Preset box, select *Box* to apply a plain border to the graphic, or *Shadow* to apply a shadow border

Figure 11.9   **Moved graphic**

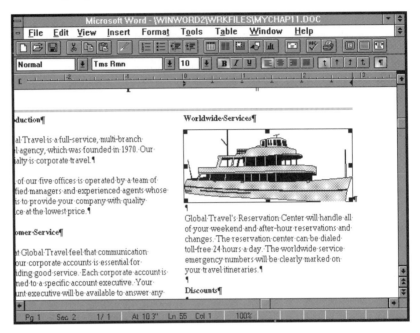

- In the Line box, click on the desired line thickness of the border

- Click on *OK*

Before closing the dialog box, you can observe the sample diagram in the Border box to see the effect of the border that you selected. By default, the shadow is applied to the right side and the bottom of the graphic. You can increase the amount (thickness) of shadow by increasing the width of the line type in the Line box.

Let's add a shadow border to the graphic:

1. Verify that the graphic is selected.

2. Choose **Format, Border** to open the Border Picture dialog box.

3. In the Preset box, select **Shadow** (see Figure 11.10). The diagram in the Sample box displays the effect of the shadow.

4. Click on **OK**.

5. Deselect the graphic and compare your screen to Figure 11.11. A thin shadow is displayed at the right and bottom edges of the graphic. Depending on how the graphic is positioned in

Figure 11.10   Selecting a shadow border

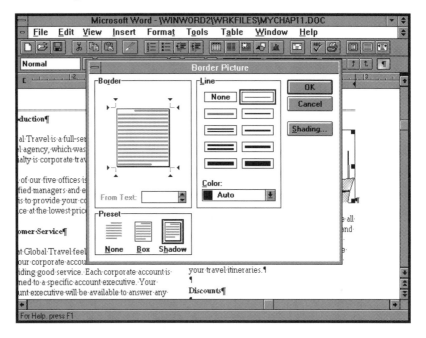

Figure 11.11   Added shadow border

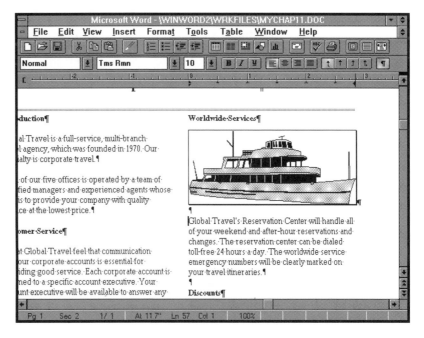

your document window, you might need to scroll to view the bottom of the graphic.

MODIFYING A GRAPHIC BORDER

After you have applied a border to a graphic, you can change its appearance (or remove it altogether).

To modify the border

- Select the graphic

- Choose *Format, Border*

- In the Border box, click on the side of the sample diagram that you want to modify

- In the Line box, select the line type that you want (you might need to continue in this manner, trying various combinations of sides and line thicknesses, until you have achieved the desired effect)

- Click on *OK*

Let's modify our graphic's border to increase the size of the shadow:

1. Select the graphic.

2. Choose **Format, Border** to open the Border Picture dialog box.

3. In the Border box, click on the right edge of the sample.

4. In the Line box, select the fourth line style from the top in the second column. This will apply a thicker line style to the right edge of the graphic border.

5. Observe the change in the border sample. The right side of the border sample displays a thicker line.

6. Click on the bottom edge of the border sample to apply a thicker line style to the bottom of the graphic frame. Compare your screen to Figure 11.12.

7. Click on **OK**.

8. Deselect the graphic and compare your screen to Figure 11.13.

9. Observe the larger shadow on the right and bottom edges of the graphic.

Figure 11.12   **Modifying the shadow border**

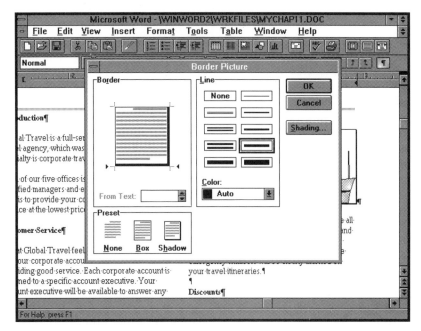

Figure 11.13   **Completed graphic border**

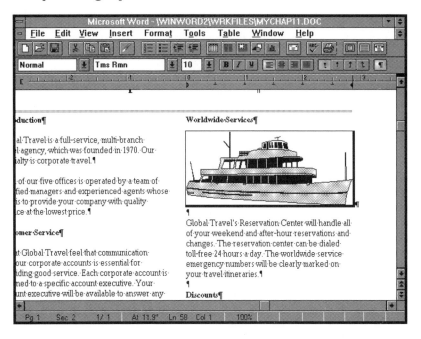

10. Print or Print Preview the completed document, shown in Figure 11.14.

11. Cancel Print Preview.

12. Save the disk file and close the document.

SUMMARY

In this chapter, you learned how to create newspaper-style columns of text. You learned how to import Word graphic images into your document, how to move and size the graphic, and how to change the style of the graphic border.

Here is a quick reference guide to the Word features introduced in this chapter:

Desired Result	How to Do It
Create newspaper-style columns	Place the insertion point where you want the columns to begin; choose **Format, Columns**; specify the desired number of columns in the Number of Columns text box of the Columns dialog box; in the Apply To drop-down list box, select the portion of the document you wish to affect; click on **OK**
Display multi-column text	Choose **Print, Preview** or **View, Page Layout**
Change the space between columns	Place the insertion point in the section containing the columns to be affected; choose **Format, Columns**; in the Space Between box, type the desired value, or use the increment arrows; click on **OK**
Insert a line between columns	Place the insertion point in the desired section; choose **Format, Columns**; check **Line Between**; click on **OK**
Insert a graphic	Place the insertion point where you want to insert the graphic; choose **Insert, Picture**; select the drive and directory where the graphic is stored; select the file name of the desired graphic; click on **OK**

Figure 11.14   Completed MYCHAP11.DOC document

Global Travel
Complete Travel Services

Introduction

Global Travel is a full-service, multi-branch travel agency, which was founded in 1970. Our specialty is corporate travel.

Each of our five offices is operated by a team of qualified managers and experienced agents whose goal is to provide your company with quality service at the lowest price.

Customer Service

We at Global Travel feel that communication with our corporate accounts is essential for providing good service. Each corporate account is assigned to a specific account executive. Your account executive will be available to answer any questions and provide you with any information that you request.

The corporate travel division of global Travel is designed to offer the best and most professional service available to your business travelers. We encourage you to tour our facility and meet our staff at your convenience.

International Travel

We offer complete international itinerary assistance. We maintain a supply of passport and visa applications so that we can provide the necessary papers to our clients with minimum delay. Our International Rate Program guarantees your fast and accurate pricing, no matter how complicated the itinerary.

Corporate Profiles

Your company profile will be stored in our computer, and individual profiles will be maintained on each frequent traveler. Each profile will contain information regarding passport information, seating preference, car rental preference, frequent-flyer membership number, and corporate discount numbers. This information ensures that we can provide frequent travelers, fast, cost-effective itineraries.

Worldwide Services

Global Travel's Reservation Center will handle all of your weekend and after-hour reservations and changes. The reservation center can be dialed toll-free 24 hours a day. The worldwide service emergency numbers will be clearly marked on your travel itineraries.

Discounts

Global Travel guarantees the lowest air fares available. Due to the volume of tickets that we issue, several of the large air carriers offer us special discounts that we can pass on to our clients. The table below lists the current discounts available through Global Travel.

Our quality-control specialists check each of your tickets to guarantee that you have received the lowest rate available. In addition, each ticket is checked to ensure that it includes seating assignments and boarding passes before it is delivered to you.

Desired Result	How to Do It
Size a graphic	Select the graphic and drag the middle handle on the left or right edge of the graphic frame to affect the width; drag the middle handle on the top or bottom edge to affect the height; or drag one of the corner handles to increase or decrease the width and height proportionally
Restore a graphic to its original size	Select the graphic; choose **Format, Picture**; click on **Reset**; click on **OK**
Move a graphic	Select the graphic; drag it to the desired location, using the dotted rectangle as reference; release the mouse button
Add or modify a graphic border	Select the graphic; choose **Format, Border**; click on the top, bottom, left, or right boundary in the Border box to select it; in the Preset box, select the desired type of border; in the Line box, click on the desired line thickness of the border; click on **OK**

In the next chapter, you will learn how to create form letters.

IF YOU'RE STOPPING HERE

If you need to break off here, please exit Word. If you want to proceed directly to the next chapter, please do so now.

CHAPTER TWELVE: CREATING FORM LETTERS

Components of a
Form Letter

Attaching the
Data File to the
Main Document

Generating Your
Form Letters

Sorting the
Information in a
Data File

To help you distinguish between steps presented for your general knowledge and steps you should carry out at your computer as you read, we have adopted the following system:

- A bulleted step, like this, is provided for your information and reference only.

1. A numbered step, like this, indicates one in a series of steps that you should carry out in sequence at your computer.

In word processing, merging or *mail-merge* is the process of transferring selected information from one document to another document. For example, you can write a form letter and instantly merge it with your mailing list to produce a customized letter for everyone on the mailing list. Other common mail-merge documents include mailing labels, interoffice memos, and reports.

Word's File, Print Merge command enables you to take information from two documents—for example, a form letter and a list of names and addresses—and combine them into a single document. Of equal importance, perhaps, is the ability to sort the information in the mailing list, say, in alphabetical order by last name using the Tools, Sorting command.

When you're done working through this chapter, you will know

- How to create and attach the components of form letters
- How to generate form letters
- How to sort data in a table

COMPONENTS OF A FORM LETTER

Before using Word's Print Merge feature, you should be familiar with three important terms that correspond to the three main components of the merge process: the main document, the data file, and the merged document.

THE MAIN DOCUMENT

The *main document* contains normal text plus *field names,* which contain the instructions for carrying out the merge. The basic information in the main document remains the same. For example, a letter of invitation could be a form letter. The main document would contain the invitation text and various field names that would cause Word to retrieve names and addresses from a data file (discussed after the next section). Word would then insert the names and addresses in specific places in the merged document. However, before you can instruct Word to merge documents, you must have inserted field names in your main document.

FIELD NAMES

In the main document, field names are used to indicate where variable information is to be inserted. In the data file (discussed next), field names indicate the category of information in each column. The field names inserted in the main document must match the field names in the data file. You can insert field names in your document before the data file is attached; however, this would cause you to have to enter field names twice. For this reason, it is easier to insert the field names *after* the two files have been attached (you'll learn how to attach files later in this chapter).

THE DATA FILE

The *data file* stores information to be brought into the main document. You can think of the data file as a name-and-address list from which the program gets what you want to include in the main document. However, not only can you store names and addresses in the data file, you can also use it to store sentences, whole paragraphs, as well as any text or data you expect to use repeatedly. You can set up your data file as ordinary paragraphs or as a table. In this chapter, we use a table to compile data file information. In Chapter 10, you saw how compiling data in a table is an efficient way to keep the data organized. For this reason, it is recommended that you set up your data files as tables.

The data file consists of a *header record,* which is a group of field names, data records, and fields. The header record is the first row of the table. It contains field names, which indicate the type of information in each column. Except for the header record, each additional row of the table contains a set of related information, known as a *record*. Each record includes all of the information for one person in the name-and-address list. The various types of information in each record are known as *fields*, which are the equivalent of cells in a standard table.

There are several important guidelines for naming fields in data files:

• Each field name must be unique

• It must begin with a letter

• It can contain up to 32 characters

• It can contain letters, numbers, and underscore characters; however, it cannot contain spaces

Let's open a data file with missing records and then complete it:

1. Open **ch12data.doc**.

2. Change to Normal view.

3. Observe the header record, located in the top row of the table.

4. Observe the data records, located in the rows below the header record.

5. Place the insertion point in the first field of the last row.

6. Type **Dudley** and press **Tab**.

7. Type **Long** and press **Tab**.

8. Type **Unique Rugs** press **Tab**.

9. Type **125 North Road** and press **Enter**. Then type **Suite 3904**. You can press Enter to force information to a separate line in the record. The second line of information remains within the same record.

PRACTICE YOUR SKILLS

1. Complete the table with the following information:

Yuma	**AZ**	**85365**	**Beijing**

2. Save the disk file as **mydata** and compare your screen to Figure 12.1.

Figure 12.1   **Completed MYDATA.DOC document**

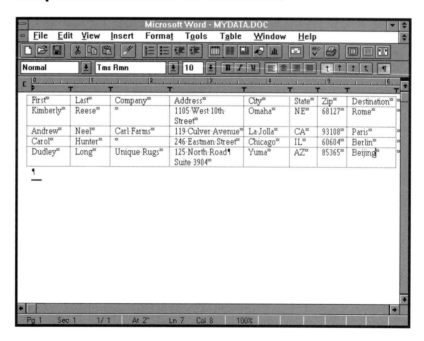

3. Close the document.

ATTACHING THE DATA FILE TO THE MAIN DOCUMENT

Attaching the data file to the main document identifies the data file as the one to be used for the variable information when the two documents are merged. Make sure that the main document is open when you attach the data file.

To attach a data file to a main document

- Make the main document the active window

- Choose *File, Print Merge*

- Click on the *Attach Data File* button

- Specify the location and the name of the data file

- Click on *OK*

When you attach the data file, the *print-merge bar* is displayed above the ruler. The print-merge bar enables you to quickly and accurately insert the field names.

To insert field names in the main document by using the print-merge bar

- Place the insertion point where you want to add a field name

- Click on the *Insert Merge Field* button

- In the *Print Merge Fields* list box, select the desired field name

- Click on *OK*

Once the field name is inserted in the main document, it is enclosed by chevrons—for example, *<<First>>*, which represents the first-name field.

To enter a field name in the main document without using the print-merge bar, press Ctrl+F9 and type the field name between the braces ({}) that appear. Be sure to use the exact same field names used in the data file. If you are unsure of the field names, you can click on the Edit Data File button in the print-merge bar to display the data file.

Let's view the main document, attach the data file, and then complete the main document:

1. Open **ch12main.doc**.

2. Observe the field names in the document.

3. Choose **File, Print Merge** to open the Print Merge Setup dialog box, shown in Figure 12.2.

Figure 12.2   **Print Merge Setup dialog box**

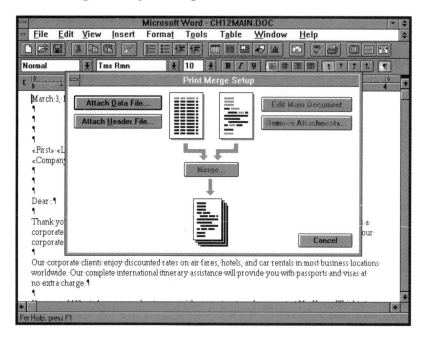

4. Click on the **Attach Data File** button to open the Attach Data File dialog box.

5. In the File Name list box, select *mydata.doc* (see Figure 12.3).

6. Click on **OK** to attach the file to the current document.

7. Observe the change in the ribbon. The print-merge bar is now displayed above the ruler (see Figure 12.4).

8. Place the insertion point on the first blank line below the <<*Company*>> field.

Figure 12.3   **Attaching a data file**

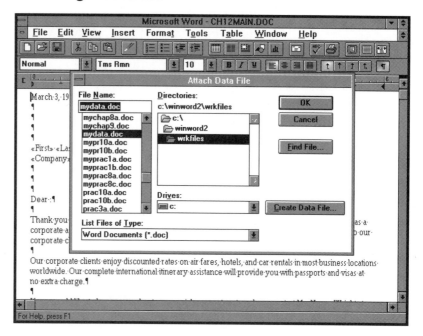

Figure 12.4   **Displayed print-merge bar**

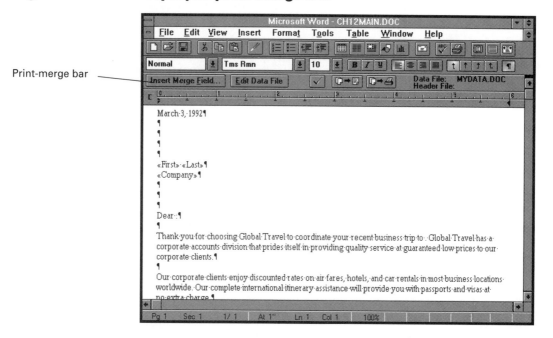

9. Click on the **Insert Merge Field** button to open the Insert Merge Field dialog box.

10. In the Print Merge Fields list box, select *Address* (see Figure 12.5) to place the information from the Address column in the completed form letter.

Figure 12.5   **Inserting the address field**

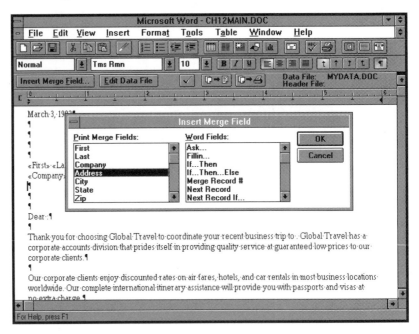

11. Click on **OK**. The address merge field is inserted in the document.

12. Press **Enter** so that three blank lines will remain between the address and the greeting.

13. Click on the **Insert Merge Field** button to open the Insert Merge Field dialog box. Notice that the Print Merge Fields list box contains a number of fields to choose from.

14. In the Print Merge Fields list box, double-click on **City** to place the information from the City column in the completed form letter.

15. Type **,** and press the **spacebar** to place a comma and space after the city name.

PRACTICE YOUR SKILLS

1. Complete the form letter contained in the ch12main.doc disk file, using Figure 12.6 as a guide. Be sure to include the *Destination* merge field at the end of the first sentence of the letter and insert any spaces where necessary.

Figure 12.6   **Merged form letter**

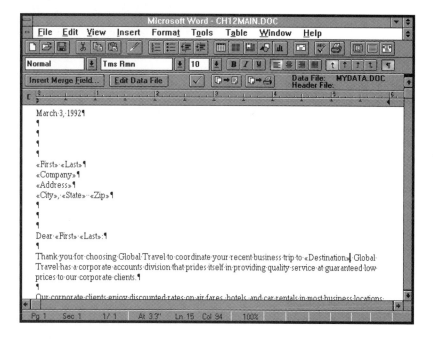

2. Save the disk file as **mymain**.

GENERATING YOUR FORM LETTERS

After you have completed and attached the data file and the main document, you can then merge the two documents. To merge the documents, click on the Merge To New Document button in the print-merge bar.

When you merge the documents, a new document is created with the name Form Letters1. If you merge another document before you exit Word, the new document's name will be Form Letters2, and so on. A form letter is created for each record in the data file. You can print the form letters just as you would print any other document. You can merge directly to the printer without creating a new document by clicking on the Merge To Printer button, the rightmost button in the toolbar.

Note: By default, Word deletes any blank lines in the merged document that are created by empty fields in the data file. For this reason, records should not be left blank (see step 4 in the following exercise).

Let's merge the main document and the data file to create our form letters:

1. Observe the name of the current document, *MYMAIN.DOC.*

2. Click on the **Merge to New Document** button in the print-merge bar, the fourth button from the left. MYDATA.DOC and MYMAIN.DOC are now merged.

3. Observe that the new document is named *Form Letters1.* Each letter is placed on a separate page within the document.

4. Use Go To in order to view the three remaining form letters. A letter has been created for every data record in the MYDATA.DOC file. Notice that the first and third letters do not have a company name, and the fourth letter has a two-line address.

5. Close all of the documents without saving them as disk files.

SORTING THE INFORMATION IN A DATA FILE

There will probably come a time when you will need to arrange a list of data, such as an address list, in alphabetical or numerical order. For example, you might want your data file records to appear in ascending alphabetical order by last name, or in descending numerical order by zip code.

You can use Word's Tools, Sorting command to sort columns of text in tables alphabetically, numerically, or by date. If you want to sort by a column other than the first one, you need to specify the column number. Columns are numbered from left to right.

To sort data in a table

- Select all of the text in the column that you want to sort; do not select headings or blank lines

- Choose *Tools, Sorting*

- In the *Sorting Order* box, select the desired order—*Ascending* or *Descending*

- In the *Key Type* drop-down list box, select the type of sort— *Alphanumeric, Numeric,* or *Date*

- In the *Field Number* box, select the number of the column by which to sort

- Click on *OK*

Let's experiment with sorting the records in a data file a couple of different ways:

1. Open **ch12list.doc**.

2. Observe the second column, which contains last names. The last names are not arranged alphabetically.

3. Select all of the rows except the header record (see Figure 12.7).

4. Choose **Tools, Sorting** to open the Sorting dialog box.

5. In the Sorting Order box, verify that **Ascending** is selected, in order to sort the last names from A-Z.

6. In the Key Type drop-down list box, verify that **Alphanumeric** is selected.

7. Double-click in the Field Number box and type **2** to instruct Word to sort by the second column of the table. Compare your screen to Figure 12.8.

8. Click on **OK** to begin the sort.

9. Deselect the records and observe that they have been sorted, and that the last names in column 2 are listed in ascending alphabetical order (see Figure 12.9).

10. Observe that the zip-code data are not sorted in any particular order.

Figure 12.7   **Selected records to be sorted**

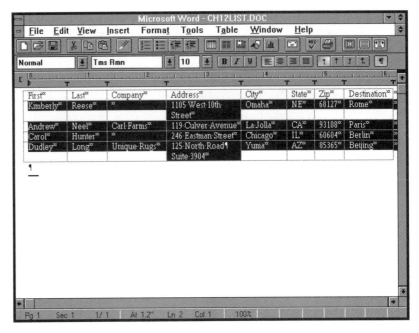

Figure 12.8   **Specified sort criteria**

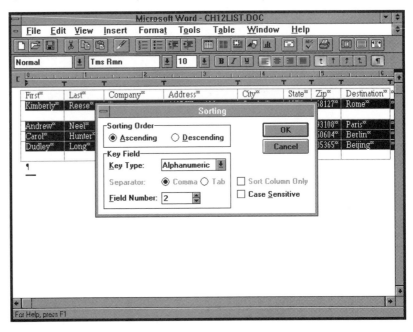

Figure 12.9   **Records sorted by last name**

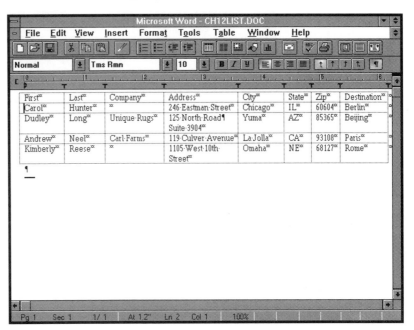

11. Select all of the rows of the table except for the header record.

12. Choose **Tools, Sorting** to open the Sorting dialog box.

13. In the Sorting Order box, select **Descending**, to sort the zip codes from 9-0.

14. In the Key Type drop-down list box, select **Numeric**, to sort only numeric data.

15. Double-click in the Field Number box and type **7** to sort by the seventh column of the table. Compare your screen to Figure 12.10.

16. Click on **OK** to begin the sort.

17. Deselect the data and observe that the zip code data are sorted in descending numeric order (see Figure 12.11).

PRACTICE YOUR SKILLS

1. Sort the table by zip code in ascending order.

Figure 12.10   Specifying new sort criteria

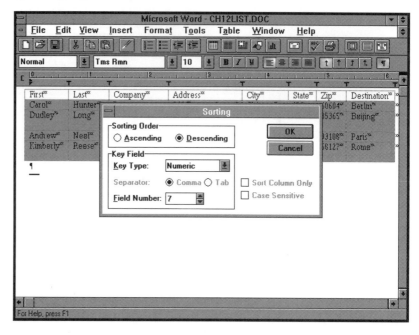

Figure 12.11   Records sorted by zip code

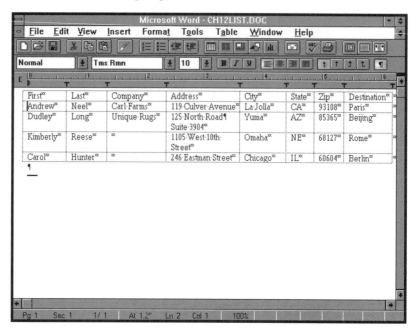

2. Save the disk file as **mylist**.

3. Deselect the records and compare your screen to Figure 12.12.

Figure 12.12   **Completed MYLIST.DOC document**

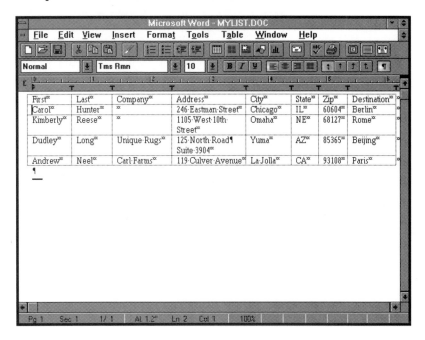

4. Close the document.

PRACTICE YOUR SKILLS

This exercise gives you the opportunity to practice the skills you just learned. The following instructions lead you through the steps necessary to complete and attach the components of a form letter.

Follow these steps at your computer:

1. Open **prc12df.doc** (Chapter 2).

2. Enter the data shown in Figure 12.13 (Chapter 10, this chapter).

3. Save the disk file as **myp12dfa** (Chapter 1).

Figure 12.13   Completed data file

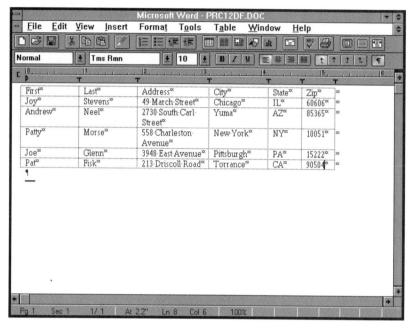

4. Open the disk file **prc12mda.doc** (Chapter 2).

5. Attach the data file myp12dfa.doc (this chapter).

6. Enter the field names shown in Figure 12.14 (this chapter).

7. Save the disk file as **myp12mda** (Chapter 2).

8. Merge the files to create a new document (this chapter).

9. Print the merged form letters (Chapter 1) and compare them to Figure 12.15.

10. Close all of the documents (Chapter 1) without saving them as disk files.

If you have finished the activity, you might like to try a more challenging one requiring similar skills. In this activity, you will create a data file, complete a main document, and merge the files to create form letters.

Follow these steps at your computer:

1. Open a new document (Chapter 2).

Figure 12.14 **Entered fields**

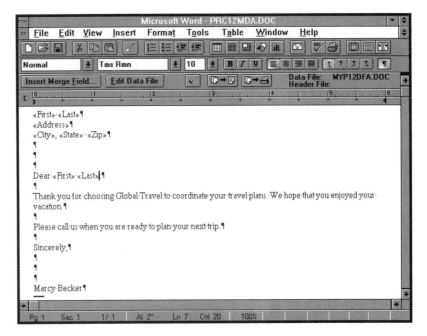

2. Create a table with six columns and four rows (Chapter 10).

3. Enter the data shown in Figure 12.16.

4. Save the disk file as **myp12dfb** (Chapter 1).

5. Open the document **prc12mdb.doc** (Chapter 2).

6. Attach the data file myp12dfb.doc (this chapter).

7. Enter the field names shown in Figure 12.17 (this chapter).

8. Save the disk file as **myp12mdb** (Chapter 2).

9. Merge the files to create a new document (this chapter).

10. Print the merged form letters and compare them to Figure 12.18 (Chapter 1).

11. Close all of the documents without saving them as disk files (Chapter 1).

Figure 12.15   Merged form letters

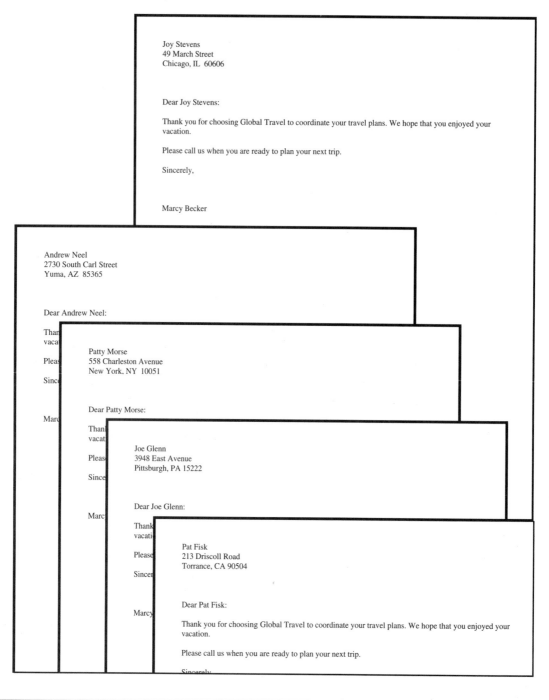

Figure 12.16   Completed data file

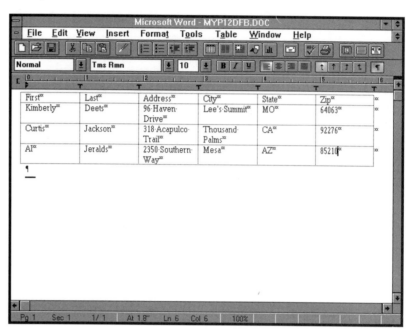

SUMMARY

In this chapter, you learned how to create form letters by merging the main document and the data file. You learned how to insert merge fields in a main document, then attach the corresponding data file. You also learned how to sort a list of data in alphabetical and numerical order.

Here is a quick reference guide to the Word features introduced in this chapter:

Desired Result	How to Do It
Attach a data file to a main document	Activate the main document window; choose **File, Print Merge**; click on the **Attach Data File** button; select the desired data file; click on **OK**

Figure 12.17   **Entered field names**

Desired Result	How to Do It
Insert field names in the main document	Place the insertion point in the desired location; click on the **Insert Merge Field** button; select the desired field name; click on **OK**
Merge documents	Attach the data file; activate the main document window; click on the **Merge to New Document** button
Sort text in a table	Select all the data to be sorted; choose **Tools, Sorting**; select the desired sort order; select the type of sort; in the Field Number text box, type the number of the column by which to sort; click on **OK**

In Chapter 13, you will work with templates and styles.

IF YOU'RE STOPPING HERE

If you need to break off here, please exit Word. If you want to proceed directly to the next chapter, please do so now.

Figure 12.18   Merged form letters

Global Travel Announcement

We are happy to announce that

**Kimberly Deets
of
Lee's Summit, MO**

has won a three-week, all-expenses-paid vacation to Europe.

Your 21-day European vacation will include seeing the sights of France, England, Switzerland, Germany, and Italy. You will stay at the most luxurious European hotels, and dine at the finest restaurants.

Please contact your nearest Global Travel office for more information about this terrific prize!

Global Travel Announcement

We are happy to announce that

**Curtis Jackson
of
Thousand Palms, CA**

has won a three-week, all-expenses-paid vacation to Europe.

Your 21-day European vacation will include seeing the sights of France, England, Switzerland, Germany, and Italy. You will stay at the most luxurious European hotels, and dine at the finest restaurants.

Please contact your nearest Global Travel office for more information about this terrific prize!

Global Travel Announcement

We are happy to announce that

**Al Jeralds
of
Mesa, AZ**

has won a three-week, all-expenses-paid vacation to Europe.

Your 21-day European vacation will include seeing the sights of France, England, Switzerland, Germany, and Italy. You will stay at the most luxurious European hotels, and dine at the finest restaurants.

Please contact your nearest Global Travel office for more information about this terrific prize!

CHAPTER THIRTEEN: USING TEMPLATES AND STYLES TO AUTOMATE YOUR WORK

Using the NORMAL Template

Using the MEMO2 Template

Using Styles

Each time you instruct Word to create a document, the program does so according to a template. A *template* is a stored file that contains boilerplate text and/or special formatting information. It serves as a kind of skeleton, providing your documents with an underlying structure. Templates also include styles, which contain special character and paragraph formats. (You were introduced to character styles and paragraph formats in Chapters 4 and 5, respectively.) Each style is stored under a specific name—for example, *heading 1.*

Word comes with a number of useful templates, each designed for a specific kind of document. For example, the NORMAL template is used to create a standard document, while the MEMO2 template can be used to create a business memo.

The primary benefit of using a template is that all, or at least some, of the document's characteristics have been defined in advance. This enables you to create documents that have similar character and paragraph formats, as well as similar page setups, without having to specify each parameter for each individual document.

When you're done working through this chapter, you will know

- How to create a document using the NORMAL template
- How to create a document using the MEMO2 template
- How to use styles
- How to create and modify styles

USING THE NORMAL TEMPLATE

Every document that you create in Word uses a template. By default, Word uses the NORMAL template for each new document. You can select a different template for a new document by choosing File, New to open the New dialog box and selecting a template in the Use Template list box.

To attach a different template to a document

- Choose *File, Template*
- In the *Attach Document To* box, select the desired template
- Click on *OK*

Let's create a memo using the NORMAL template:

1. Choose **File, New** to open the New dialog box, shown in Figure 13.1.

2. Observe the Use Template list box. The NORMAL template is selected by default.

3. Click on **OK**.

4. Type **Interoffice Memo** and press **Enter** twice.

5. Type **To:** and press **Tab**.

6. Type **Ruth Allen** and press **Enter**.

7. Type **From:** and press **Tab**.

8. Type **Nancy Wright** and press **Enter**.

9. Type **Date:** and press **Tab**.

Figure 13.1   **The New dialog box**

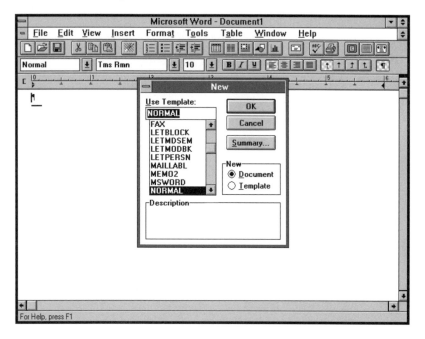

INSERTING THE CURRENT DATE

Rather than typing the current date in every document that you create, you can have Word enter your computer's current system date.

To insert the current date

- Place the insertion point where you want to add the date

- Choose *Insert, Date and Time*

- In the *Available Formats* list box, select the desired format

- Click on *OK*

Let's insert your computer's current system date:

1. Choose **Insert, Date and Time** to open the Date and Time dialog box.

2. In the Available Formats list box, select the third option (see Figure 13.2), which gives the full month, followed by the day, followed by the full year. (The date displayed is the current date.)

Figure 13.2   **Selecting a date format**

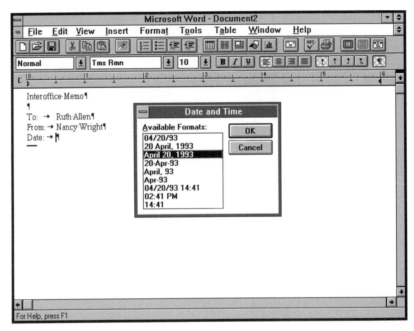

3. Click on **OK**. The system date is displayed in the document.

4. Press **Enter**.

5. Type **Subject:** and press **Tab**.

6. Type **Change in Additional Services** and press **Enter** twice.

 INSERTING A FILE

In Chapter 8 you learned how to use the Edit, Copy and Edit, Paste commands to copy and move selected text from one document to another document. However, the easiest way to insert the entire contents of one document in another document is to use the Insert, File command.

To insert an entire file

• Place the insertion point where you want the document to appear

• Choose *Insert, File*

- Select the desired disk file
- Click on *OK*

Note: If you have more than one window open, remember to activate the window of the document receiving the inserted disk file before you choose Insert, File. The inserted file is always placed in the active window.

Let's insert the contents of the CHAP13A.DOC disk file in our memo:

1. Choose **Insert, File** to open the File dialog box.

2. Double-click on **chap13a.doc** in the WRKFILES directory to place the contents of the file in the current document.

3. Verify that the insertion point is at the end of the document.

4. Press **Enter** twice.

5. Type **cc:** and press **Tab**.

6. Type **Grace Berg** and press the **spacebar**.

7. Type **Keith Donnelly**.

8. Save the disk file as **mych13a.doc**.

9. At the top of the document, select **Interoffice Memo**.

10. Apply the bold character style and change the point size to **12**.

11. Select the four paragraphs beginning with **To:** and ending with **Subject:**.

12. Set a left-aligned tab at the 1" mark.

13. Deselect the text.

14. Select **To:** (do *not* select the entire line) and apply the bold character style.

15. Apply the bold character style to *From:*, *Date:*, and *Subject:*.

16. Select *Additional Services*, after the *Subject* line, and apply the bold character style. Change the point size to **11**.

17. Select *Newsletter* and apply the bold character style.

18. Select *Telex* and press **F4** to repeat the character formatting. Compare your screen to Figure 13.3.

Figure 13.3   **Formatting the memo**

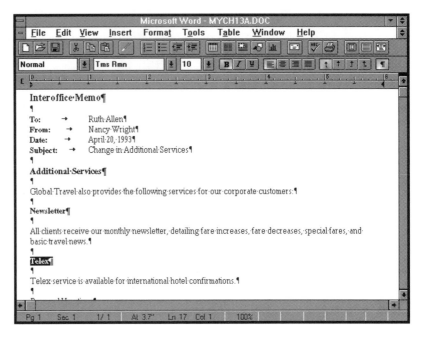

PRACTICE YOUR SKILLS

1. Apply the bold character style to the *Personal Vacations*, *Flight Insurance*, and *Fax* headings.

2. Print Preview the document.

3. Save the disk file and close the document.

USING THE MEMO2 TEMPLATE

Earlier, you learned how to create a memo using the NORMAL template. However, you can also create a business-style memo by using Word's MEMO2 template, which is a special template created specifically for this purpose. This template enables you to create and maintain a distribution list of people to whom you regularly send memos. Using the distribution list helps to reduce repetitive typing.

When you open the MEMO2 template, Word displays the Distribution List Manager. You can add names to the distribution list by clicking on Add Name and typing the desired name. When you are finished entering names, click on Close.

The MEMO2 template enables you to select the name of the memo recipient from the distribution list, as well as the names of those people receiving copies. You will also be prompted to enter the name of the sender and the subject.

Let's create a memo using the MEMO2 template:

1. Choose **File, New** (Do *not* click on the New button in the tool-bar; it does not open the New dialog box.)

2. In the Use Template list box, select **MEMO2** (see Figure 13.4; the files in your list box may differ from those shown in Figure 13.4). Notice that the message in the Description box states that this template is designed for creating business memos.

Figure 13.4   **Choosing the MEMO2 template**

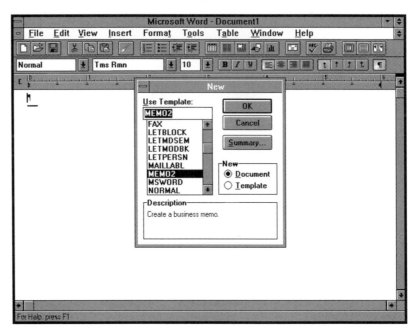

3. Click on **OK** to display text at the top of the document. The Memo Template dialog box is displayed (see Figure 13.5).

Figure 13.5 **Memo Template dialog box**

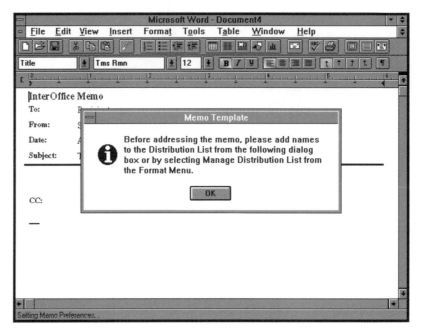

4. Click on **OK**. The Distribution List Manager dialog box is displayed.

5. Click on **Add Name** to add a name to the distribution list.

6. Type **Allen, Ruth** and click on **OK**.

7. Click on **Add Name** to add another name to the distribution list.

8. Type **Berg, Grace** and click on **OK**.

9. Click on **Add Name** to add another name to the distribution list.

10. Type **Donnelly, Keith** and click on **OK**. Compare your screen to Figure 13.6. Notice that Word automatically arranges the list of names in alphabetical order.

11. Click on **Close**. A message box is displayed, telling you to use the Format, Manage Distribution List command if you want to update the distribution list.

Figure 13.6 **Memo distribution list**

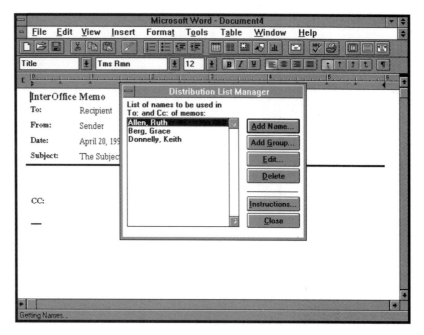

12. Click on **OK**. Notice the message

    Do you want to draft a new memo?

13. Click on **Yes** to begin a new memo. The To dialog box, which you will use to name the recipient, is displayed.

14. In the Address Memo to list box, verify that *Allen, Ruth* is selected (see Figure 13.7).

15. Click on **Select** to specify that Ruth Allen's name will appear on the *To* line of the memo. Notice that an arrow is displayed next to *Allen, Ruth*, indicating that it is selected.

16. Click on **Done**.

17. In the Address Memo from Whom list box, type **Nancy Wright** (see Figure 13.8) and click on **OK**, to place Nancy Wright's name on the *From* line of the memo.

18. In the Subject text box, type **Change in Additional Services** (see Figure 13.9), and click on **OK**.

Figure 13.7   **Naming the recipient**

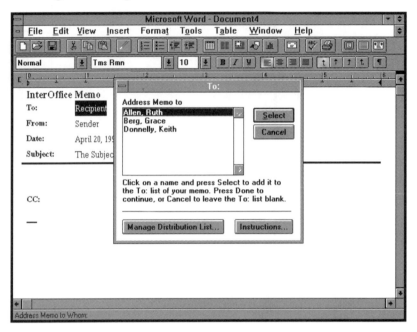

Figure 13.8   **Naming the sender**

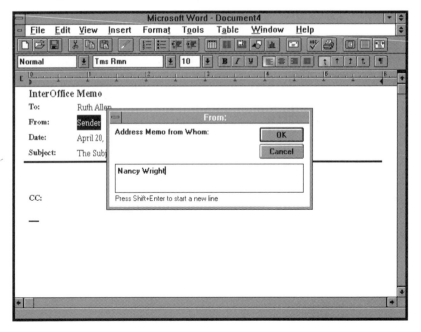

Figure 13.9   **Specifying the subject of the memo**

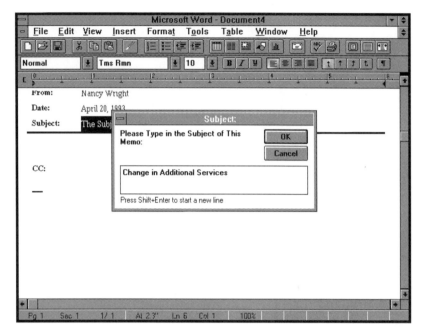

19. In the Carbon Copy Memo To list box, select **Berg, Grace** (see Figure 13.10).

20. Click on **Select** to place Grace Berg's name in the carbon copy section of the memo.

21. In the Carbon Copy Memo To box, select **Donnelly, Keith**.

22. Click on **Select** to also place Keith Donnelly's name in the carbon copy section of the memo (see Figure 13.11).

23. Click on **Done**. The Memo Template dialog box informs you that you can start typing the body of the memo (see Figure 13.12).

24. Click on **OK** to begin inserting text for the memo.

25. Choose **Insert, File**.

26. Double-click on **chap13b.doc**.

27. Observe the cc list at the bottom of the document. All the names that you chose appear in the list.

28. Save the disk file as **mych13b**.

Figure 13.10   **CC: Memo dialog box**

Figure 13.11   **Carbon copy memo list**

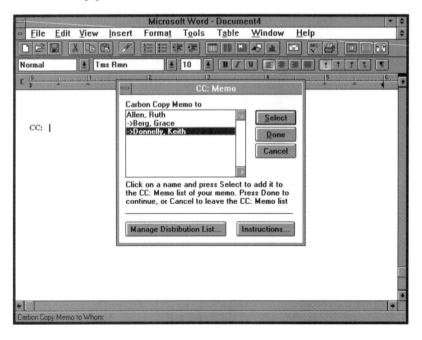

Figure 13.12   Memo Template dialog box

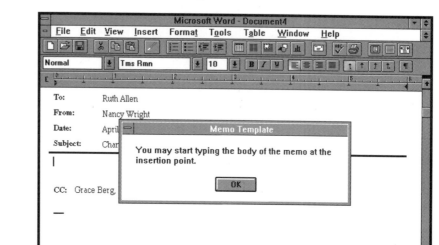

USING STYLES

Templates contain styles, which are named sets of formatting instructions. Styles enable you to quickly and easily format the paragraphs in a document. You can use the styles included in the templates, or you can create your own.

Note: These styles differ from the ones you learned about in Chapter 4 in that here each style might contain a set of instructions, as opposed to a single instruction. For example, in Chapter 4 you saw how a word can have the bold character style applied to it. As it is used here, a style might refer to bold, 10 point, Times Roman, *and* underline. Furthermore, these styles are applied to whole paragraphs. All of the paragraphs using the same style will contain the same formatting.

The Style drop-down list box, at the left end of the ribbon, lists all of the styles included in the template of the current document.

To apply a style to one or more paragraphs

- Select (or place the insertion point in) the appropriate paragraph, or, for more than one paragraph, select the paragraphs
- Open the *Style* drop-down list box
- Select the desired style

Let's examine styles that have already been applied, and then apply some of our own:

1. Place the insertion point anywhere in *InterOffice*, at the top of the document.

2. Observe the Style list box. The style applied to *InterOffice* is *Title*.

3. Observe the point size and bold character style. The Title style applies the 12-point type size and the bold style to the text.

4. Place the insertion point anywhere in the name *Allen*.

5. Observe that the current style name applied to Allen is *To*.

6. Observe the point size. The To style applies the 10-point size to the text.

7. Place the insertion point in *Global Travel*, below *Additional Services*.

8. Observe that the current style applied to *Global Travel* is *Normal*.

9. Observe the point size. The Normal style applies the 10-point size to the text.

10. Place the insertion point in the *Additional Services* heading.

11. Open the Style drop-down list box and select the **heading 2** style. The heading 2 style applies the 11-point type size and the bold character style to text.

12. Place the insertion point in the Newsletter heading.

13. Open the Style drop-down list box and select the **heading 3** style. This style makes text bold.

14. Place the insertion point in the *Telex* heading and press **F4** to apply the heading 3 style. Compare your screen to Figure 13.13.

Figure 13.13   Applied heading styles

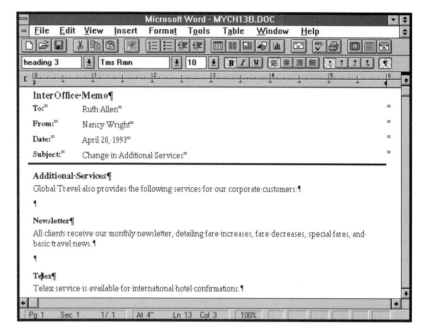

PRACTICE YOUR SKILLS

1. Apply the heading 3 style to the *Personal Vacations*, *Flight Insurance*, and *Fax* headings.

2. Print Preview the document.

3. Save the disk file and close the document.

CREATING STYLES

You now know how to select an existing style from the Style list box. However, you can create your own customized styles. The first step in doing so is to apply the desired formatting to text, or place the insertion point in text that already has the desired formatting applied to it. Then, either choose Format, Style from the menu or use the Style list box in the ribbon. We recommend using the Style list box, as it is simpler and faster.

To create a style based on a formatted paragraph

• Select the formatted paragraph

- Select the style name in the Style list box (or press *Ctrl+S*)
- Type the new style name
- Press *Enter*

Style names can contain up to 24 characters. They can include any combination of characters and spaces, except the backslash (\).

When you create a new style for a document, it is saved whenever you save the disk file. You can create up to 220 styles for a single document. The styles created in a document can be used only in that document. If you create a style in a template, it can be used in any new documents that are based on that template.

Let's examine the styles in the NORMAL template and then create our own style:

1. Open **chap13c.doc**.

2. Select the *Introduction* heading, near the top of the document.

3. Observe the ribbon. The Normal style applies the Tms Rmn font and the 10-point size to the paragraph.

4. Apply the **heading 1** style (or any heading style that your printer can support). The heading 1 style applies the Helv font and the bold and underline character styles to the paragraph.

5. Apply the **heading 2** style. This style applies the Helv font, the 12-point type size, and the bold character style.

6. Apply the **heading 3** style. This style applies the Tms Rmn font, the 12-point type size, the bold character style, and a 0.25" indent.

7. Apply the **Normal** style.

8. Verify that *Introduction* is selected.

9. Use the ribbon to change the point size to 12 and make the heading bold and italic. These formats will be used in the new style.

10. Use the I-beam to drag across the style name *Normal* in the Style list box (or double-click on Normal) in order to select it.

11. Type **Subhead** to name the new style (see Figure 13.14).

12. Press **Enter**.

Figure 13.14   **Naming a style**

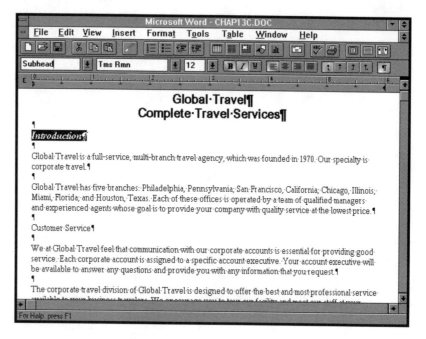

13. Open the Style list box and observe the list of styles. The Subhead style is included at the bottom of the list.

14. Close the Style list box.

15. Apply the Subhead style to the *Customer Service* heading.

PRACTICE YOUR SKILLS

Apply the Subhead style to the following headings:

International Travel

Corporate Profiles

Worldwide Services

MODIFYING STYLES

Using styles to format a document is an easy way to make formatting changes. For example, if you format the Subhead style to include bold and italics, and then want to remove the italic character style and add underlining, all you have to do is redefine, or modify, the style. When you modify a style, all of the paragraphs that have the Subhead style applied to them will be updated with the new formatting.

To modify a style

- Apply the formatting changes to a paragraph containing the desired style
- Select the paragraph
- Select the style name in the Style list box
- Click on *Yes* in the resulting message box

Let's modify our Subhead style:

1. Select the *Introduction* heading.

2. Use the ribbon to remove the italic character style and apply the underline character style.

3. Open the Style list box and select **Subhead**. A message box is displayed which asks

   ```
   Do you want to redefine the style "Subhead"
   based on the selection?
   ```

4. Click on **Yes** to update all of the headings that have the Subhead style applied to them.

5. Observe that all of the headings are updated. Scroll to view all the headings with the Subhead style.

6. Save the disk file as **mych13c**.

7. Print the document and compare your printout to Figure 13.15.

8. Close the document.

Figure 13.15   **Completed MYCH13C.DOC document**

Global Travel
Complete Travel Services

Introduction

Global Travel is a full-service, multi-branch travel agency, which was founded in 1970. Our specialty is corporate travel.

Global Travel has five branches: Philadelphia, Pennsylvania; San Francisco, California; Chicago, Illinois; Miami, Florida; and Houston, Texas. Each of these offices is operated by a team of qualified managers and experienced agents whose goal is to provide your company with quality service at the lowest price.

Customer Service

We at Global Travel feel that communication with our corporate accounts is essential for providing good service. Each corporate account is assigned to a specific account executive. Your account executive will be available to answer any questions and provide you with any information that you request.

The corporate travel division of Global Travel is designed to offer the best and most professional service available to your business travelers. We encourage you to tour our facility and meet our staff at your convenience.

International Travel

We offer complete international itinerary assistance. We maintain a supply of passport and visa applications so that we can provide the necessary papers to our clients with minimum delay. Our International Rate Program guarantees your fast and accurate pricing, no matter how complicated the itinerary.

Corporate Profiles

Your company profile will be stored in our computer, and individual profiles will be maintained on each frequent traveler. Each profile will contain information regarding passport information, seating preference, car rental preference, frequent-flyer membership number, and corporate discount numbers. This information ensures that we can provide frequent travelers, fast, cost-effective itineraries.

Worldwide Services

Global Travel's Reservation Center will handle all of your weekend and after-hour reservations and changes. The reservation center can be dialed toll-free 24 hours a day. The worldwide service emergency numbers will be clearly marked on your travel itineraries.

SUMMARY

In this chapter you learned how to create documents using the templates provided with Word. You also learned how to use existing styles, as well as how to create your own styles and apply them to your documents. Finally, you learned how to modify styles.

Here is a quick reference guide to the Word features introduced in this chapter:

Desired Result	How to Do It
Attach the NORMAL template to a file	Choose **File, New**; click on **OK**
Insert the current date	Position the insertion point where you want the date to appear; choose **Insert, Date and Time**; select the desired date format; click on **OK**
Insert a file	Activate the destination document window; place the insertion point at the desired destination; choose **Insert, File**; select the name of the file to be inserted; click on **OK**
Attach the MEMO2 template to a file	Choose **File, New**; select **MEMO2**; click on **OK**; click on **OK** again; click on **Add Name**; type as many names as desired, clicking on **OK** after each name is typed; click on **Close**; click on **OK**; click on **Yes**; select the name of the desired recipient(s); click on **Select**; click on **Done**; in the Address Memo from Whom list box, type the sender's name; click on **Done**; in the Subject text box, type the subject of the memo; click on **Done**; in the Carbon Copy Memo To box, select the desired name(s); click on **Select**; click on **Done**
Apply a style	Place the insertion point in the desired paragraph or select the desired paragraphs; open the Style drop-down list box and select the desired style

Desired Result	How to Do It
Create a style	Format a paragraph as desired; select the formatted paragraph; select the style name in the Style list box; type the new style name; press **Enter**
Modify a style	Apply the formatting changes to a paragraph containing the desired style; select the paragraph; select the style name in the Style box; click on **Yes**

Congratulations! You have now learned how to use many of Word's features. You are now prepared to take all that you've learned and apply it to your own documents. Remember, in order to master the skills that you've acquired, you must supply the most important ingredient—practice. Only through practice will you be able to get beyond the techniques themselves. Good Luck!

APPENDIX A: INSTALLATION

Before You Begin
Installing

Installing Word on
Your Computer

Selecting a Printer
for Use with Word

This appendix contains instructions for installing Word for Windows 2.0 on your computer and for selecting a printer for use with Word.

BEFORE YOU BEGIN INSTALLING

Please read through the following two sections before beginning the installation procedure.

PROTECTING YOUR ORIGINAL INSTALLATION DISKS

Word comes with several floppy disks that you'll need to install the program on your computer. Before you begin, you should protect your original installation disks from accidental erasure. When a disk is protected, its data can be read, but not modified.

To protect a 5 1/4-inch disk

- Place a write-protect tab over the notch on the edge of the disk

To protect a 3 1/2-inch disk

- Slide the plastic locking button in the corner of the disk to its uppermost position

REQUIRED HARD-DISK SPACE

You need to have at least 15Mb (15,000,000 bytes) of free hard-disk space to install Word for Windows 2.0. If you do not have at least 15Mb of free hard-disk space, you must delete enough files from your hard disk to bring the total free space up to 15Mb. For help in doing this, please refer to your DOS or Windows manuals.

Note: Remember to back up (copy to a floppy disk) any files that you wish to preserve *before* deleting them from your hard disk.

INSTALLING WORD ON YOUR COMPUTER

Follow these steps to install Word for Windows 2.0:

1. Turn on your computer and start Windows. (If you have not already installed Windows on your system, please do so now; for help, see your Windows reference manuals.)

2. Insert the installation disk labeled *Setup - Disk 1* in the appropriately sized disk drive.

3. Choose **File, Run** from the Windows Program Manager menu.

4. Type **a:setup** (for drive A) or **b:setup** (for drive B), and then press **Enter** to start the Word installation program.

5. If you are prompted to enter your name and organization, follow the on-screen directions to do so. Click on **Continue** when you are done.

6. When you are prompted to specify the hard-disk directory where you want to install Word, click on **Continue** to accept the default directory, C:\WINWORD. If asked whether you want to create this directory, click on **Yes**.

7. A dialog box appears showing the available types of installation (see Figure A.1).

   In order to complete the hands-on activities in this book, you must select Complete Installation; the other installations do not provide the necessary Word options.

8. Click on the **Complete Installation** button.

9. You will be asked whether you want to see more information on a tool that helps WordPerfect users learn Word for Windows. Click on **No**; having this option enabled will interfere with your ability to complete the exercises in this book. If you are a WordPerfect user and wish to use this tool after you finish the book, you can enable it at that time.

Figure A.1   **Installation types**

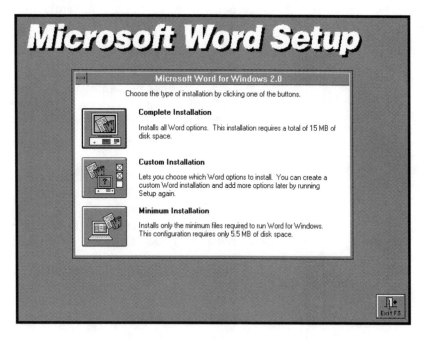

10. You will be asked whether you want Setup to make changes to your AUTOEXEC.BAT file. Click on **Do Not Update**.

11. A dialog box appears, informing you of the installation procedure's progress; 100% means that the installation is complete. When you are asked to insert a new Setup disk, please do so.

Note: You can click on Cancel at any time to cancel the entire installation.·

12. When the installation procedure is complete, you are returned to Windows. To start Word, simply double-click on the newly created Microsoft Word icon (located in the newly created group Microsoft Word 2.0).

SELECTING A PRINTER FOR USE WITH WORD

Before you can print from Word, you must select a printer. To do so, follow these steps:

1. Start Word for Windows 2.0.

2. Choose **File, Print Setup**. A dialog box appears, displaying a list of the printers that are currently installed on your system.

3. If your printer appears on the list (you may have to scroll), select it and click on **OK**. You can now use this printer with Word.

4. If your printer does not appear on the list (even after scrolling), install the printer on your system (for instructions, refer to your Windows documentation), then repeat this printer selection procedure from step 1.

Note: The printed examples shown in this book were all printed on a PostScript laser printer. Your printouts may differ somewhat, depending on which printer you are using. Printer choice also affects how text appears on your screen. If you are using a non-PostScript printer, your screen typestyles and sizes may differ from those shown in this book's figures.

APPENDIX B: KEYSTROKE REFERENCE

Insertion Pointer Movement

Text Selection

Text Entry and Formatting

Text Editing

Character Formatting

Paragraph Formatting

File and Window Management

Field Management

Miscellaneous

This appendix lists the keystrokes that you can use to issue Word commands.

INSERTION POINTER MOVEMENT

Move	Key/Key Combination
One character to the left	Left Arrow
One character to the right	Right Arrow
One line up	Up Arrow
One line down	Down Arrow
One word to the left	Ctrl+Left Arrow
One word to the right	Ctrl+Right Arrow
To the end of a line	End
To the start of a line	Home
Down one screen	Pg Dn
Up one screen	Pg Up
To the start of a document	Ctrl+Home
To the end of a document	Ctrl+End
To any page of a document	F5
Back to last insertion point location	Shift+F5

TEXT SELECTION

Select	Key/Key Combination
Left character	Shift+Left Arrow
Right character	Shift+Right Arrow
Previous line	Shift+Up Arrow
Next line	Shift+Down Arrow
Extend selection	F8
Shrink selection	Shift+F8
Column	Ctrl+Shift

TEXT ENTRY AND FORMATTING

Format	Key/Key Combination
Start new paragraph	Enter
Start new line	Shift+Enter
Insert hard page break	Ctrl+Enter
Insert column break	Ctrl+Shift+Enter
Insert normal hyphen	Hyphen
Insert optional hyphen	Ctrl+Hyphen
Insert hard hyphen	Ctrl+Shift+Hyphen
Insert hard space	Ctrl+Shift+Spacebar

TEXT EDITING

Edit	Key/Key Combination
Move selected text	F2
Copy selected text	Shift+F2
Delete character to the right	Del
Delete character to the left	Backspace
Delete word to the right	Ctrl+Del
Delete word to the left	Ctrl+Backspace

CHARACTER FORMATTING

Format	Key/Key Combination
Increase point size	Ctrl+F2
Decrease point size	Ctrl+Shift+F2
Change point size	Ctrl+P
Change case	Shift+F3
Remove formatting	Ctrl+Spacebar
Capitalize	Ctrl+A
Capitalize (small caps)	Ctrl+K
Bold	Ctrl+B
Underline	Ctrl+U
Underline words, but not spaces	Ctrl+W
Double underline	Ctrl+D
Enlarge font	Ctrl+F2

Format	Key/Key Combination
Shrink font	Ctrl+Shift+F2
Change font	Ctrl+F
Hidden text	Ctrl+H
Italic	Ctrl+I
Subscript	Ctrl+Equal sign (=)
Superscript	Ctrl+Plus sign (+)

PARAGRAPH FORMATTING

Format	Key/Key Combination
Single-space lines	Ctrl+1
Double-space lines	Ctrl+2
1 1/2-space lines	Ctrl+5
Center lines	Ctrl+E
Left-align lines	Ctrl+L
Right-align lines	Ctrl+R
Justify lines	Ctrl+J
Remove paragraph formatting	Ctrl+Q

FILE AND WINDOW MANAGEMENT

Format	Key/Key Combination
Save As	F12 or Alt+F2
Save	Shift+F12 or Alt+Shift+F2
Open	Ctrl+F12

Format	Key/Key Combination
Close document window	Ctrl+F4
Restore document window	Ctrl+F5
Maximize document window	Ctrl+F10
Close Word window	Alt+F4
Restore Word window	Alt+F5
Maximize Word window	Alt+F10
Minimize Word window	Alt+F9
Next window	Ctrl+F6 or Alt+F6
Previous window	Ctrl+Shift+F6 or Alt+Shift+F6
Next pane	F6
Previous pane	Shift+F6

FIELD MANAGEMENT

Function	Key/Key Combination
Next field	F11 or Alt+F1
Previous field	Shift+F11 or Alt+Shift+F1
Toggle field	Shift+F9
Update field	F9
Insert field	Ctrl+F9
Unlink field	Ctrl+Shift+F9
Lock field	Ctrl+F11
Unlock field	Ctrl+Shift+F11

MISCELLANEOUS

Function	Key/Key Combination
Help	F1
Help pointer	Shift+F1
Glossary	F3
Repeat command	F4
Repeat Find/Go To	Shift+F4
Insert bookmark	Ctrl+Shift+F5
Spelling checker	F7
Thesaurus	Shift+F7
Menu	F10
Print	Ctrl+Shift+F12

APPENDIX C: DIFFERENCES BETWEEN WORD 2.0 AND WORD 1.0

Word for Windows 2.0 represents a major upgrade from Word 1.0. Word 2.0 provides significant enhancements that can make your everyday word processing tasks faster and easier to perform. Table C.1 lists some of the major differences between Word 2.0 and Word 1.0.

Table C.1   **Differences between Word 2.0 and Word 1.0**

Feature	Description
Dialog boxes	Virtually every dialog box displays more options in Word 2.0 than in Word 1.0.
Edit, Find	In Word 2.0, the Find dialog box remains open until you close it. In Word 1.0, the corresponding dialog box (called Search) closes automatically after every search.
Edit, Select All	Edit, Select All is a new menu command in Word 2.0, allowing you to select the entire document from the menu. Word 1.0 methods of selecting entire documents are still available.
Menu commands	Commands in Word 2.0 have been redistributed throughout the menus. Although virtually all menu commands are still available, they often are found in new locations or have different names.

Feature	Description
Ribbon and ruler	The ribbon and the ruler have changed dramatically from Word 1.0. Formerly, the ribbon was used only for character formatting, and the ruler was used only for paragraph formatting. In Word 2.0, many options available on the Word 1.0 ribbon and ruler have been consolidated onto the ribbon. Other options have been left off completely, including Small Caps, Word Underline, Double Underline, Superscript, Subscript, and the three options for line spacing.
Show/Hide	In Word 1.0, the Show All option includes showing field codes, such as page-number codes. In Word 2.0, showing field codes is a separate option from Show/Hide.
Toolbar	The toolbar is completely new in Word 2.0, providing quick access to some of Word for Windows's most frequently used commands. Options include New, Open, Save, Cut, Copy, Paste, Undo, Spelling, Print, and three modes of Zoom.
Tools, Grammar	The grammar checker is new in Word 2.0, giving you the ability to check your documents for grammar and style.
View, Zoom	Zoom is a new feature in Word 2.0, allowing you to view your document at any magnification level from 25% to 200%. Unlike Print Preview, the Zoom mode allows you to edit and format text at any magnification.

APPENDIX D: EXCHANGING DOCUMENTS WITH OTHER PROGRAMS

Opening Non-Word
2.0 Files

Saving Non-Word
2.0 Files

Word for Windows 2.0 is compatible with many popular word processing and spreadsheet programs. You can open a non-Word 2.0 document (disk file), edit and print it, and then save it in its original file format or as a Word 2.0 file. Or, you can open a Word 2.0 document and then save it in a file format that can be used with a non-Word 2.0 program. This appendix lists the various formats in which Word can open and save files, and shows you how to make your desired file conversions.

OPENING NON-WORD 2.0 FILES

To open a non-Word 2.0 file

- Choose *File, Open* (or click on the toolbar Open button) to display the Open dialog box.

- If necessary, select the desired drive in the Drives list box.

- If necessary, select the desired directory in the Directories list box.

- Select the desired file in the File Name list box. Or, type the desired file name (with extension) in the File Name text box.

- Click on *OK* (or press *Enter*). A Convert File dialog box appears, listing the file formats that Word 2.0 can convert from (that is, the file types that it can open). The format of the file you specified in the previous step is highlighted. (**Note**: If the file format of your specified file does not appear in this box, but does appear in Table D.1, exit this procedure, run the Word Setup program to add the missing file-format converter, and then repeat this procedure.)

- Click on *OK* (or press *Enter*) to convert your file from the highlighted format to Word 2.0 format.

Once you've opened a non-Word 2.0 file, you can edit, print, save, or close it exactly as you would any standard Word 2.0 file. If you want to save the file in Word 2.0 format, use Save (to keep the same name and location) or Save As (to change the name and/or location). If you want to save the file in its original format (for example, as a WordPerfect 5.1 file), please refer to the procedure presented in the next section, "Saving Non-Word 2.0 Files."

Table D.1 lists the types of non-Word 2.0 files that can be opened.

Table D.1   **File Types You Can Open from Word 2.0**

File Format	Type of File
BIFF	Microsoft Excel 2.0 and 3.0 worksheets
DCA/RFT	DisplayWrite and IBM 5520
File Templates (.DOT)	Microsoft Word for Windows
Microsoft Word for DOS	All versions
Rich Text Format (.RTF)	Microsoft standard file interchange
Text Only	Without line breaks
DOS Text Only	For opening plain text files created from a DOS-based product (for example, Microsoft Word for DOS or WordPerfect)
Text with Layout	Restores text to paragraph form, including indents and paragraph spacing
DOS Text with Layout	For opening plain text files created from a DOS-based product (for example, Microsoft Word for DOS or WordPerfect)
Microsoft Word for Windows	Versions 1.0, 1.1, and 1.1a

File Format	Type of File
Microsoft Word for the Macintosh	Versions 4.0 and 5.0
WordPerfect	Versions 4.1, 4.2, 5.0, and 5.1
Lotus 1-2-3	Worksheet formats, WK1 and WK3 files
WordStar	Versions 3.3, 3.45, 4.0, 5.0, and 5.5
dBase	Versions II, III, and IV

You can also open the following types of files. But, in order to do so, you'll have to obtain the necessary file-format converters by sending in the Special Offer coupon included in your Word for Windows 2.0 package.

- Microsoft Works for DOS

- Microsoft Works for Windows

- Microsoft Windows Write

- Multimate versions 3.3, Advantage 3.6, and Advantage II

- Microsoft Multiplan versions 2.0, 3.0, 4.0, and 4.2

SAVING NON-WORD 2.0 FILES

To save a file in a non-Word 2.0 file format

- Choose *File, Save As* to display the Save As dialog box.

- If necessary, select the desired drive in the Drives list box.

- If necessary, select the desired directory in the Directories list box.

- Select the desired file format in the Save File as Type list box. (**Note:** If your desired file format does not appear in this box, but does appear in Table D.2, exit this procedure, run the Word Setup program to add the missing file-format converter, and then repeat this procedure.)

- Type the desired file name (without extension) in the File Name text box.

- Click on *OK* (or press *Enter*).

Once you've saved a file in a non-Word 2.0 file format, you can open it from the program that uses this file format (for example, WordPerfect 5.1) and then edit, print, save, or close it exactly as you would any standard file in that program.

You can save a file in the non-Word 2.0 file formats listed in Table D.2.

Table D.2 **File Types You Can Save from Word 2.0**

File Format	File Type
DCA/RFT	DisplayWrite and IBM 5520
File Templates (.DOT)	Microsoft Word for Windows
Microsoft Word for DOS	All versions
Rich Text Format (.RTF)	Microsoft standard file interchange
Text Only	Without line breaks
DOS Text Only	For saving plain text files to be opened by a a DOS-based product (for example, Microsoft Word for DOS or WordPerfect)
Text with Layout	Creates a text file while maintaining columns, line spacing, tabs, text frames, paragraph spacing, indents, and tables
DOS Text with Layout	For saving plain text files to be opened by a DOS-based product (for example, Microsoft Word for DOS or WordPerfect)
Text Only with Line Breaks	Inserts a carriage return at the end of each line
DOS Text Only with Line Breaks	For saving plain text files to be opened by a DOS-based product (for example, Microsoft Word for DOS or WordPerfect)
Microsoft Word for Windows	Versions 1.0, 1.1, and 1.1a

File Format	File Type
Microsoft Word for the Macintosh	Versions 4.0 and 5.0
WordPerfect	Versions 4.1, 4.2, 5.0, and 5.1
WordStar	Versions 3.3, 3.4, 4.0, 5.0, and 5.5

You can also save files in the following formats. But in order to do so you'll have to obtain the necessary file-format converters by sending in the Special Offer coupon included in your Word 2.0 for Windows package.

- Microsoft Works for DOS
- Microsoft Works for Windows
- Microsoft Windows Write
- Multimate versions 3.3, Advantage 3.6, and Advantage II
- Microsoft Multiplan versions 2.0, 3.0, 4.0, and 4.2

INDEX

■ TO RECEIVE 5¼-INCH DISK(S)

The Ziff-Davis Press software contained on the $3\frac{1}{2}$-inch disk included with this book is also available in $5\frac{1}{4}$-inch format. If you would like to receive the software in the $5\frac{1}{4}$-inch format, please return the $3\frac{1}{2}$-inch disk with your name and address to:

Disk Exchange
Ziff-Davis Press
5903 Christie Avenue
Emeryville, CA 94608